D1213210

The Theater of JEAN GENET

The Theater of JEAN GENET

A CASEBOOK

edited by Richard N. Coe

Grove Press, Inc., New York

Library of Congress Catalog Card Number: 79-10274
Manufactured in the United States of America.

First Printing

ACKNOWLEDGMENTS. The editor is grateful to the following for permission to reprint: American Educational Theatre Association, Inc. for John Gassner's review of *The Blacks* in *Educational Theatre Journal*, October 1961. | *Aspects de la France* for Pierre Chaumeil's "Revue de la Presse," 5 May 1966. | Therese Brøndum-Pringsheim for excerpts from two letters to Dr. Friedrich Flemming, and the lecture by Lily Pringsheim, 15 September 1951. | *Drama Survey* and Thomas B. Markus for "The Psychological Universe of Jean Genet," in *Drama Survey*, vol. 3, 1964. | *Drama Survey* and Robert Nugent for "Sculpture into Drama: Giacometti's Influence on Genet," in *Drama Survey*, vol. 3, 1964. | Nicole Duault for her article on Genet at the Sorbonne, in *France-Soir*, 31 May 1968. | *L'Express* for interview with Peter Brook, 19 May 1960; excerpt from interview with Genet, 26 April 1957; Robert Kanter's review of *Les Nègres*, 5 November 1959. | *Le Figaro* for Jean-Jacques Gautier's review of *Haute Surveillance*, 4 March 1949; Producer Jean Marchat replies to the review, 7 March 1949; François Mauriac's review of *Haute Surveillance* (*Le Figaro Littéraire*), 26 March 1949; an excerpt from Jean-Jacques Gautier's review of *Les Paravents*, 23–24 April 1966. | Editions Gallimard for an excerpt from Jean-Louis Barrault, "Scandale et Provocation," in *Cahiers Renaud-Barrault*, April 1966. | Lucien Goldmann and *The Drama Review* for "The Theater of Genet: A Sociological Study," trans. Pat Dreyfus, reprinted *The Drama Review*, vol. 12, no. 2 (T38), Winter 1968. Copyright © 1968 by The Drama Review. Reprinted by permission. All rights

For Dr. Friedrich Flemming

OF BAD SEGEBERG

—to whom this book owes so much.

Contents

Editor's Foreword

The literary career of Jean Genet has, from the outset, been a battlefield. He has been insulted and reviled, censored and threatened; in compensation, he has been adulated, exalted and overpraised. He has been loved and hated; he has never left either his readers or his audiences indifferent.

And Genet, of course, has flung himself into the mêlée. When he was insulted with silence, he created scandals in such a way that he *had* to be talked about; and when, at last, he was acclaimed and accepted, he created further scandals by rejecting this acceptance and by refusing to allow his plays to be performed or his novels to be quoted. Jean Genet is an anarchist of the most obdurate and classical variety; and no amount of success has reconciled him to the claims of an ordered society.

This is not to say that there has not been, particularly in America and in England, in Italy and in Germany—rarely in France, if one excepts Jean-Paul Sartre's monumental *Saint Genet*—a fair amount of reasoned, objective academic criticism. But it is significant that, in the case of Jean Genet, the calm aura of academic judgments, of emotions "recollected in tranquillity," grows in exact proportion to the distance from the dynamic source of the disturbance.

Here, then, is the principle which has guided me in the selection of texts for the present *Casebook*. A "casebook" is—or should be—a collection of immediate, on-the-spot evidence, from which eventually, at a decent remove in time, emotion, and space, a scholar may distill his sober and balanced opinions. In Genet's case, to present as evidence a selection consisting predominantly of such already precooled judgments would falsify the picture. When audiences at *The Screens* were hurling missiles—ranging from rotten eggs to steel bolts and Bengal lights—at the actors, a level-headed appraisal of the aesthetic theories underlying Genet's later dramas would have been not only premature, but positively misleading. Such valuable and lasting academic judgments exist; I have quoted a few of them, and the remainder may be located through the bibliography; but in the text, by and large, I have tried to recapture above all the ephemeral and white-hot urgency of immediate reactions: the muddled honesty of many people doing—or at least saying—the wrong thing for the right reason.

Where I have not had the space to quote, I have given my own summary of events and opinions; and, wherever possible, I have indicated sources which can be located. All prose quotations have been rendered into English; the occasional quotation in verse has been left in French unless I have been able to locate an acceptable version in translation. As far as possible, articles have been given their original titles; when these were either nonexistent, however, or else hopelessly unrevealing (e.g., *Last Month in the Theater*, or *French Literature Today*), I have invented my own, normally using a phrase or a sentence from the article quoted. Throughout the *Casebook*, I have regularized the spelling of Genet's name; it is worth recording, however, that the variants "Genêt" and "Genest" appear to be used quite deliberately in some cases by the more openly malevolent critics.

R.N.C.

Thief into Poet

Jean Genet was born in Paris on 19 December 1910, the unwanted child of a common whore. Brought up, first by the Assistance publique, *later by foster parents in the Morvan, he was soon packed off to reform school, and the years he spent there completed his degradation. He became a petty racketeer, a common thief, a male prostitute; he joined the army, only to desert a few days later; and as beggar and bum, he saw the inside of most of the larger prisons in Europe . . . or such, at least, is the story of his early life, as he weaves it into the legend that he calls* The Thief's Journal.

Is this story true? And if so, how did such a man become a poet? Illiterate adolescent gangsters and layabouts do not commonly grow up into masters of style. It is of the essence of the "legend" that this transmutation was sudden, unexpected, and quasi-miraculous. Jean Genet was thirty-two years old and, as usual, in prison—and to him came Poetry like a Pentecostal flame, a gift of Grace that was to lead him to salvation:

THOSE LINES BETWEEN MY FINGERS

JEAN GENET

I received another note from Bulkaen in exchange for mine. It was written in the careful handwriting which was used for penning the petition for reprieve in which, owing to his ignorance, he got entangled in barbarous sentences and pointed words and, before writing, in movements of the hand that were like sweeps of the leg in dancing, movements in which the clumsiness of his imagination tried to hide behind the agility

---

From *Miracle of the Rose*, trans. Bernard Frechtman (New York: Grove Press, 1965), p. 108. Reprinted by permission.

and elegance of the hand. He asked me to write a few lines of verse about a subject which he gave me: "Jean, would you write a few lines of verse about two friends who loved each other a lot in prison? One of them goes away. The one who's left behind writes to him to say that he'll always love him and that he's waiting to join him, even in the penal colony, where they'll be happy." And he added: "Believe me, lots of men think that way in prison."

Those lines between my fingers! Ever since then, I can't help seeing Bulkaen in the penal colony where he should have been (for though I was robbed of my death, his death stole his destiny; it was Bulkaen whom I envisioned amidst the ferns when I wrote *The Condemned Man*). . . .

The Condemned Man *is Genet's first published poem. In conversation with Jean-Paul Sartre, Genet gave an alternative version of the same episode—a version which, although it differs in every detail from the story as told in* Miracle of the Rose, *is none the less identical in spirit:*

THEY CHALLENGED ME . . .

JEAN GENET

"I was pushed into a cell where there were already several prisoners in 'city' clothes. You're allowed to wear your jacket while you're still awaiting trial. But though I had filed an appeal, I was made, by mistake, to wear the prisoner's outfit. That weird get-up seemed to be a jinx. They despised me. I later had the greatest difficulty in overcoming their attitude. Among them was a prisoner who composed poems to his sister, idiotic, sniveling poems that they all admired. Finally, in irrita-

---

Quoted by Jean-Paul Sartre, in *Saint Genet*, trans. Bernard Frechtman (New York: George Braziller, 1963), p. 427.

tion, I said that I could do just as well. They challenged me, and I wrote *The Condemned Man*. I read it to them and they despised me even more. I finished reading it amid insults and jeers. A prisoner said to me, 'I write poems like that every morning.' When I got out of jail, I made a particular point of finishing the poem, which was all the more precious to me for having been despised."

If the critics have accepted and embellished the legend, Genet himself is largely responsible, for he has never done anything to contradict it:

A VOLUME OF PROUST . . .

ROBERT WERNICK

. . . Beckett and Ionesco were reading the French classics, Racine and all that, when they were in school. Genet never read anything, really, till he was in his thirties and a jailbird of long standing. It was World War II, and the jails of France were filling up with a new type of prisoner—educated, law-abiding citizens who had been arrested for resisting the Germans. One of these prisoners gave Genet, an almost illiterate thief, a volume of Proust. Genet expected to make fun of the big words, but he had only to read one page of the voluptuous prose and he was caught forever in the toils of literature. . . .

Hidden away behind the legend, however, lies the truth: a truth which, on the rare occasions when it can be glimpsed, appears to be at once less romantic and at the same time more

---

From "The Three Kings of Bedlam," *Life*, 2 February 1968.

intriguing. For there seems to be no doubt that Genet did learn his trade as poet and writer, not in some instant of inspired revelation, but, like any other artist, only in infinitely less favorable circumstances, by years of hard work, practice, self-discipline, and self-education.

An episode which, significantly, does not appear in The Thief's Journal concerns the period—toward the year 1926 or thereabouts—when for a short while Genet seems to have served as human "guide dog" to the strange, forgotten figure: the "blind bard," René de Buxeuil. De Buxeuil was a facile, sentimental, and at one time popular versifier, who specialized in religio-moralistic ballads, touching lyrics for calendars, and who, as the supreme achievement of his career, composed the marching song for the right-wing, royalist legion, the Camelots du Roi. How long Genet stayed with him is not known: but it is almost certainly from him that he learned at least the primary elements of versification.

At all events, it is clear that by 1937—that is, some four years before The Condemned Man—Genet was not only a highly literate and memorable autodidact, but had already written a good deal. It is fascinating to compare his own account of his residence in Brno and of his subsequent adventures in Hitler's Germany[1] with the account which follows—the earliest account that I have discovered by a person who actually knew him before the War: Frau Lily Pringsheim.

TOWARD THE END OF 1937 . . .

LILY PRINGSHEIM

Who is Jean Genet, and why can this Frenchman, now forty-two years old, not be disregarded?

---

1. See *Journal du Voleur* (Paris: Gallimard, 1949), pp. 98 ff., *The Thief's Journal,* trans. Bernard Frechtman (New York: Grove Press, 1964), pp. 82 ff.

In its original form, this essay was the text of a lecture delivered, without notes, by the late Frau Pringsheim to an audience at the

Unquestionably, a legend has grown up around the figure of Jean Genet, for rarely has a writer attained such a notorious degree of significance in so short a time. And this significance has its roots not only in his unique destiny, which was to be obliged to live continuously behind prison walls; it is also of incalculable social import. There has been published a volume of his Collected Works, all of which were composed either in prison, or in some cases even while he was still a state reform school pupil in various institutions for juvenile and adolescent delinquents. Outside prison he wrote, in 1945, the novel—or rather the diary, or confession—called *J'étais un voleur* ["I was a thief"]. This term "confession" must not be misunderstood. Genet does not confess anything because, according to any customary conception, he repents of it; nor has he anything in common with Jean-Jacques Rousseau, who, in his *Confessions,*

Volkshochschule in Darmstadt on 15 September 1951. About a year or so later she revised it, in the form here reproduced, apparently intending it for publication. For reasons unknown, however, it remained in MS. until after her death [28 September 1954—see *Darmstädter Tagblatt,* 29 September 1954]; and it was finally published in an abridged version in the *Programm-Heft des Darmstädter-Theaters,* No. 15, 1966–1967, under the simple heading: "Jean Genet." The recovery of the original typescript is due to the efforts of Dr. Friedrich Flemming, and of Dr. Michel, Principal of the Darmstadt Volkshochschule. It is translated by R.N.C., and reprinted by permission of Frau Therese Brøndum-Pringsheim.

Lily Pringsheim, born at Königsberg on 7 February 1887, was a writer and journalist who had settled in Darmstadt in the 1920s. In the early thirties, she was a Social-Democratic Deputy to the *Landstag* of Hesse; but in 1933 she was forced to emigrate, first to Czechoslovakia, later to England and America. She returned to Darmstadt in 1945, where she lived until her death.

The date which she gives for Genet's arrival in Brno appears to be inaccurate. All evidence suggests that Genet spent part of the winter 1936–1937 in Vienna, and arrived in Brno in the early spring of 1937, having crossed the frontier at Retz/Znaim. He spent several months in the town, earning a living by giving French lessons to the daughter of the leading gynecologist and perhaps to others as well; but he appears to have left, heading for Katovice in Poland, toward the beginning of June. [Ed.]

"confesses" simply in order to achieve a degree of degrading self-pity and, in the concluding chapters, to launch forth in the wildest accusations against his erstwhile friends—with the consequence that, save on rare occasions, Rousseau does not tell the truth at all. Genet has no interest in making himself out better than he was, because he refuses to accept "morality" in this sense. Genet is simply resolved to portray things *as they are*, and to tell them to others, knowing full well that these same "others" would much rather not listen. Genet himself was a so-called "juvenile delinquent," he was a thief all his life up to his middle thirties, and he has committed almost every crime in the calendar, excepting only murder. He was forever escaping from prisons, making his way surreptitiously across frontiers, stealing; he had been in Morocco and in Spain, and had finally reached the very nadir of degradation. When he tried the experiment of returning to France, he was promptly arrested[2] and—O irony of fate!—sent to a barracks for military training. He promptly had a row with his superior officer, and beat him up, after contemptuously telling him what he thought of the system that first locked criminals in prison and then proceeded to deem them good enough to serve as soldiers in defense of a "country" they had never known and of "ideologies" of which they had no notion. Yet once more, by the skin of his teeth, he succeeded in getting out of the military prison and made his way secretly to Czechoslovakia where, toward the end of 1937, he was picked up and, since he claimed to be an army deserter, was brought to the League for Freedom and Peace [*Liga für Freiheit und Frieden*].[3] It was here, as I translated the frenzied

2. After leaving Katovice (where, in prison, he heard of the fall of Blum's Popular Front government, and lamented the fate of socialism), Genet went to Berlin, and thence, via Brussels and Antwerp, to Paris, where he arrived in the latter part of August 1937. Here, after a few weeks, he was arrested for issuing forged passports and during the inquiry which ensued, the story of his previous desertion came to light. Frau Pringsheim is wrong when she situates this episode *before* his arrival in Brno. [Ed.]

3. Another slight error: the *Liga für Freiheit und Frieden* was specifically a women's organization. It was in fact the much more important

torrent of explanations that poured forth from his lips in extraordinarily rapid French, that I got to know him, covered in rags as he was, and crawling with lice.

Genet was a foundling child who had been left on the steps of the *Assistance publique*. This was the beginning of his existence as an outcast. I have no wish, at this juncture, to indulge in any of the shallow sentimentality to which, perhaps, I might be tempted by this fact. None the less, Jean-Paul Sartre is probably right when today, in the great, detailed study which has just been published by Gallimard in Paris and is entitled *Saint-Genet comédien et martyr*, he attributes the whole of Genet's atrocious life to this instant, when his mother abandoned him and vanished forever.

The League for Freedom and Peace in Brno was run by a group of quite remarkable people who lived for their convictions and who later—all save three—were murdered for them. . . . Unlike so many others in Germany, not a single one among them was ever induced to betray his principles; not one made an about-face to meet the advancing hordes of Hitler. Nor was anyone put off by the external appearance of this rather undersized, indeed almost dainty, vagabond. He seemed pleased at this, and also by the way I interpreted. It was instantly apparent that in him we had to deal with a truly astonishing intelligence and a quite remarkable talent. I could scarcely believe the extent of his knowledge of literature, since, except for a few short breathing spaces, he had been continually in jail; nor was it highly likely that as a child in the reform schools he should have picked up knowledge of this description.

Genet came many times—in fact, constantly—to see us. Often we would let him have his way and sleep on the very narrow projecting ledge of a balcony. He was glad to have the stars to look at, and was wholly unaccustomed to a bed, or to any of the "normal" comforts of life, which indeed never

---

Liga für Menschenrechte that rescued Genet in Czechoslovakia. Its founder in Brno was Dr. Otto Schütz, later a well-known figure in innumerable campaigns for human liberties and civil rights, who now works for the United Restitution Office in New York. [Ed.]

failed to astonish him. I must explain that we had very little in common with the "bourgeois" variety of Social Democrats: we were old hands at emigration, not new to the game, like so many since 1945, who simply learn the jargon by heart, and who, either for reasons that have nothing to do with the matter or because they get paid for it by the day, or else simply to swim with the current, have joined the German Socialist Party. We were very poor refugees, and we had already wandered over a great part of the world, scaling the barriers of frontiers and meeting with all sorts and conditions of men. Need forges bonds, creates perceptiveness and understanding. Consequently, we came forward to meet Genet without the slightest doubt or hesitation; and even if he was—or alleged himself to be—a thief, it seemed to us that, by comparison with the atrocities which were being perpetrated in Germany by the criminals of National Socialism, *his* criminality was shadowy and small. In Genet, one immediately sensed a great moral need for form; his language assumed rare and strange shapes, and his delight in everyday objects that totally failed to strike the attention of others was almost childlike in its fantasy. In that time of Germany's infamy, and in the face of those daily repeated threats that Hitler was screaming over the radio at the Czechoslovak Republic, all petty calculations were foreign to us. We lived with the presupposition that all of us had one foot in jail, and nobody worried or cared whether we had landed there because we had been driven to crime by sheer necessity, as with some, or as victims of political persecution, as with others, or for racial reasons, as with others again, or, like Genet, because he had been swindled out of his youth. We were united in our horror of Hitler, and in our burning desire to help the brave people of the Czechoslovak Republic in their struggle to defend themselves.

Then circumstances grew more difficult still and Genet left us, with the bold intention of making his way somehow through Germany back again to France, there to sleep out the nights once more beneath his beloved Seine bridges and, by dint of sheer watchfulness, to keep out of the hands of the police. He begged me to store away a number of manuscripts which he had written during his most recent term of imprisonment. I gave him the Berlin address of Wilhelm Leuschner,[4] with whom the SS were playing cat-and-mouse, repeatedly releasing him from prison one day only to pull him in again the next. Genet shared with Leuschner an uncontrollable thirst for knowledge, for Leuschner, like Genet, carried books about with him everywhere he went: Shakespeare, language textbooks, scientific treatises. Both read and learned on every possible occasion—it used to infuriate the SS whenever, during intervals in interrogation, anyone buried himself in a book, and the text would be snatched away in a storm of jeering. Indeed, Genet *did* venture secretly as far as Berlin, and *did* meet Leuschner, armed with a variety of recommendations from us, which he had learned by heart, for he would carry nothing with him in writing when he dodged across frontiers. Leuschner must have realized immediately that Genet was to be judged by standards other than those applying to ordinary beings, and received him with remarkable friendliness. It is an eternal pity that Genet was not the person destined to murder Hitler. As an unknown vagabond and beggar, who was politically nonsuspect and who, on top of everything, was a foreigner, *he* could have got away with it.

I received one further letter from Genet, censored by the prison authorities in Marseilles. There, things were going so badly for him that he thought he would probably die. I managed somehow to get money to him. He never forgot this, for he had not a friend in the world, save the companions of his cell: murderers and thieves.

---

4. Wilhelm Leuschner: German trade-union leader, sculptor, and Social Democrat. After a series of quarrels with Robert Ley, founder of the Nazi Labor Front, Leuschner became the center of opposition to Hitler inside Germany. He was the inspiration behind the so-called "Generals' Plot" which, in July 1944, attempted to murder Hitler; the attempt failed, and he was arrested and hanged. [Ed.]

Later, in the United States and then in Peru, I read that Jean Genet was living with Cocteau in his famous "Existentialist Côterie," and that he was an up-and-coming genius. They soon fell out—inevitably, given their mutual tastes and inclinations. Genet parted from Cocteau, his writings were published and his talks on the radio were feared, for in them he mercilessly revealed the conditions in which "child criminals" were made to live, while at the same time he took sides, exclusively and unconditionally, with these same adolescents, who symbolized his own life and his own destiny. Many people felt nauseated when they read his works. Many rejected them as absurd and criminal "glorifications of crime." Yet it would be wrong to look for pornographic tendencies in these books, however shatteringly gruesome Genet may be in his revelation of the passionate sexuality of prisoners among themselves. One should read them—if one can bear it—because these things are so, and because such conditions do prevail, whereas normally we become upset if dinner is burned or if we think we've been cheated out of half-a-dollar.

It is equally wrong to read them—thereby emphasizing our own highmindedness—as the "misshapen brainchildren of a common criminal." Claudel, the great French Catholic poet, finds Genet's writings, like his very existence, wholly intolerable. There have been too many violations and desecrations by this lost sheep of a thief, who at the outset, in his childhood, was a faithful Catholic! . . . There have been too many revelations of what really goes on inside *Catholic* reform schools! . . . Claudel cries aloud, and writes and publishes that Genet should be forbidden to utter a word. In vain!

And yet, today, Genet writes no longer. For the time being, outside the prison walls, the stimulus has evaporated. I met him again in Paris a short while ago, and he was beside himself that he had known nothing of my arrival; he had already given us up for lost, although only fifteen years had passed [. . .]. Now, however, he writes to us continually. My daughter Heidi, who is temporarily visiting Europe from Peru, and who, in the old days in Brno, was scarcely more than a child, spent several days with me in his company in Paris in July [1952], and, save for his external appearance, he has scarcely changed at all. The rags have vanished, he earns enormous sums of money and gives it all away, he has established a family life for one of his homosexual friends, whom he allowed to marry, and to whom he makes an allowance and has given a house in the South of France. He is very proud of the three children of his former "friend." Apart from this, however, he thinks of himself as dead [*mort*], because he no longer writes anything, and because the marvels of freedom outside the prison walls, together with the world of the bourgeoisie, have nothing more to offer him. In Hamburg, he went through the experience of a soirée given by his publisher, who held a cocktail party in honor of poor little Genet, at which—once again—the ladies, all in bewitching party hats with veils, crowded around him, and found him *frightfully* interesting and *frightfully* famous . . . and one after the other felt socially obliged to describe not only their husbands, but themselves too, as criminals, in order to impress him![5] The exercise misfired completely. Everyone knows Goethe's parody *Satyros*, in which the crowd all run madly after Satyros and end up by singing "Und rohe Kastanien, die ess ich so gern." . . .

—But I am the only one who really knew him when he was a lost thief and a vagabond.

The late Frau Pringsheim had two daughters, Therese (referred to above as "Heidi," and now Frau Brøndum-Pringsheim) and Marianne (now Frau Roessink-Pringsheim). In 1937, Marianne was already married and living in Peru. Genet did not meet her until very much later, in Paris, and the outcome of the

5. This anecdote suggests a later addition to the MS. Genet was not published in Germany until 1955. [Ed.]

meeting was intense dislike on both sides from the first moment. But "Heidi" was still a school-girl, and remembers Genet well:

A BALCONY, A BLACK WOMAN, A BURIAL, AND A BATH

THERESE BRØNDUM-PRINGSHEIM

. . . As far as I can recall, Genet handed no manuscripts over to my mother. We got to know him in Brno, in 1937—at that time he was about twenty-six years old. A number of ladies belonging to the League for Human Rights [*Liga für Menschenrechte*] asked my mother, who was half-French, to come to their aid to try and make something out of this peculiar Frenchman. My mother agreed to do so, and promptly installed him on our balcony, since there was no space anywhere else in our one-and-a-half-room flat.[6] My mother was always sheltering the oddest characters in our various attics, cellars, and miscellaneous spooky cubbyholes.

At that time, Genet used to wear a brown corduroy suit with a black turtleneck sweater, which he never once took off in three months. His whole luggage consisted of a cowhide folder full of manuscripts and writing materials. He had come straight from the Balkans, or rather, straight out of a series of Balkan jails. You probably know that, as a young man, he had been

---

6. In Brno, we used to live on the Dlouhá (the "Long Street"), I don't remember the number. The balcony was on the opposite side of the house from the entrance, or street front. My mother used to insist that Genet had always climbed down with a rope; even as a child, however, this struck me as an exaggeration, since we lived on the third floor. But if not, then he would have had to pass through our bedroom, which is equally difficult for me to imagine. So the rope-and-balcony story *is* possible, after all.

I thought at first that it was *this* balcony which might have inspired his play of the same title; but after I had seen it I realized my mistake.

Extracts from two letters, dated 5 November and 17 December 1968, written by Frau Brøndum-Pringsheim to Dr. Friedrich Flemming. Passages selected and translated by R.N.C. Reprinted by permission of Frau Brøndum-Pringsheim.

forced to quit France because during his military service he had boxed an officer on the ears. In those days, I was just a schoolgirl, and I can remember only feeling very proud that a real *man* used to come every day to take me home. He further promised me to blow the teachers—whom I couldn't stand—sky-high!

One day, he took me with him down to the river, carrying a big parcel under his arm. When I asked him about it, he told me that he was going to bury the parcel in the river. I felt sure that, at the very least, he had chopped "la Négresse" (a friend of his, who used to live in some park or other) into little pieces, and I was delighted at the prospect of the burial, since I must have been a bit jealous of her. We came to the river, he made a moving funeral oration, possibly even *I* managed to squeeze out a tear or two for the Negress, and then the parcel went flying into the river. It turned out later, unfortunately, that the contents were much more innocent: it was the underclothes of a wealthy Jewish industrialist, to whom Genet had given lessons in French, and who, from humanitarian motives and with the greatest of tact, had made Genet a present of some of his choicest underwear. Unhappily, he was at least three times as broad around the waist as Genet; besides which, Genet never accepted anything from anyone, except later from my mother, and that under very different circumstances.

My mother used to tell the story (I can no longer swear today whether it is true or not) about how this same Jewish family had, with immense cunning, planned that Genet should take a bath. The bath tub was so excitingly, so appetizingly prepared with perfumed bath salts! And then Jean was enticed into the bathroom, and the door was shut behind him. . . . An hour later, when they knocked gently and inquired after his postbalneary condition, Jean opened the door, still fully dressed in his corduroys and turtleneck sweater, the bathroom was full of steam, and on the surface of the crystal-clear bath water there sailed lots of toy boats, which he had concocted out of toilet paper. . . .

From Brno, Genet made his way illegally back to Paris,

lived for a while under one of the Seine bridges, and then landed again in prison. There, my mother often used to send him parcels—something which he never forgot. Later, he and she often met in Paris; but by then he was already pretty famous, and no longer the undersized, filthy tramp in whose writings, as early as 1937, my mother had already discerned a great genius. Later still, I myself used to meet him there frequently, and as a special, exciting treat, he once took me in a luxury taxi to the *marché aux puces*. I found this "flea market" dirty and boring, and we quarreled about it—as we always did quarrel until we finally parted.[7] At that time, he lived in a flat near the Sacré Cœur, and was generally in an evil temper because summer in Paris is stifling, and also because his Italian "friend" hadn't written to him.

And that was the end of our acquaintance. My mother saw him on one last occasion in Darmstadt, where he made himself pretty unbearable and was continually making insulting remarks about her "bourgeois" friends. He was determined that his play *The Blacks* should be performed only by a Negro cast; and, when this proved impossible, he left the city. . . .[8]

Genet's writings in prison (La Santé and/or Fresnes) appear to have included The Condemned Man *and* Our Lady of the

---

7. In June 1952 [?], Lily Pringsheim wrote to her daughter "Heidi" that she had had a letter from Genet: "He asked after you, after 'Heidi who always mistrusts me,' and so I wrote to him: 'Heidi has married a Dane, and the result is three little she-Danes.' Here is what he answered: 'You tell me that Heidi has married a *Dane*. Since there is a race of creatures called *Great-Danes*, I assumed that Heidi, who was always odd, even as a little girl, had married a great Dane, and given birth to three little pups. But perhaps I'm wrong . . . or am I?' " [Ed.]

8. The German première of *Die Neger* took place on 30 May 1964 at the Landestheater Darmstadt, produced by Samy Molcho and Gerhard F. Hering with a white cast. Genet did everything in his power to prevent the performance, and left in disgust when he was legally advised that he could do nothing about it. [Ed.]

Flowers—possibly some of the other poems as well. In all likelihood it was Olga Barbezat, wife of Marc Barbezat the Lyon publisher, and at that time a prison visitor, who "discovered" Genet, and who showed some of his manuscripts to Jean Cocteau. At all events, by 1942/43, Cocteau had become Genet's most fervent advocate. On the occasion of Genet's next arrest, it was he who sent a letter to the presiding judge of the 19e cour correctionnelle, pleading for clemency and referring to the poet as "the greatest writer of our time"; and he was constantly insisting on the quality of Genet's genius to anyone who was prepared to listen—even if the listener belonged to the forces of the German Occupation:

A GERMAN OFFICER HEARS OF GENET

ERNST JÜNGER

Paris, 20 July 1943

Lunch with Florence [Gould]. Cocteau told us that he had been listening in court to the case against a young man charged with stealing books. One item in the haul had been a rare edition of Verlaine, and the magistrate had asked:

—Did you know the cost of that book?

To which the accused had replied:

—I had no idea of its cost, but I knew its value.

Further items included books by Cocteau himself, and another question followed:

—What would you say if someone were to filch a book that you had written?

—I should be very proud indeed!

From the *Diaries* of Ernst Jünger: *Strahlungen II*, in *Werke*, vol. III (Stuttgart, 1962), pp. 220–221. Translated by R.N.C.

As far as I can trace, this is the earliest reference to Genet in German. A variant of the same story will be found in *Poésie 43*, vol. 15, July-Sept. 1943, pp. 74–75, signed "P.S." [Ed.]

Cocteau himself does not appear to have actually published very much about Genet until the early fifties; from then onward, however, references abound. In particular, Cocteau returns again and again to the paradox that Genet, the apparent immoralist, is in reality the very opposite:

GENET THE MORALIST

JEAN COCTEAU

5 July 1946

. . . Jean Genet who, one of these days, will have to be thought of as a moralist, however paradoxical that may seem, since normally we confuse a moralist with a man who moralizes —Jean Genet, a few weeks ago, spoke the following haunting words to me: "It is not enough to watch our heroes live and to feel sorry for them. We must take their sins upon our own shoulders and bear with the consequences."

Who are my true heroes? Emotions. Abstract figures who are none the less alive for all that, and who are outrageously demanding. This is what I came to realize as I listened to Genet and as I grew aware of the extent to which his own soul had been ravaged by the crimes of the Egyptian Querelle. He knew that *he* was responsible, and thrust aside any excuses which might render him less so. He was prepared not so much to contemplate having to face the legal proceedings which might be taken against the audacities of his book, but rather to answer the charges which a higher justice would bring against his characters.[9]

The date which is given (1942) for the trial at which Cocteau entered a plea on Genet's behalf is probably wrong. All other sources suggest that this event took place in July 1943. [Ed.]:

9. "In order to make it clear to the tribunal who Genet was, when he was up before the Assises (1942), I declared that I considered him to be the greatest writer in France. I leave you to imagine the wild hilarity with which this statement was greeted in the press under the Occupation. But Parisian magistrates go in constant fear of repeating some immortal blunder—of sentencing another Baudelaire. I saved Genet. Nor do I withdraw a single word of my statement."

In that instant he suffused with a sudden brightness the dark, interminable lawsuit in whose toils I am caught. In a flash he explained to me why it is that I cannot find it in me to rebel against it. These charges brought against words, attitudes, and dreams—it is both right and proper that the writer should stand forth and answer them, and that he should himself appear in court, with a policeman at either hand. Totally false is the position of the writer who sets himself up as judge, who takes his seat among the magistrates presiding at his own trial, and who glances down pityingly upon the accused. A man must be either in the dock or on the bench. This is the very foundation of our commitment.

Had I not belonged to that race of men who are always in the dock, and who know no better than to mumble and stutter in their own defense, how ashamed I must have felt in the presence of Genet, as he entrusted me with the secret of his own torment. Besides, though, would he have entrusted me with it in the first place had he not recognized me long ago, spotted me at first glance, known me by those secret signs which enable outlaws to recognize each other? I had already watched Genet refusing to be introduced to a famous writer [Gide?] whose immorality seemed suspect to him. . . .

From Jean Cocteau, *La Difficulté d'Être* (Monaco: Editions du Rocher, 1953), pp. 242–245. Reprinted by permission. Translated by R.N.C.

See also: *Maalesh; Journal d'une tournée de théâtre* (Paris: Gallimard, 1949; trans. Mary C. Hoeck, London; Peter Owen, 1956, pp. 14–15); and various passages in the *Journal d'un Inconnu* (Paris: Grasset, 1953).

AT THE CAFÉ DE FLORE

SIMONE DE BEAUVOIR

Paris, Spring 1944

For some months we had been hearing about an unknown poet whom Cocteau had discovered in prison, and whom he maintained to be the greatest writer of his age. At any rate, this was how he had described him in July 1943, when composing a letter to the presiding magistrate of the police court in the nineteenth *arrondissement*, before whom the poet, one Jean Genet, was up for sentence, with nine previous convictions against him for theft already. Barbezat intended to publish some of his poems and an extract from a prose work in *L'Arbalète*, and his wife Olga—brunette Olga, that is—occasionally went to see him in prison. It was from her that I had learned of his existence, and discovered one or two facts concerning his life. He had been placed with foster parents, a peasant family, soon after birth. The larger part of his childhood he had spent in reformatories. His career as burglar and pickpocket had taken him all around the world, and he was, on top of all this, a homosexual. He had taken up reading in prison; this had led to his writing poems and, subsequently, a book. Olga Barbezat was ecstatic about his talent, but I was less impressed than I might have been in my youth. The gutter-Bohemian of genius seemed to me a somewhat stereotyped figure; and knowing Cocteau's taste for the offbeat, not to mention his passion for discovering people, I fancied he might be overboosting his protégé's claims. But when the first section of *Notre-Dame des Fleurs* appeared in *L'Arbalète*, we were very much impressed. Genet had obviously been influenced by Proust and Cocteau and Jouhandeau, but he nevertheless possessed a voice of his own, a quite inimitable style of utterance. It was a most uncommon occurrence nowadays for us to

---

From Simone de Beauvoir, *The Prime of Life*, trans. Peter Green (New York: World Publishing Co.; London: André Deutsch Ltd., 1962), pp. 579–581. Reprinted by permission.

read anything that renewed our faith in literature: these pages revealed the power of words to us as though for the first time. Cocteau had read the situation aright: a great writer *had* appeared.

We were told he was now out of prison; and one afternoon in May, when I was at the Flore with Sartre and Camus, he came over to our table. "You Sartre?" he inquired brusquely. With his close-cropped hair and thin, tight lips and suspicious, rather aggressive expression, he struck us as a pretty hard case. He sat down, but stayed only a moment. But he came back on other occasions, and we saw a good deal of each other. Hard he certainly was; an outcast from the day he was born, he had no reason to respect the society that had rejected him. But his eyes could still smile, and a child's astonishment lingered about his lips. Conversation with him was easy: he was a good listener, and quick to respond. One would never have guessed he was a self-taught person: he had the boldness of judgment, the sweeping prejudices, the unself-conscious attitude characteristic of those who take a cultured background completely for granted. He also possessed remarkable powers of discernment. His whole demeanor reminded one irresistibly of the Poet with a Mission; he affected to despise the elegant luxury of salon society, and castigated it for its snobbishness. But he did not keep up this pose for long, he was far too passionate and inquiring a person. His range of interests, nevertheless, was strictly circumscribed: he detested anecdotes and had no time for the merely picturesque. One evening we went up to the penthouse terrace of my hotel, and I showed him the view over the neighboring rooftops. "What the hell am I supposed to make of *that?*" he asked me testily, and went on to remark that he was far too busy with his own reactions to waste time on mere external spectacle.

In actual fact he was an excellent observer when he chose; if an object or person or event had some positive meaning for him, he would find the most appropriate and direct language in which to describe it. On the other hand, he was not uncritically receptive. There were certain truths he was after, and he would seek, even in the oddest byways, for any key that might unlock them. He conducted this quest in a spirit of sectarian fervor, yet also brought to it one of the keenest intelligences I have ever known. The paradoxical quality about him during this period was that though he ran to certain set attitudes, which camouflaged his true nature, he remained nevertheless wholly attached to freedom. The whole basis of his fellow feeling for Sartre was this idea of liberty they shared, which nothing could suppress, and their common abhorrence of all that stood in its way: nobility of soul, spiritual values, universal justice, and other such lofty words and principles, together with established institutions or ideals. In conversation, as in his writings, he was deliberately offhand, and asserted that he would never hesitate to rob or betray a friend; yet I never heard him speak ill of anyone, and he would not permit attacks on Cocteau in his presence. We took his personal behavior more seriously than his declarations of aggressiveness, and became very attached to him from the first moment of our acquaintanceship.

About the time we got to know Genet we conceived the idea of throwing another fiesta, to which I would have willingly invited him; but Sartre objected on the grounds that Genet wouldn't care for such an occasion. There was some truth in this. It suited middle-class people, solidly established in the world, to lose themselves for a few hours in a noisy alcoholic haze; Genet, on the other hand, had no taste for such dissipations. He had started off lost, and now preferred to feel solid earth beneath his feet. . . .

THIEF INTO POET . . . INTO DRAMATIST

EDWIN MORGAN

Genet's poetry, which belongs to the forties, is no doubt the least important part of his work, but it raises questions of considerable interest. There can be few writers more able to persuade us that "poetry," however we define it, may emerge through prose. Uneasy as we may be before the occasional overlush flowers (both real and figurative) he scatters in his novels, it is not the rhetoric of "prose poetry" as such that he is concerned with, but rather his own distinctive idea of a poetry that inheres in obsessional objects and situations and is released—like a vapor, a fragrance, an essence, a melody—only by the hand of the writer to whom the obsessions are necessary, for whom they are within the fabric of his personal legend. Hence in Genet the poetry of the prison cell, the handsome young thug, the sailor's trousers, the dust of Spain. There is, he says, only one criterion for judging the beauty of any such manifestation: "The song which it excites in me, and which I translate into words to communicate it to you—my lyricism."[10]

In his prose we have no difficulty in accepting the truth of this, but in his verse his touch is much less certain. Yet the verse has a continuity of themes with the prose: homosexual love, crime and punishment, apotheosis of the criminal. The same symbolic images are used (roses, jewels, angels, darkness, water, blue, masks, blood, iron). The same persons reappear—*The Condemned Man* and *Funeral March* are dedicated to Maurice Pilorge, *The Galley* to Harcamone, *A Love Song* and *The Fisherman of Le Suquet* to Lucien Sénemaud—all of whom are in the novels or in *The Thief's Journal*. But Genet's poetic models held back his development as a poet. They were mostly half a century out of date, and the regular rhyming stanzas he tended to use made it too hard for him to achieve any of the extraordinary combinations of lyricism and slang which characterize his novels. Sartre in his *Saint Genet* nippily calls him a "*voleur*" [thief] for his multiple echoes (from Coppée and Mallarmé to Baudelaire and Rimbaud), and argues that his main shortcoming as a poet is the lack of lucidity that goes with the hieratic use of poetic diction and a floundering among mixed metaphors which gradually cancel each other out.

10. *L'Enfant Criminel.*

There is truth in this, but it is not the whole story, as Sartre himself seems on the point of recognizing. Even in the early poems, which are the least surefooted, one finds passages that are far from negligible in the way they unroll the typical bold erotic *élan* of Genet:

We hadn't talked our love out yet.
We hadn't rolled our last fag yet.
Why do the courts hurry away
A killer who outshines the day?

Love come to my mouth! Love open your doors!
Come down, step lightly, cross the corridors,
nimbler than a shepherd whirl down the stair,
safer than a whirl of dead leaves in the air.

O pierce these walls: if you should need to, fight
by rooftops, oceans: fight disguised in light:
use menaces, pray on your knees and cry,
but O my frigate come, one hour before I die.[11]

And although there are plenty of piled-up romantic properties and gestures and stiff or faded phraseology ("*posez votre air d'apache,*" "*les yeux bleus d'un bel indifférent,*" "*ces flammes cruelles,*" "*tes pieds inhumains,*" "*quelque dur amant*"), there are also some impudently evocative stanzas that issue Genet's direct-languaged challenge to the reader's responses, as, in the following passage, the easy romance of the objects evoked is nicely dried off by the neoclassical snap of the rhymes with their provocatively apt collocations of ideas:

Les matins solennels, le rhum, la cigarette . . .
Les ombres du tabac, du bagne et des marins
Visitent ma cellule où me roule et m'étreint
Le spectre d'un tueur à la lourde braguette.[12]

---

11. From *The Condemned Man*, translated by Edwin Morgan.
12. From *The Condemned Man*.

One significant fact which emerges from all the poems is that they are less pornographic than the prose. This, far from being in their favor, seems to point to an inhibition, and the inhibition must be related to Genet's conception of verse-writing and what could and could not be done with it. Only *The Condemned Man* has much that is explicitly pornographic, and the material comes across with a heavy hand and at times topples over into the ludicrous. After that early experiment, Genet seems to have felt that the rather bediamonded and sonorous poetic language he most wanted to use, and the indulgently sprawling symbolism which in his poems he was never able to harden into a structural device, were incompatible with sexual realism, and although the poems are (obviously) of sexual import, his later methods are less brandishing. The occasional mild shock tactics (rhyming "main bleue" with "queue," or "étrangleur" with "fleurs") are throwaways, and not much more than tics of style.

What is more interesting, in the last and by far the best poem in the series, *The Fisherman of Le Suquet*, is Genet's decision to make the still reasonably outspoken homosexual drive of the work secondary to a more universally appreciable, almost shy and sad, quasi-pastoral love narrative that escapes momentarily from the mesh of the criminal underworld. He tells us, in *The Thief's Journal*, "with what tenderness I love my little fisherman from *Le Suquet*" and how "the more I love Lucien the more my taste for theft and thieves recedes." Without weakening into complete decriminalization, Genet allows human regret and a human awareness of change to open up his eroticism, and with it the too rigid idea of the poem he had held till then. *The Fisherman of Le Suquet* is no longer afraid to seem "modern": it uses prose and vers libre as well as meter and rhyme, dramatic dialogue as well as monologue. The gain in interest and immediacy is striking. If Genet had not turned to drama, the signs are that he might have made something of his poetry. But who can deny the rightness of his move toward the "embodied poetry" of *Deathwatch* and *The Blacks?*

TO THE PRESIDENT OF THE REPUBLIC

Jean Cocteau has taken the initiative in addressing an appeal to the President of the Republic, begging him to grant a free pardon to Jean Genet, who, in consequence of his latest sentence, has incurred the penalty of perpetual preventive detention.

The editors of the Literary Page of Combat *wish to associate themselves with Jean Cocteau and Jean-Paul Sartre in making this approach.*

Monsieur le Président.[13]

We are resolved to appeal to your supreme authority, begging you to intervene most exceptionally in the case of a writer whom we all admire and whom we all respect: Jean Genet. We are well aware that his work lies beyond the range of conventional literature, and should not be put into the hands of all and sundry. But the examples of Villon and Verlaine have determined us to implore your clemency on behalf of a very great poet.

Over and above this we have learned—for all that Jean Genet himself has not mentioned the fact—that his latest, definitive sentence was pronounced as the result of his having taken upon himself a crime committed by Jean de Carnin, who died on the barricades during the Liberation, in order that the name of Jean de Carnin should live unsullied in our memories.

For this we cannot but esteem him the more highly; and we are thereby the more encouraged in our appeal.

The whole of Jean Genet's literary career is serving to wrench him away from a past whose faults were flagrant; a definitive condemnation would plunge him right back into the depths of that evil from which his writings have managed at long last to redeem him.

---

13. The President of the French Republic at this date was M. Vincent Auriol, and the free pardon was granted. [Ed.]

From *Combat*, 16 July 1948, p. 4. Translated by R.N.C.

We implore you, M. le Président, to reach a rapid decision, and thus to rescue a man whose life henceforward is destined to be wholly devoted to his work.

We beg to assure you, M. le Président, of our deepest gratitude and of our profoundest respect.

JEAN COCTEAU
JEAN-PAUL SARTRE

The Plays and the Critics

The Maids

Les Bonnes was presented for the first time at the Théâtre de l' Athénée (Théâtre Louis Jouvet) in Paris on 19 April 1947, in the same program as Giraudoux' L'Apollon de Marsac.

More or less simultaneously, the text of the original version was published in the review L'Arbalète (no. 12, May 1947, pp. 47–92).

The cast included Yvette Etiévant (Claire), Monique Mélinand (Solange), Yolande Laffon (Madame). Production by Louis Jouvet, décor by Christian Bérard. The play ran for about eighty performances. The maids were played as adolescent girls, and the action was set in 1900. When Les Bonnes was revived in a different version in 1954, the setting was contemporary, and the maids were played as middle-aged women.

The following preproduction announcement is the earliest introduction to Genet as a dramatist that I have been able to discover in the popular press:

THE UP-AND-COMING DRAMATIST

"M.D."

We have survived the Jean-Paul Sartre season.

We have survived the invasion from the stables of Monsieur Duhamel.

I have to announce that, shortly, there will be a further revelation.

Stronger meat than ever.

Monsieur J.-P. Sartre: white-hot existentialism—that passing fashion, that ephemeral philosophy.

From *Le Grelot* (Paris), 8 April 1947. Translated by R.N.C.

Finished, forgotten, dead-and-done-with.

Duhamel and his Americans: old-hat naturalism, sired by the *Théâtre Libre* after touring the slums of Brooklyn, Chicago, and San Francisco.

But now . . . the quintessence, the ultimate distillation, the up-and-coming writer, the man whose name is on everybody's lips, the Revelation simmering in the saucepan.

Never before performed, but published . . . published in a deluxe edition.

As for his prose, we have already had specimens in *Les Temps Modernes*.

A writer not to be put into the hands of all and sundry.

A writer whose own hands, however, tend to stray here, there, and everywhere.

A writer to be watched.

Especially if you invite him into your house.

In a word . . . Monsieur Jean Genet, lately of La Santé, Fresnes, and other desirable residences which are sure springboards to fame and fortune.

François Villon—precursor—finished up on the gallows.

Jean Genet—profiteer—is likely to finish up in an Academy.

Monsieur Jean Genet has had illustrious sponsors: MM. André Gide, Jean Cocteau.

It should be added that Monsieur Jean Genet is a homosexual.

Monsieur Louis Jouvet, ever on the watch for the latest fashion, is rehearsing his coming play.

Monsieur J.-L. Barrault, our most notable producer of the commercial avant-garde, has first option on another.

Obviously, there is one snag. Monsieur Jean Genet, recipient of numerous sentences, thief, stool pigeon (on his own admission), is ineligible for the *Société des Auteurs*.[1]

But that can be fixed.

In a word, Monsieur Genet, professional burglar, proposes to turn an honest penny; he intends to join the ranks of the

1. An institution which watches over authors' royalties. [Ed.]

honest rate-payers, give interviews, sip tea with fashionable hostesses without snitching the spoons.

Apotheosis or downfall?

Wait and see.

What was Jean Genet? An unsmirched virgin of impurity? Or a racketeer in the reekiest of rackets? The future will decide.

Or could it be that he is just a dramatist? Nothing more, nothing less . . . ?

"M.D." followed up this "introduction" with one of the earliest reviews of the play:

REVIEW OF THE MAIDS *(1947)*

"M.D."

I have already introduced Monsieur Jean Genet to my readers. Only one question remained unsettled—was he a writer? Answer: No. Not even a gutter poet.

Monsieur Genet is making a bad mistake by swapping trades. I would suggest an immediate burglary at Jouvet's private residence, just to teach him to stop taking the mickey out of the general public. And after that, let Monsieur Genet return to his original vocation.

Jean Genet might have written *Fric-Frac;* however, a professional dramatist, who happens also to be an honest man in the most bourgeois sense of the term, got in first with the idea.

The Maids will probably get Monsieur Genet into hot water with the National Union of Domestic Employees. The whole business is a matter for discussion between house servants and cat burglars; it lies outside the competence of the ordinary dramatic critic, it has nothing to do with theater.

From *Le Grelot,* 22 April 1947. Translated by R.N.C.

Two young actresses, each in a thoroughly ungrateful part, reveal an impressive mastery of technique and many promising qualities—Mlles Mélinand and Etiévant. The latter has the further advantage of being decidedly attractive. Mlle Yolande Laffon speaks her lines in imitation of Jouvet, doubtless inspired thereto by the Master himself, who produced the whole caboodle. The outcome leaves no room for argument: it is *bad*.

The décor is exquisite. Or horrific. The choice is yours. Horribly thrilling or exquisitely horrible. It is signed by that fashionable scene painter, Christian Bérard, the most lionized among the brotherhood of the ill-washed, the most woolly-bearded among the Honorable Confraternity of Queers.

In short, a typically Parisian personality.

In the audience, on the first night, we observed, among those who had come to applaud Genet's first venture, Marcel Carné and spouse, together with a number of other connoisseurs. An audience of queers counts double.

Jean Cocteau sent his apologies.

In bed with boils, probably. . . .

Early reviewers of Les Bonnes *included J.-J. Gautier in* Le Figaro *(20/21 Apr. 1947: "impressive"); André Ransan in* Ce Matin *(22 Apr.: "excellent"); "E.H." in* Le Parisien Libéré *(22 Apr.: "disgusting"); Philippe Hériat in* La Bataille *(23 Apr.: "boring"); G. Joly in* L'Aurore *(24 Apr.: "densely tragic"); Jacques Lemarchand in* Combat *(24 Apr.: "brilliant"); Georges Huisman in* La France Hebdomadère *(24 Apr.: "masochistic"); Roger Lannes in* Le Figaro Littéraire *(26 Apr.: "sordid melodrama"); Maxime Belliard in* La France Libre *(27/28 Apr.: "unhealthy"); René Lalou in* Gavroche *(1 May: "corrupt and corrupting"); "R.K." in* La Gazette des Lettres *(3 May: "good"); Hervé Lauwick in* Noir et Blanc *(4 May: "absurd verbal hysteria").*

The three reviews which follow represent the most serious assessments by well-known critics and writers:

CRIME IS SUPPOSED TO BE SILENT

ROBERT KEMP

Sganarelle used to complain about Don Juan; Figaro used to wonder how many masters would have enough intelligence to make good servants; while, speaking from the other side of the barricades, Boileau summarized the whole problem in one-and-a-half (very bad) alexandrines:

> *. . . souvent voleurs ou traîtres,*
> *Et toujours à coup sûr ennemis de leurs maîtres.*

Moreover, there are maids and maids. Both in the naturalist novel and in the slice-of-life theater. A whole thesis could be written on the subject. Yet I can recall nothing quite so unreal, quite so hysterical, as M. Jean Genet's *The Maids*. I am aware that, here and there, people will applaud them. In the existentialist camp, for instance, where eloquence is fashionable. Or among the proselytes of a "dynamic" theater—so-called—which flies with a battering ram against gates which are already wide open. Of course, the social status of immature female domestics is one which may well awaken our sympathies—yesterday, perhaps, rather than today, since today the "servant problem" is one in which the servants, not the masters, invent the rules of the game—and well deserves serious dramatic treatment; but it were better handled in the manner of Flaubert or of Maupassant, of Henri Monnier or of Courteline, or more seriously still, in that of Le Play. . . . *Not* in terms of a sequence of surrealist hallucinations. One must draw the line somewhere.

The maids in question, a pair of adolescent sisters, Claire and Solange, spend their time waiting for their mistress to go

---

From *Une Semaine dans le Monde*, 26 April 1947. Translated by R.N.C.

out, whereupon they try on her dresses, ape her manners, invent conversations between mistress and maid . . . and get drunk on language. What floods of eloquence pour forth from those childish lips! I wonder what they have been reading? Charles Mérouvel? Céline? Sartre? . . . all higgledy-piggledy. But the mixture goes to their heads. Already their games have led them into crime. They have contrived an anonymous letter denouncing their mistress' lover to the police. But now things are going wrong. Monsieur rings up, to say that he has just been let out of jail. Madame, hawk-eyed, spots signs of the crazy play-acting that has been going on while she was out. The two accomplices lose their heads, hurl insults at each other. One half-strangles her sister; the sister, half-strangled, recovers sufficiently to gulp down the cup of lime-tea-and-gardenal which she herself had brewed in order to poison her mistress. . . .

Crime is supposed to be silent. But here it can scarcely get by without a positive brass band of high-flown literary language. Artistically speaking, this is pure *grand-guignol* stuff. Not for a single instant did I feel that tormented atmosphere, nor the impact of that dramatic intensity, which I had been promised. My skepticism remains as it was, undiminished. Tinged, however, toward the end, with boredom and exhaustion.

DARK INTIMATIONS OF ANOTHER WORLD

THIERRY MAULNIER

. . . Jean Genet's *The Maids* has been, and will continue to be, received by the audience with what are known as "diverse reactions." Some think the play "boring"; others see it as a brilliant literary exercise; while still others are all but exasperated by the almost unbearable atmosphere of *malaise* which is deliberately sought and provoked in the audience by the author

From *Le Spectateur*, 29 April 1947. Translated by R.N.C.

of this astonishing tragedy of servitude. I am quite well aware that henceforward anyone who speaks highly of Jean Genet is liable to appear merely to be embracing the latest whim of snobbery; and that a writer whose past happens to include a number of prison sentences has no greater right to serious critical consideration than does one whose career has been that of an honest citizen and paterfamilias. I am further fully conscious of the fact that the stir created by Jean Genet's "scandalous" novels, published in limited editions, was not entirely due to their sheer literary quality. None the less, *and all allowances made*, this literary quality is quite outstanding; and it is, of course, still perfectly legitimate to regret that *The Maids* was not written by some highly respected citizen, honest, law-abiding, the apple of the Internal Revenue's watchful eye. Be that as it may, however, the fact remains that *The Maids* is a play that reveals a genuinely original dramatist, of unquestioned mastery, and perhaps also gives us a glimpse of a new dramatic style.

It is no small achievement to have created what one can only call tragic grandeur out of elements which, in the context of our present society, might appear to be as sordid, as mediocre, and as downtrodden as possible. Nor is it any meaner achievement, on the part of an author who has deliberately chosen to weave his play about two criminally intentioned servants, to have rejected all the facile temptations of melodramatic social protest. I was unable to detect anywhere in Jean Genet's play the least hint of social commitment; and yet his drama remains a positively atrocious indictment of modern society. And this very atrocity—however vaguely it may be felt—is perhaps not without influence in inspiring that *malaise* which disturbs certain well-dressed ladies in the audience . . . ladies who, themselves, have "maids." Jean Genet's play puts a finger straight on the sore spots of our social guilt complexes. [. . .] What the audience finds so disconcerting in a play of this kind is, first and foremost, the intimation that it brings them, the dark intimation of another world which it understands no more than Madame understands Claire and Solange. "But it's just not *true*," commented one of the well-dressed ladies leaving the theater, "my maids *adore* me." Plainly, this lady had not the slightest suspicion that her words might have been spoken by Madame. A further element which disconcerts the audience, moreover, is that Jean Genet has deliberately used a style that is the diametrical opposite of realism. His maids, unquestionably, do *not* talk like real maids; but why should they talk like "real" maids, when here at hand we have precisely a poet who can transmute into clear and memorable language those feelings of which "real" maids are no more than obscurely aware, experiencing them only as hot wafts of love or hate exhaled from the abysses of the subconscious? It is this transposition, this sudden "gift of tongues" loaned unexpectedly to the eternally tongue-tied, which constitutes the essential style of the play. . . .

THE TRUE ROOTS OF THE SCANDAL

JEAN TARDIEU

[The audience was enthusiastic in its praise for Giraudoux' "Apollon de Marsac."] Why, I wonder, if not the better to signify by contrast the indignation that choked it at having to sit through the previous play, Jean Genet's *The Maids*, whose loquaciousness, strikingly different from Giraudoux', is at its happiest exploring the most disturbing and debased realms of experience.

Now, I would gladly sympathize in this with the average member of the audience, were I not all too well aware what depths of hypocrisy lie hidden beneath this virtuous disapproval. At all events, *The Maids* is a worrying play, and one is entitled

---

From *Action*, 2 May 1947. Reprinted by permission. Translated by R.N.C.

to ask where the true roots of the scandal are to be found. In the basic fact of having tackled such a subject? Or in the fact of having treated it in this particular manner? So much for the author's contribution. As for the audience, again one asks, wherein lies the scandal? In applauding the play? Or in *not* applauding it?

Is there not something admirable, and even useful, in choosing precisely such scabrous subjects—subjects which normally cause all well-bred and right-thinking people to cast down their eyes in a fit of cowardice? Genet has set his action in the year 1900, which makes it possible for him to exaggerate the characteristics of his nightmare creatures; and yet, for all that, even in the transitional society in which we live, maids still exist and, despite certain mitigating circumstances, this type of social oppression exists unquestionably as a fact, and may well induce in certain weak-minded victims complexes similar to those which we observe in the heroines of the play.

Having said this, however, the fact remains that, from a purely human point of view, the theme is treated most unrealistically, and that this conscious and deliberate distortion is, in itself, a singularly unpleasant phenomenon.

Indeed, this ancillary tragedy has been accused of being "unhealthy"; and I agree that nothing is more repulsive than the repressed atmosphere in which Claire and Solange evolve as soon as Madame leaves the house and they are able to return to their habitual "ceremony" [. . .]. Doubtless the evocation of the nauseating smells of the kitchen sink, intermingled with the cloying perfumes of a boudoir in the 1900's, the curious mixture of pure hatred and unbalanced admiration which the maids feel toward their mistress, crimes-of-violence and prison-with-forced-labor considered as patents of nobility, as the only conceivable means of escape from this ultimate degradation, the contemptuous "kindness" of Madame, who is in fact nothing but a kind of expensive whore and whose elegant "husband" is a burglar, the scene, finally, where Solange pushes the "ceremony" to its logical conclusion by giving Claire—

who willingly consents to the "game"—the cup of poisoned tea which, together, they had prepared for Madame: all this, taken together, constitutes an experience which is literally nauseating. On the other hand, this atmosphere of repression, which has its roots in a social fallacy, this repression, together with everything that it implies in terms of semimania, submarine lighting, hellish waking nightmares, and noxious exhalations—this *is* the subject of the play; and given such a subject, a running social sore, would it have been right to describe it in pale pastel-colored language?

As I was suggesting earlier, in *The Maids* all the dramatic action lies in the use of language; and indeed, it is language used with its full force of hypnotic persuasion, since it leads on inexorably to an Act—the poisoning—which is at once a reality and a symbol. This kind of dialogue-litany, always in the minor key, transforms a plain and commonplace news item into a species of tragedy, and it is difficult to deny the beauty, admittedly high-flown and slightly artificial, of the dramatist's style, despite the fact that some of the scenes seem to drag and come dangerously close to boring the spectator. . . .

In spite of the interest awakened by the initial production of Les Bonnes, *followed by that of* Deathwatch *in 1949, it was the revival at the Théâtre de la Huchette on 13 January 1954 which established Genet's reputation as a dramatist, not only in France, but on an international scale. In this production,* Les Bonnes, *produced by Tania Balachova, shared a double bill with* La Matinée d'un homme de lettres, *a drama adapted from three short stories by Chekhov. Tania Balachova herself played the part of Solange; Alberte Taillade, that of Madame; while that of Claire was to alternate between Tatiana Moukhine and Anne Reinerg. According to the chronicler of* Libération *(12 Jan. 1954), Mlle Reinerg was so annoyed at this arrangement that she attempted to commit suicide on the evening of the dress rehearsal.*

In this production, a revised version of the text was used, and the two versions were published side by side by J.-J. Pauvert. What is not clear is whether the "revised version" was in fact the original text as written by Genet which, in 1947, had been modified by Louis Jouvet for his production; or whether both original and Jouvet-modified versions had been discarded, and the "revised version" was in fact a third rewriting of the same play.[2]

It was this performance which occasioned one of the earliest American reviews of the play:

REVIEW OF THE MAIDS *(1954)*

THOMAS QUINN CURTIS

Jean Genet is the strangest and perhaps the most compelling figure to have appeared on the French literary scene during the past decade. Jean Cocteau has christened him "The Black Prince of French Letters," and Jean-Paul Sartre has devoted a whole book to a study of his works.

Genet is the poet of the lower depths. A Gorky without the Russian's belief in social reform, he is a philosophic anarchist. He knows the Paris underworld and the inside of jails from personal experience, having served some long sentences for theft as a young man. As an adolescent, his heroes were the great law-breakers, and he is proud of his acquaintance with Maurice Pilorge, who was beheaded at Saint Brieuc for a sordid murder in the late thirties [. . .].[3]

---

2. See Jacqueline Michel in *Le Parisien Libéré*, 7 January 1954. [Ed.]

3. Genet refers frequently to Maurice Pilorge, but whether he ever knew him in fact is open to doubt. He mentions the date of Pilorge's execution as one of the fateful dates in his life; but (as Philip Thody points out in his *Jean Genet: A Critical Appraisal*, p. 11) he consistently gets that date wrong by some six weeks! [Ed.]

Thomas Quinn Curtis, in *New York Herald Tribune*, 18 January 1954.

The chilly terror evoked by *The Maids* is the terror, not of the *grand-guignol* horror play, but of something grander. It crackles with a satanic fury as the flame of true drama rises. A more experienced playwright might have made it a perfect specimen of construction, an exercise in suspense technique, but conventional technique is of little interest to Genet. Its dialogue is often repetitious, and the squeamish may take offense at its brazen language, but Genet gives here to an ignoble tale a touch of genuine tragedy.

Three further productions of The Maids *deserve special attention.*

In May 1961, while Jean-Louis Barrault was on tour, he "lent" the state-subsidized Odéon–Théâtre de France to Jean-Marie Serreau for a season of contemporary plays. Ionesco and Beckett had already received the consecrating honor of a production at the Odéon: now Genet was to join them. Les Bonnes appeared in a double bill with Ionesco's Amédée ou comment s'en débarrasser: production by Jean-Marie Serreau, costumes and décor by Léonor Fini; with Tatiana Moukhine once more as Claire, Reine Courtois as Solange, and Yvonne Clech as Madame. In the almost unanimous view of the critics, this was a well-nigh perfect production of the play, against which all subsequent productions are to be measured.

Later producers, faced with a play which was recognized as a "modern classic," have tended to seek for off-beat variants in order to establish their originality. The first of these was a catastrophic but fascinating failure, the more so in that it was produced by the same Jean-Marie Serreau who had triumphed at the Odéon.

In September 1963, Serreau produced the play at the Théâtre de l'Oeuvre with an entirely Negro cast (Danielle Van Bercheycke as Claire, Toto Bissainthe as Solange, and Moréna

Casamance as Madame). The reasons for the failure of this experiment were best analyzed by Gilles Sandier:

REVIEW OF THE MAIDS (1963)

GILLES SANDIER

. . . in 1961, Jean-Marie Serreau gave us a production of *The Maids* which, together with the original production by Jouvet in 1947 and the revival by Tania Balachova in 1954, will be remembered as one of the most significant dates in the history of a play which, in my opinion, together with Ionesco's *The Chairs* and Beckett's *Godot*, stands out as one of the three most representative works, one of the three essential dates in the contemporary theater.

[. . .] But now Serreau's mistake appears to have been to have tried to squeeze *The Blacks* inside the framework of *The Maids*. In casting Negro actresses for the parts in the play, he has committed a disastrous pleonasm: Claire and Solange become social outcasts on two scores simultaneously—both as "maids" and as "blacks." With the result that, paradoxically, the play collapses into a sort of smug and facile realism which is diametrically opposed to the true dramatic mood of the work—a work which, in Genet's original conception, was intended so sharply to emphasize the "fakeness and artificiality" of any theatrical performance that he even urged the parts be played by young men dressed up as women, the better to increase the effect of distanciation. And it is precisely this distanciation which is annihilated by the fact that the actresses are Negro. . . .

Jean Genet's recommendation that Claire and Solange be played by male actors was in fact taken up in the third of these

---

From Sandier, "Jean-Marie Serreau ou le Démon de l'invention," in *Arts*, no. 928 (18–24 September 1963), p.7. Translated by R.N.C.

notable productions of the early sixties. In October 1964, The Maids *was given at the La Mama Experimental Theatre Club, New York, in a production by Tom O'Horgan, with Steve Ghare as Claire, R. Clay Haney as Solange, and Tilla Petra as Madame:*

THE MAIDS *PERFORMED BY MEN*

SYDNEY S. WALTER

. . . The play has always seemed to me tedious and overlong, and with the roles of the maids played by women, I think a production must inevitably grow boring. Initially, it is fascinating to watch Genet's sleight-of-hand as he illuminates the situation by having the maids adopt roles within the world of the play. Long before the playwright's lengthy speeches have all been delivered, though, even the most superb actresses must have squeezed all the dramatic juices from the device of having Solange play Claire and Claire play Madame.

Performed by women the play offers two levels of insight into a situation; we see the situation alternately as Solange and Claire see it, and then as Solange and Claire think Claire and Madame see it. Performed by men the play becomes an intriguing, if bewildering, dissection of reality. Performed by women the basic reality is one of two maids who, in the safety of Madame's absence, play out a fantasy. Performed by men the basic reality is one of two transvestites who, in the safety of a theatrical convention, play out a fantasy within a fantasy.

More is involved here than simply introducing another level of reality, for if the audience can believe that the actors are really transvestites who are using this theater and this audience to achieve a status which society denies them, then both theatrical conventions and the security of the audience will be profoundly disturbed.

The play on the level of maids impersonating their mistress

From *The Village Voice*, 29 October 1964. Reprinted by permission.

says that society, in relegating certain of its members to a lowly status, excludes these unfortunate ones from participation in the emotional experiences of love and charity, experiences taken for granted by society's favored ones. "Filth can't love filth." The maids' fantasy is a struggle to enjoy the emotional responses which they envy Madame. By extension, the play on the level of transvestites impersonating women shows an audience two men trying to achieve certain emotional experiences in the permissive convention of a theatrical production.

An irony is introduced when we realize that the audience, whose approval is necessary if the fantasy is to generate a valid experience, is representative of that society which has disinherited the men. If these men are really transvestites, then the audience is being tricked into fulfilling those whom it has denied by participating in the fantasy. Disturbing.

All this, and ramifications too devious to explore here, is suggested simply by having men play the roles of the maids. To develop these ideas, though, requires a director and actors of great skill and understanding. For example, there is certainly a place for conventional, indicative acting within the play. There is no reason why roles once and twice removed from reality must be believably acted. Somewhere, however, we must catch glimpses of the real agony of the unfulfilled transvestites. Without this the phoniness of the role-playing is not the comment it might be, but only a demonstration of inadequate skill. . . .

The success of the set also depended on members of the audience being able to believe that they were being used to fulfill socially thwarted men. A bed made of a board over two stools and garish but flimsy set pieces could have worked if the audience had seen the men trying to make inadequate materials serve their fantasy. We should have seen transvestites transforming whatever they used into ritualistic devices, not actors asking us to suspend our disbelief in makeshift props. The difference is implicit in the level of reality on which the production is based. If we are to see the actors as real transvestites, then the production must show us glimpses of their dissatisfaction with their shabby set. We must see the properties being transformed in order to understand the ritual aspect of the play. In order to see this we must see the properties before their transformation, or at moments when they revert to clumsy constructions.

Why was Madame played by a woman? Genet wrote, "If I were to have a play put on, in which women had roles, I would demand that these roles be performed by adolescent boys. . . ." Although Tilla Petra turned in the best performance of the evening, her presence on stage was ultimately confusing. Was the actress an accomplice in the ritual? Did Madame think her maids were really women?

Tom O'Horgan should be commended for using Genet's suggestion. Unfortunately, the lack of a clear directorial viewpoint made the evening a camp instead of an illumination.

The most striking of all early interpretative analyses of The Maids *was that given by Jean-Paul Sartre in Appendix III of his* Saint-Genet comédien et martyr.[4] *When the play was published in America,*[5] *this Appendix, in a slightly modified form, was used as an introduction to the volume; with the result that from the first American critics, much more than their French or English counterparts, have tended to consider the play in terms of Sartrean existentialism:*

SARTRE AND GENET

ROBERT CHAMPIGNY

Sartre's introduction is an adaptation of Appendix III in *Saint-Genet comédien et martyr*, a voluminous and somewhat

4. *Œuvres Complètes de Jean Genet*, I (Paris: Gallimard, 1952), pp. 561–573. This brilliant essay is too well known to be included in the present *Casebook*. [Ed.]

5. *The Maids and Deathwatch: Two Plays*, with an Introduction by Jean-Paul Sartre, trans. Bernard Frechtman (New York: Grove Press, 1954). [Ed.]

From *Accent*, Summer 1954, pp. 222–224.

indigestible existential analysis of Genet. Without the context of this book, a few remarks in the introduction remain enigmatic. For example, the *rapprochement* between the criminal and the saint and, in the last lines, the metamorphosis of being and nothingness into Good and Evil.

This passage from an ontological to an ethical vocabulary has been the main concern of Sartre since *L'Etre et le néant*. It was already conspicuous in *Les Mouches*. In *Le Diable et le bon Dieu* and in *Saint-Genet comédien et martyr*, Sartre expatiates on the same theme.

Being and nothingness are two limiting concepts. Sartrean consciousness is ambiguously both. The main precept of Sartrean ethics is to assume this ambiguity. Otherwise, one forsakes the human condition. The morals of authority and passivity propose a set of stereotyped conducts. Value is reduced to abstract or concrete being. What is is good. In a social context, the assimilation between Good and Being is effected by the conservative elements, that is, in so far as French society is concerned, the bourgeois class.

Nonbeing, for Sartre, is active: it is the power of negation. It is because we are not, at the same time that we are (something), that we can enter the realm of value: value should be, thus is not. But in a society in which the Good has been identified with actual conditions by the dominant class, nonbeing appears purely destructive (instead of permitting creation) and is thus identified with evil (the devil in *Le Diable et le bon Dieu*). Not only this, but nonbeing is shorn of most of its destructive power and is permitted to manifest itself only in marginal, ineffectual activities.

Human existence is cut in two. The bourgeois embodies being, hence the good. In the margin of his conservative society, certain scapegoats are entrusted with "incarnating" nonbeing, that is, evil. Such safety valves are the Christianity of the saint (in opposition to the Christendom of the pharisee), the irony of the aesthete (see the romantic and surrealist futile criticism of the bourgeois), certain types of criminality.

According to Sartre, this regrettable parallelism reflects a radical split between being and nonbeing and an identification of the Good with being. Sartre's Baudelaire, an aesthete and would-be mystic, entitles his poems *Les Fleurs du mal* because he accepts the bourgeois definition of the Good, hence his own activity as manifesting the unreal *and* evil. Sartre finds in Genet an even better example. In the latter's works, there is a perpetual shift between the aesthete, the criminal, and the mystic (or saint), a shift which is half-ironical (Genet knows what he is doing: he is a *comédien*) and half-serious (he is nailed to the condition which society has imposed on him when he was a child: he is a *martyr*).

Thus the main theme in Genet's work, particularly in *The Maids* and *Deathwatch*, is alienation. The man who is integrated in a society may sleepily believe that he finds there a justification of his existence. He finds reality in his role, he coincides with his role; his existence is realized, redeemed in routine activities. But the man who has been given *and* who has accepted a marginal role is deprived of this easy justification. His incarnation remains gratuitous, absurd; he remains in the situation which Sartre has described in *Nausea*.

This is the meaning of the obscenity which, in Genet's works, is not intended to titillate the "normal" reader, but to nauseate him. For the obscene is the concrete manifestation of the absurd, of the gratuitous. The *body* justifies us, realizes us, for the body is active. *Flesh* permits only exhibitionism. Genet's homosexuality is likewise linked by Sartre to social conditions. Genet has spent most of his life in prison and the living conditions in prison tally nicely with the fact that bourgeois ethics frown on homosexuality.

When contingent existence cannot find a realization, when flesh cannot be justified, assumed and effaced by action, we are dealing with alienation. Genet's homosexuals play at being what they are not: "normal" men and women. In *Deathwatch*, the imprisoned criminals try to form a society; but the society of criminals is counterfeit; it is a revealing reflection of the "normal" society from which it draws its meaning and its very substance. In *The Maids*, the two maids (whom Genet wanted to be played by male actors) exist, in their *own* eyes, only with reference to their bourgeois mistress. In order to see themselves as they have agreed to be, in order to realize themselves, one of them has to play the role of the mistress when the latter is out. At the end, the maid who plays this role kills herself, thus trying at last to establish a reciprocity in the master-slave relationship. She is the saint, but an inverted saint, an inverted martyr: she kills herself in order to annihilate her god.

Now and then, anyone may experience alienation. In pain, the body ceases to be a tool to become a stranger; the body becomes gratuitous, unjustifiable flesh. The potency of the Christian myth comes from the fact that it promises a justification even for raw incarnation, even for the scandal of suffering. Sartre has stressed, and overstressed, the alienation which the glance of another person may suffice to produce. In *Huis Clos*, the three characters, who are in "hell," would need new actions to justify their past. But they are dead, have no future, and they try to make each other the judge, to make the other justify their existence. The structure and atmosphere of *Huis Clos* are strikingly, and even suspiciously, similar to those of Genet's plays.

What is generally a transient experience is an obsession with Genet's characters. They are alienated, possessed by the other. Unlike the well-adjusted man of magazine psychologists, they know it. Unlike the man who tries to assume his existence, not only do they know it, but they remain fascinated by this alienation: they play the alienated beings that they are.

There is no salvation for Genet's characters, but Genet himself takes advantage of the perdition of his characters: since he is an artist. He finds a justification, a realization, he appropriates his alienated past by making words what was flesh, what could not be body. The central implicit symbol in his works is the rose on the dunghill, in the center of the cross. But Genet's aesthetic salvation cannot make us quite forget that for even more unlucky people, there is no such rose. Genet's work is an emetic. Let it not be an opiate.

Genet has written poems, but it seems that in this respect,

Cocteau's teaching has not yielded remarkable results. Genet's particular brand of "poetry" finds a better field of expression in his novels. These novels, which are in fact hagiographies in the ambiguous meaning of the word (sacred-devilish, pure-obscene), are unfortunately as tiresome as Henry Miller's exhibitions, even though Genet's vision and talent are far more rich and potent than Miller's. Among Genet's works, my preference would thus go to these two plays, or rather to *The Maids,* for *Deathwatch* is but a rough copy of *The Maids.* The task of writing a play has made Genet strive toward a terseness and an intensity from which his art, essentially the art of the conjurer, benefits greatly.

The English translation, through no fault of the translator, stresses what may appear a flaw: the juxtaposition of conventional slang and sophisticated psychological analysis. This makes Genet's characters unlikely, especially in the second play: one of them, in particular, is very literate about his illiteracy. But then Genet himself is an unlikely character; his works are self-portraits (which may or may not detract from the value of his plays). Bourgeois aesthetics are based on likelihood. It is fitting that Genet's aesthetics should be based on unlikelihood, should be anticlassic rather than affirmatively romantic. Unlikelihood may be a revealing reflection of what passes for likelihood, in the same way that evil may be a revealing reflection of what passes for good.

ECSTASY THROUGH COMPULSION

LAWRENCE LEIGHTON

. . . Starting from Genet's wish that the sisters in *The Maids* should be played by male actors, Sartre finds in the play an elaborate counterpoint of appearance which aims at the annihila-

From *Kenyon Review* (Autumn 1955), pp. 639–642. Reprinted by permission.

tion of reality. The "let's pretend" ritual, which is not apparent to the spectator as pretense until some time after the play starts, establishes characters who are only projections of the consciousness of others and yet are trying to become those others. As Sartre sees it, "appearance is revealed at the same time as pure nothingness and as cause of itself. And being, without ceasing to set itself up as absolute reality, becomes evanescent."

This Pirandello-like kaleidoscope may be Genet's intention or Sartre's ingenuity. The ordinary reader is more likely to be impressed by Genet's preoccupied sensitiveness to domination and submission in human relations, the creation of the pecking order in the human hen coop. It is this preoccupation which supplies the nerves for whatever dramatic strength these plays possess. If that strength is weak, it comes from the fact that out of the viciousness of his life Genet can distill only a lyrical contemplation. He has abjured conflict.

Genet has written nothing since the *Journal* seven years ago and the furor and the prestige have died down which caused Cocteau, Claudel, Sartre, and Gide to petition the President of the French Republic to save him from life imprisonment following his tenth conviction for theft. He has been compared with Villon and Rimbaud, but such comparisons are biographical and extraliterary. The equation which has been made with Sade is more serious, but equally false. Sade attempted to objectify his fantasies and failed even to suggest actual experience. Genet's writing comes from what he has known and done. The hatred of the maids for their mistress comes from his own experience as a servant and from his animosity toward people who want to do him good. His feeling about the prisoners of *Deathwatch* resembles Hemingway's about bullfighters and boxers.

Actually, if literary affiliation is demanded, it is most easily sought with Céline. The inversion of values which was inherent in the older man's writing became patent in his later life. Céline subjects us to his filth and degradation, rubs our faces in it, with a compulsion deriving from his hysteria. Grotesque incongruities, maniac obsessions break the reader's frame of reference and distort his perspective. He does not know whether he is in contact with his "real" world or Céline's hallucination. Consequently moral and aesthetic judgment are in abeyance.

The metamorphoses which Céline effected from frenzy Genet induces by ecstasy. His characters exhibit compulsion, but it is the compulsion of ritual. Their patterns of conduct are not formed to correspond with the rhythm of ordinary living. By incantation they pass out of themselves. The ritual of dressing up as the mistress, Solange's soliloquy after her sister's death, Green Eyes' spiral dance when he tries to go backward in time, all these gestures attempt to undo reality.

For Genet's revolt against the society which treats him as an outcast takes the form of an effort to cast out society. Far from being a simple nihilist he practices a transversion of values which erects the thief, the traitor, the murderer into objects of admiration. The "real" world of the bourgeois is subject to every form of attack, the inversion of the moral scale, the ridicule of its structure of pretense, as in *The Maids*, the demonstration of aesthetic values implicit in a criminal's domination of other criminals by virtue of personality, as in *Deathwatch*.

In the years of silence which have followed the publication of the *Journal* in 1949, Genet may have attained the saintliness which he had proclaimed himself as seeking, even if it was incapable of description, but it is hard for the ordinary reader to conceive of it in other than terms of insanity. The bourgeois world had already had its revenge if only in the literary flaws of Genet's work.

His procedure of affirmation has been purely lyrical. He had accepted when young the stigmata with which society had branded him and later used the resources of a sensitive vocabulary to adorn this fictitious character with the excitement of ecstasy. His associates in the *Journal* are cognizable only as lyric emanations of his own sensitiveness and imagination. Their reported actions and speech are banal. His descriptions and analyses glow, but they depend upon his words.

In the same way in these plays, where there is little room for description or analysis, his characters are puppetlike. There is the momentary impact of comic shock from their outrage to accepted behavior. Nothing remains except the uneasy, subterranean recognition that these Punch and Judy shows relate themselves to the worlds of our unguarded fantasies.

In opposition to ordinary moralists who find an act detestable by the harm it does, Genet claims that his concern is to judge its beauty or its elegance by the song which it raises in him, "le chant qu'il soulève en moi." Presumably the murder that climaxes *Deathwatch* is incapable of inspiring a song. It rings false, or as Sartre says, it is faked. Green Eyes, whose own murderous action was an act of compulsion and who is trying to convert his misfortune into heaven, is shocked by the act and tells Lefranc that he is cheating his way to exaltation.

In this world of aesthetic judgment the plain reader can detect the affinity with Huysmans and Wilde, with Gide when he was being sheerly perverse, and confess to disappointment. The publishers inform us that Genet has been acclaimed the greatest French writer of his generation. In sober truth American readers have encountered little postwar French literature, outside of Sartre and Camus, which has been serious enough to compare with Genet. Yet, even though he is something more serious than the writers of the *roman noir*, a category to which a recent critic in the London *Times Literary Supplement* relegated him, this book does little more than to demonstrate that the recent French theater can show other fantasies besides those of Anouilh.

Deathwatch

Haute Surveillance *(written earlier than* Les Bonnes*) was given for the first time at the* Théâtre des Mathurins *in Paris on 26 February 1949, in the same program as* Feydeau's Léonie est en avance, ou Le Mal joli. *It had previously been published in the review* La Nef, *March-April 1947.*

The cast included Tony Taffin (Yeux-Verts); Claude Romain (Maurice); *Robert Hossein* (Lefranc); *Jean-Marc Lambert* (Le Surveillant). *Production by Jean Marchat in collaboration with Jean Genet; décor by André Beaurepaire.*

Early reviewers of Haute Surveillance *included Henri Spade in* Paris-Presse-Intransigeant *(24 Feb. 1949: pre-announcement); Robert Kemp in* Le Monde *(4 Mar.: "prolix, driveling, boring"); G. Joly in* L'Aurore–France Libre *(4 Mar.: "interesting"); J. Lemarchand in* Combat *(4 Mar.: "a genius in the romantic tradition"); "L.E." in* La Croix *(6/7 Mar.: "nauseating . . . execrable"); F. Ambrière in* Opéra *(9 Mar.: "unspeakable imbecility"); G. Lerminier in* L'Aube *(9 Mar.: "good"); M. Beigbeder in* Le Parisien Libéré *(10 Mar.: compares Genet with* Racine*).*

The fluctuations in Genet's early reputation as a dramatist are well illustrated by the following controversy:

"UNDILUTED FILTH"

JEAN-JACQUES GAUTIER

Faced by Monsieur Genet on this occasion, we can react in one of two ways: with a laugh or with indignation.

From *Le Figaro*, 4 March 1949. Reprinted by permission. Translated by R.N.C.

We are entitled to laugh, because this so-called *magnum opus* of his never for one instant rises above the level of Théâtre de Belleville melodrama, adapted to the tastes of a fashionable clientèle, of that clique of snobs without whose approbation no reputation can be manufactured, least of all a reputation for sophisticated smut.

Precisely: we ought to laugh—for all this business of tough guys wallowing in the lush lyricism of crime, " 'tis wondrous, yet 'tis true" . . . 'tis plain, downright ludicrous as well! These high moral tones arising out of Fontevrault and Fresnes and Clairvaux, this state penitentiary mysticism ("ad augusta per angusta")—all this gives scope enough for laughter. And the clean breath of laughter being that which distinguishes man most characteristically from the beasts, at least a good laugh might introduce *something* clean into the affair. And that would already make a noticeable difference. For in the matter of degradation, hooliganolatry, and general sewage—we've had a bucketful!

The themes of the play are nauseating. The tone is abominable. For forty-eight minutes (which seem like twenty-four hours) we are subjected to a drenching in undiluted filth. One word caught my attention in passing: "garbage" . . . in the last analysis, this is what it is: garbage raised to the status of a philosophy. The essence of the evening consists in immoral propositions lingeringly dissected, pulped and kneaded with loving, disgusting, complacent relish, by an author who, I suppose, is never happier than when wallowing in the observation of "beings rotten to the core." You may, I suppose, meet people who will come up to you and blather about "poetry." Don't you believe it. Literature—yes. And of the nastiest variety: the kind that feeds on the carcasses of crawling meat and the leprosy of souls.

We have had our bellyful of these nauseous exhalations from the kitchen sink, of these self-satisfied stinks from intellectual latrines. We have had our bellyful of these murderers enthroned in the seat of kings and bearing Apollo's lyre, of these gallows birds escaped from Sacred Groves, of these jail cells full of perverts elaborating a Philosophy for Our Time, of the stench of these tales from the looney bin, and of these downright bad plays which are to the legitimate theater what bad coinage is to true currency. . . .

THE PRODUCER REPLIES

JEAN MARCHAT

Dear Sir,

This is the first occasion—you may take my word for it—on which I have felt impelled to rise in revolt against a piece of criticism; but the tone of your entire article this morning on *Deathwatch* is wholly unacceptable.

It never occurred to me (for I know you reasonably well) to hope that you could find it in you to appreciate or to understand Jean Genet's play. It would have been easy enough, however, for you to say as much in polite and moderate terms. Yet it is quite conceivable that the flood of abuse you have spewed up may induce your readers to believe that the Théâtre des Mathurins has in all reality put on a piece of "undiluted filth," and even that we were deliberately counting on the prospect of a scandal sufficiently resounding to attract an audience of snobs with a taste for pornography.

Modesty makes it somewhat awkward for me to be obliged to remind you that our theater, given its record both for producing new plays and for "discovering" new actors, perhaps deserves some greater degree of consideration.

May I be allowed further to point out to you that the fact that you happen not to understand the first thing about a play, or even the fact that you positively loathe it, does not

---

From *Le Figaro*, 7 March 1949. Reprinted by permission. Translated by R.N.C.

necessarily prove that it is a piece of sheer stupidity or of "garbage."

Nothing, however, can disturb your "superior incomprehension."

That this play should have been put on by a theater such as ours; that the production, the décor, the performance of each actor should have been handled with the most scrupulous attention; that it should have aroused the admiration and the enthusiasm of personalities as widely differing as Thierry Maulnier, Jacques Lemarchand, Jean Cocteau, Jean-Paul Sartre, Georges Auric, Stève Passeur, Simone de Beauvoir, J.-J. Rinieri, Paul Abram, Marie-Laure, J.-M. Beigbeder, Lise Deharme—I skip the rest, there are too many of them—that options on the production rights should have been instantly taken out in both North and South America, in Italy and in England—all this leaves you serene and untroubled. Your mind is made up; and so you snigger.

But your snigger is nothing new; it will warm the hearts of those who uttered an identical snigger at the first performance of plays such as *L'Annonce faite à Marie*, or *Le Roi Candaule*, or *The Playboy of the Western World*, or *Le Malentendu*, or in general, at all such mature, violent, and unusual dramas which, at the outset, demand for their appreciation and understanding a healthier and a purer outlook on life than you, Sir, have at your disposal. And greater serenity as well.

When *Le Roi Candaule* was republished, André Gide had the delightfully sadistic notion to include, at the end of the preface, a certain number of extracts from the critics who had witnessed the first production. I cannot too warmly urge you to read these pages.

In a few years' time, when Jean Genet's play comes up for reprinting, we propose to include a careful selection of passages taken from our most *understanding* critics. Your article contains a number of pearls, whose place in this context is already reserved.

Yet all such revenge must of necessity prove a waste

of breath; for if, in a few years' time, Jean Genet's fame is—as I am convinced it will be—beyond dispute, your own name, I very much fear, will have been unjustly lost in that limbo which has already engulfed the names of those critics who, once upon a time, so ponderously and yet so frivolously slashed at Gide's *Candaule*—just as you now slash at our performance.

I am, Sir,

Yours faithfully

DISILLUSIONED ROMANTICISM

GABRIEL MARCEL

A fellow critic, M. Thierry Maulnier, has, it seems, recently written that he expects yet once again to be in thorough disagreement with me, this time over Jean Genet's play *Deathwatch*, which is being performed at the Mathurins. His expectations will not be disappointed. I found *Deathwatch* an irritating play, although less so, admittedly, than *The Maids*. But *not*—and I must stress the fact—on account of the subject matter. To tell the truth, I have never had occasion to live in the company of common criminals, but I am tempted to believe that many of the details of M. Genet's characters are psychologically true. No—what horrifies me is the romantic self-satisfaction which runs riot in the play. One ought at this point to try to analyze the features of this particular romanticism—indeed, it is important that one should do so—for it has nothing at all in common with the romanticism of the nineteenth century. Our current romanticism is one of disillusion. What I mean to say is that the criminal has lost the halo that he once earned as rebel or apostle. If he is glorified, *it is as a*

From *Les Nouvelles Littéraires*, 17 March 1949. Reprinted by permission. Translated by R.N.C., quotations from *Deathwatch*, trans. Bernard Frechtman.

criminal; nor is there any trace still discernible of that aestheticism which pervaded Thomas De Quincey's famous essay.

The prestige enjoyed by Jean Genet's "Green Eyes" is rooted in something much more immediate and, in the last analysis, sexual. He is primarily a good-looking young man; his nickname used to be "Paulo with the Flowery Teeth." He has murdered a prostitute and is awaiting trial. He expects to be condemned to death. "In a month, I'll get the axe. My head'll be on one side of the block and my body on the other." He is "a terror, a holy terror"; he is hugely complacent in this desperate situation of his; he is, as it were, ecstatic with admiration at the spectacle of his own damnation. Now, I insist again, this may be psychologically true. But once more, what is inconceivable is the self-satisfaction expressed by the author—a degree of complacency which is quite sufficiently revealed in the following lines extracted from the program note, and signed by the dramatist himself:

> *An all-but-fabulous murderer dominates another, of lesser stature, who in his turn dazzles a mere burglar . . . etc. This prestige draws its strength from the very well-head of seduction: Evil itself, about which there is built a whole hierarchy of criminality. We wish—how fervently we wish!—that every prison and that every cell should echo in real life the dramatic idea which we are presenting on the stage tonight.*

This passage requires no comment. And yet, is it possible to escape our duty to add that, in the context of our author's universe, there remains no trace of any last remaining consciousness of Good or Evil? He and his like are tirelessly engaged in building up in the audience a false guilt complex which tends to taint this same consciousness—if by any chance it happens to survive—with an element of derisiveness. One shudders to think of the echo that such a theater might awaken in some fifteen- or sixteen-year-old adolescent; for I am convinced that it is only upon adolescents that this poisonous and (I insist) essentially *sexual* drama can act effectively. But what I find alarming is that such an action should find accomplices among our reputed critics and among men who, in all other respects, are very models of strong-mindedness and of notable moral honesty.

IN THE WAKE OF RACINE, BAUDELAIRE, AND PROUST

J.-J. RINIERI

. . . *The Maids* flung wide the gates that opened out on the prospect of a New Theater, the theater of true poetry; Jean Genet's latest play confirms his dramatic genius and establishes his value as a writer—a value which threatens to be misunderstood, partly because of his own singular character, partly owing to the elements of snobbery which have surrounded him. . . .

Readers of *La Nef* have already been able to enjoy the beauties of Genet's text. But the ultimate test of a play is its effectiveness on the stage; and to watch the dramatist, as I did, producing the play himself, interpreting and stressing every hidden meaning, is suddenly to grasp what theater means, and what the theater is capable of being in our time.

Indeed, the man himself is amazed to discover that his gestures, his voice, his language, and his body, each in its own way, actually compose the most authentic pages of his own history; and that his noblest dignity consists in assuming in his own person that fundamental Being whom he conjures out of the scattered fragments of his identity strewn around the four corners of a stage whose darkness is now made visible.

This is why *Deathwatch* is no ordinary play, even of the highest, most perfect variety; it is "the theater's theater," in the sense in which Heidegger described Hölderlin as "the poet's poet"; and it is among the very greatest that Genet must be ranked, in the wake of Racine, Baudelaire, and Proust. . . .

From a review of *Haute Surveillance* in *La Nef*, no. 52 (March 1949), pp. 137–138. Translated by R.N.C.

THE CASE OF JEAN GENET

FRANÇOIS MAURIAC

Jean-Jacques Gautier has made no attempt to hide the repulsion he felt at seeing a play by Monsieur Jean Genet: *Deathwatch*. In his reply to *Le Figaro*, Jean Marchat, director of the Théâtre des Mathurins, registered a great deal of dismay and irritation. Shall I confess that there are few arguments which find me so deeply divided within myself as this one? Jean-Jacques Gautier's verdict was inspired by a violent feeling of nausea, rather than by any objective and reasoned analysis; but nausea needs no excuse for its presence other than the existence of the cause that gave rise to it.

Undeniably, some while ago, I protested against the assumed relation of cause to effect that one of our colleagues was resolved to establish between the writings of Sartre and the murder of young Guyader. Every period gives rise to its own particular literary toadstools, and these in their turn proceed to breed their like. To recognize such a phenomenon is to recognize life itself, which is criminal, and we are paid to know it. I have no faith in any method of moral prophylaxis, such as is practiced in certain other countries—in Canada for instance, where virtue is, so to speak, official government policy and where it enjoys all the prestige of a law; on the other hand, faced with the play of Monsieur Jean Genet, we are confronted with a deliberate act of provocation, almost with assault and battery. At first sight it might be thought that this play simplifies the problem, in so far as its avowed object is to glorify adolescent crime and viciousness: in which case, the nation as a whole—and not merely the "virtuous" middle classes—may claim to react legitimately in self-defense. As a result, and before actually having seen *Deathwatch* in performance, I was inclined to side with Jean-Jacques Gautier, the more so since, in my eyes, the kind of pimps that send their women

---

From *Le Figaro Littéraire*, 26 March 1949. Reprinted by permission. Translated by R.N.C.

out on the streets and the youths who go around murdering weak old men constitute a breed whose unspeakable cowardice no romantic trappings have ever been able to make more acceptable . . . particularly since the events of a certain night, some two years ago, when one of my own daughters, together with her eighty-year-old grandmother found out what it felt like to be held up by the ready-cocked machine guns of a gang of these gentry.

We all used to have a soft spot for Jean Valjean, who became a convict for having stolen a loaf of bread, and for many another old-fashioned hero-criminal, shining with virtue. It is not sufficient simply to repeat that it is no longer about such "proud and generous lions" as these that today's "New Romanticism" finds its crystallizing point. Nor have these effeminate devils inherited anything from the Lucifer-genius of Balzac's Vautrin, whose fearsome grip held in awe a whole society as corrupt as himself. What Jean-Jacques Gautier is denouncing is the current glorification of thuggery considered purely and simply as thuggery—a glorification of which we, today, are all witnesses, whether horrified, indifferent, or complicitly approving.

The fact remains, however, that I knew nothing of Monsieur Jean Genet, save for a few pages that I chanced to have read in some literary magazine, and one play, *The Maids*, whose sublime qualities, I confess, had altogether escaped me. I decided to go and see *Deathwatch*. As a result, one fine Sunday in Lent, I resolved to "skip" Father Riquet's sermon, and to go instead and listen to Jean Genet's, at the Théâtre des Mathurins. I was so conscientious about it all, in fact, that I actually went out during the interval and got hold of a copy, from the theater bookshop, of *Our Lady of the Flowers*,[1] whose title should not be suffered to tempt pious persons in search of literature devoutly Marial, nor those who happen to be hunting for First Communion presents.

---

1. This seems to be evidence that Genet's "clandestine" novels were on open sale by 1949. [Ed.]

And now, having seen the play and read the book, the problem, in my opinion, has only grown more complex than ever. That Monsieur Jean Genet is a true writer—that he even has claims to the title of "poet"—of this there is no doubt whatever. And it is no use saying that you couldn't care less, that, poet or no poet, the real issues remain unaffected; this is not the case. The real issues are affected. First of all, however, we must establish some common ground for argument. I have no sympathy at all for those adulators of Monsieur Jean Genet who, calmly and coolly, equate him with Proust and Gide. From a literary point of view, it is essentially irrelevant whether a writer indulges in this vice or that, or even whether or not he has been a common criminal. What matters is that, starting out from this or that given vice, or from whatever may have been the singular accidents of his life, his work open out upon the general experience of Man. If Proust had never depicted anything save the scene of M. de Charlus being whipped in a brothel, he would be no more significant than is M. Jean Genet himself: a highly specialized writer who places a great deal of talent in the exclusive service of his speciality. Proust painted *the* world, not simply *a* world. This adventurer in the Land of Sodom has none the less left us, in *Swann in Love*, the most polished study of a "liaison," in the broadest and most commonplace sense of the term. His own homosexuality inspired in him the most extensively human views on the solitude of *all* love, on *all* unrequited passion, on *all* jealousy. He filled his novel with as many kinds of people coming from as many divergent milieux as may be discovered in Saint-Simon. Whereas M. Jean Genet, himself no less than the heroes of *Deathwatch*, goes around and around in circles like a squirrel in a cage, imprisoned in the dungeon of a vice from which he cannot escape, even through the process of literary creation, since he can conceive of nothing outside the barbed-wire perimeter of his own tiny private hell. Poet of the Central Prison, Orpheus of the Underworld, Genet is an inspired masturbator; his morbid imagination feeds greedily on pictures whose essential mechanism is related to Jean Cocteau's ingenious clockwork. His talent lies in giving permanent form to the horrifying visions essential to his own enjoyment. Nothing more, nothing less. And by this we may measure the drifting confusion of a generation whose best-accredited representatives gawp in wonder at this sinister phenomenon. It somehow reminds me of the panic that occurred when the first subway was opened, and a whole crowd lost its head and crushed itself to death against the walls of a dead-end corridor. Just so this present generation of ours, trampling and struggling for breath in the swampy cul-de-sac of eroticism.

Considered as literature, is there anything more monotonous, more short-winded, or more sterile than vice? If you happen to have *this* vice, then try at least to think of art as a way of escape and as a means of transformation. Make the same gesture that God Himself once made: O wretched Adam, wrest forth from thy ribs this woman who doth poison all thy being, and breathe Life into her—her *own* life. Or, alternatively, follow in the footsteps of the great French moralists—as the author of *L'Algèbre des Valeurs morales* has done—adopt the tradition of the classics, not in spite of what you are, but because of what you are.

It is not that M. Jean Genet, imprisoned within the sweating walls of his own solitude, fails to make any effort to move toward a more universal view of man. His inversion is not only physiological; it is completed by a corresponding spiritual inversion which never, perhaps, until now had been expounded and defended with so much passion and so much lucidity. One of M. Jean Genet's most fervid apologists, one of those who exalt him to the rank of Proust, of Baudelaire, and (God forgive him!) of Racine, M. J.-J. Rinieri, has defined with great precision the theme which M. Jean Genet is constantly developing and illustrating: "the authenticity of a vocation for Evil, the secret world of the condemned and the effulgent glory which the Heroes of the Knight-Errantry of Crime bestow upon each other." Jean Genet himself has written the following commentary on his play:

An alternative title to Deathwatch *would be* Rules of Precedence [Les Préséances]. *But status, in this case, is rooted in an infernal Order, that is to say, status is conferred, not on the grounds of well-recognized merit, but proportionately to deeds which you consider infamous. An all-but-fabulous murderer dominates another, of lesser stature, who in his turn dazzles a mere burglar. This prestige draws its strength from the very well-head of seduction: Evil itself, about which there is built a whole hierarchy of criminality.*

We are back once more with the problem which formed the starting point of this study: what M. Jean Genet really wants is to induce in the adolescent mind a prejudice in favor of vice and in favor of crime. I am well aware that in his eyes no man deliberately *becomes* a criminal; no man chooses his own crime. Green Eyes, the hero of *Deathwatch*, belongs to the Elect; he comes of a Royal race. He has received the Gift of Grace—a sort of Grace-in-Reverse, much as Saint Cyran conceived it. M. Jean Genet might well reply to me: "The fault of which you accuse me, artistically speaking—the fault of being a prisoner within my own accursèd universe, of having no window open upon the general life of Man—these very defects should in fact both reassure and comfort you, for I am writing only for those who inhabit a doomed, infernal planet whose gates are forever shut against you." As though we could forget those pages of history through which we have recently lived, and which have brought all "normal" society dangerously close to that other society whose frontiers are blurred, and in which M. Jean Genet's male angels dress up as women and cavort about with machine guns!

The fact remains, however, that Genet's talents as a writer, his qualities as a poet, leave us neatly on the horns of the following dilemma: for either we must lodge him firmly among the ranks of the pornographers—in which case we must brand as "infamous" a work which has all the qualities of true literature; or else we must shut our eyes and permit total freedom to what is a deliberate and active attempt at corruption, an attempt to bring about a complete reversal of moral values, such as the history of our times and manners has already witnessed at the hands of that generation which emerged from the "False Resistance" and the Black Market. If we should decide to discount entirely the poetic qualities of a work which, from another point of view, is undeniably crapulous, then where are we to draw the line in a general bowdlerization of literature and the theater? What rules is such moral censorship to obey? For I can ill conceive what to reply to a reader in whose opinion the degree of eroticism displayed in *Deathwatch* or in *Our Lady of the Flowers* is a good deal less provocative than that which is to be found in *Si le Grain ne meurt*, for instance, or in my own novels—why not? Any poison administered in massive doses—it stands to reason—will be rejected by the system before it can take effect. In *Our Lady of the Flowers*, M. Jean Genet gives us a hopelessly indigestible overdose. He simply makes us sick: and in this case, even the biblical dog would hesitate to return to his own vomit.

If the reading of a book of this nature constitutes any sort of test, it is above all on the metaphysical level, and because it introduces us brutally within the circles of a Hell whose existence was certainly not unknown to us, but from which we generally prefer to divert our thoughts. But M. Jean Genet forces us to think long and deep about the problem of human beings forcibly "chosen," *predestined* for crime in the juvenile penitentiaries; for the length of three hundred pages, he holds our heads under the stagnant surface of a pond whose mire were better not submitted to analysis. This is the Mystery of Evil; and to this Mystery—to the essential part of this Mystery, which is that by which children and adolescents, here and now on this earth, are damned, predestined to a monstrous pre-eminence in infamy—as Christians we must admit, in all truth and humility, that we have no answer, we know no solution. We are reduced to silence in the face of this scandal which is a calumny upon the Uncreated Love. They are what they are. They cannot be other than as Jean Genet shows them to be. Men who turn into women, into whores; angels who are born prostitutes.

And yet (so Jean Genet might retort to us)—and yet there is an answer: for, in these very creatures of damnation, I have revealed a longing for greatness and glory which, for all that it is inverted, bears witness none the less on behalf of your Faith. It is written somewhere in the New Testament—that book which familiarity has robbed, for you, of all its mystery, yet which the very descent into the depths of Hell that I shall force upon you will oblige you to take up once more and read again, and ponder in your hearts—it is written "that prostitutes and women of loose life shall enter before you into the Kingdom of Heaven."

And there is likewise that mysterious "that which was lost," which the Son of Man (He has Himself assured us) is come into the world to find again and to save. And what can be more utterly lost than these Children of Wrath, than these Sons of Perdition?

As an epigraph to *Deathwatch* there should stand half a line of Baudelaire:

> *O fangeuse grandeur!*

And more especially, it would be well to re-read—if, like me, you do not happen to know it by heart—that page from *Une Saison en Enfer* where Rimbaud condenses into a few lines of miraculous transparency and of a supernatural purity that very same secret which M. Jean Genet buries deep beneath tumbrils-ful of filth. Do you remember?

> *Encore tout enfant j'admirais le forçat intraitable sur qui se renferme toujours le bagne: je visitais les auberges et les garnis qu'il avait sacrés par son séjour; je voyais avec son idée le ciel bleu et le travail fleuri de la campagne; je flairais sa fatalité dans les villes. Il avait plus de force qu'un saint, plus de bon sens qu'un voyageur—et lui, lui seul, pour témoin de sa gloire et de sa raison!*

And all that follows. In incorruptible language therein lies all said, all graven indelibly, all of that Truth whose prophet among us M. Jean Genet is to become. Yet he has failed to understand what Rimbaud had understood—namely, that he who bears this message must not at the same time exploit it for his own vain glory. There is one thing worse than vice and crime; it is vice and crime used for the purposes of literature, it is their methodical exploitation. Your truest glory would have consisted in seeking no witnesses other than yourself. Of all his inheritance, the wretched sons of Rimbaud have rejected precisely that one quality which, among all other poets of damnation, causes his genius to shine forth brightly forever: his renunciation of literary exhibitionism and the vocation of silence to which he was to remain faithful until the very day of his death.

Entr'acte: *The Twentieth of October 1955*

When the highest literary and social homage that France has to offer was paid to Jean Cocteau, he was determined that Genet should share it with him. Not only did he invite him to the solemn ceremonial occasion of his installation at the Académie Française, but he was defiantly resolved that the assembled Immortals should be made to hear and to respect the name "Jean Genet." In consequence, he made plans, not only to introduce the name into his great formal Discours de Réception, but to introduce it at one of the most significant and dramatic moments: namely, at the beginning of the final peroration.

This deliberate challenge to the Establishment was more easily conceived than realized. Five days before the event, Paul Léautaud noted in his diary:

15 October 1955

It is Cocteau himself who has sent me an invitation to his reception at the Academy. [Jean] Denoël is going to arrange for a car belonging to Mrs. [Florence] Gould—who will be in Paris then, and who is also going to Cocteau's reception, accompanied by Pierre Benoit—to pick me up at Fontenay and to take me back again later.

Cocteau is sixty-seven. Denoël tells me that his reception

Paul Léautaud, *Journal Littéraire*, 18 (Paris: Mercure de France, 1964), p. 280. Translated by R.N.C.

speech, and the gestures that go with it, are dazzling. This speech, as originally written, contained the name of Jean Genet. The committee, meeting to hear a preliminary reading of the speech before the actual occasion, has ordered him to cut it out.

What happened next is not clear. Later on, when the text of the famous "Discours" was published, the terrible name appeared in full, in the place where it was intended; and it contrasted sharply, indeed flamboyantly, with that of the obscure Jérôme Tharaud, Cocteau's predecessor among the Immortals, whose qualities and achievements he was, by tradition, supposed to be enumerating, but whose works, by his own confession, he was happy scarcely to have read:

But . . . a glance at my watch! Time, as I am perfectly well aware, gentlemen, is nothing but a phenomenon of perspective; but this knowledge does not alter the fact that Time is none the less our master, imposing on ourselves restrictions of his own. To tell the truth, though, I am grateful to these very restrictions; for they release me from the task of having to pass judgment on a man's work. Belonging by birth to the tribe of the accused, I cannot aspire to take my seat among the judges—least of all among those whom Jean Genet accuses of bending lingeringly and lovingly over the prisoner at the bar. . . .

If these words were actually spoken, the effect must have been electric; but it seems likely that a compromise was reached, and

---

Discours de Réception de M. Jean Cocteau à l'Académie française et réponse de M. André Maurois, prononcés à l'Académie française, le jeudi 20 octobre 1955 (Paris: Gallimard, 1955), p. 56. Translated by R.N.C.

a way found to placate Jean Cocteau's passionate integrity without actually provoking a riot in the presence of royalty:

A few days before, [Cocteau] sent in the final text of his discourse, but for the address, the Committee of Censorship requested him to remove his comments on the events in Morocco during the rule of Maréchal Lyautey, himself a member of the Académie Française, and also to suppress the name of Jean Genet for which Cocteau wickedly substituted the words: "The poet canonized by Jean-Paul Sartre." . . .

A little before 3 P.M. Cocteau got out of the Rolls-Royce with Madame Weisweiller, to be welcomed by Jean Marais, who had just arrived in his sportscar. A few minutes later, Queen Elizabeth of the Belgians arrived. Picasso was not present, but Jean Genet, with his shaven head, was seen entering the Académie. . . .

Very often, during the address, the minds of the audience turned toward Jean Genet, and in his reply, André Maurois smilingly echoed the new Academician: "You may wish for the best to be summoned here. This is my wish too, and if you bring us a François Villon, I promise to vote for him . . . provided he has written *Le petit Testament*."

To date, Genet has still not written Le petit Testament *(although* Notre-Dame des Fleurs *has often been compared to it), and André Maurois was never called on for his vote.*

Elizabeth Sprigge and Jean-Jacques Kihm, *Jean Cocteau, the Man and the Mirror* (London: Gollancz, 1968), pp. 216–219.

The Balcony

Although the first French edition of Le Balcon (original version) was published in 1956, the play was not produced in France until four years later. The world première was given at the Arts Theatre in London on 22 April 1957, in an English translation by Bernard Frechtman. The director was Peter Zadek, and the part of Madame Irma was played by Selma Vaz Diaz. In spite of the sensational "incidents" that marked the dress rehearsal and the first night, the press as a whole was not hostile. The Daily Mail urged its readers to boycott the play altogether; but the Times referred to it as "a serious work of dramatic art"; and the Observer described the first half, at least, as "flawless":

THE IMAGE OF POWER

KENNETH TYNAN

. . . The great virtue of Jean Genet's *The Balcony* is that it seeks to relate sexual habits to social institutions. According to M. Genet, the Bishop's miter, the Monarch's scepter, the Judge's robes, and the General's jackboots are symbols that inspire common men to sexual fantasies of domination and submission. In Madame Irma's House of Illusions their dreams become facts. The man from the gas company, episcopally garbed, forgives a penitent her sins; a repressed bank clerk defiles the Virgin Mary, while other clients prefer to disguise themselves as flagellant judges or victorious warriors. M. Genet

---

From "Something for Everybody," *The Observer* (London), 28 April 1957. Reprinted by permission.

regards these scabrous rituals with a sort of furious pity. What else, he implies, can we expect of a society whose only absolute values are those of conquest and authority?

That is the indictment. M. Genet dramatizes it by setting his quaint bordello in the midst of a revolution that has already wiped out all the real holders of power save one, the Chief of Police, who now enlists the regular customers to play out their fantasy roles in earnest. Overnight, the revolt is quelled; and soon afterward a new figure takes its place in the mythology of the brothel. A stranger asks permission to dress up as the Chief of Police, in which guise he promptly gelds himself. This horrific act completes M. Genet's argument. The image of power is erotic; but power itself is sexless. The reality survives by enslaving mankind to the symbol.

To object that the play's view of life is extremely personal is merely to say that only one man could have written it. Some power symbols are clearly more erotic than others. I myself would not place Sir Winston's cigar in quite the same category as Mussolini's fasces, but Baldwin's pipe is a disquieting thought; and the histories of Roman Catholicism and English Protestantism alike attest to the fact that the idea of female virginity is a potent and highly seductive thing. Nor can one rationally object to the violence of M. Genet's language: only dolts would contend that playgoers, who are numbered in thousands, should be protected against words and situations with which library subscribers, who run into millions, have long been familiar. The true objection to the play is that, although nobody but M. Genet could have written the first half at all, almost anyone else could have written the second half better.

The first, or expository, half is flawless; out of an anarchic, unfettered imagination there emerges a perfect nightmare world. But the second half is argumentative, and logic is necessarily a fettered thing, bound by rules to which M. Genet, who has flouted rules all his life, is temperamentally opposed. Just when the play cries out for an incisive, satiric mind like

M. Sartre's, it branches off into a confusion so wild that I still cannot understand what the scenes in the rebel camp were meant to convey. As an evoker, M. Genet is magnificent: as an explainer, he is a maddening novice. He cannot think in cold blood; as witness his statement that the Arts Theatre had coarsened his play, when in fact (if Bernard Frechtman's translation is to be trusted) it had softened it. Apart from Selma Vaz Diaz and Hazel Penwarden, Peter Zadek's cast is shamelessly feeble; but many good actors, one guesses, took one look at the text and turned it down in a huff. For all its faults, this is a theatrical experience as startling as anything since Ibsen's revelation, seventy-six years ago, that there was such a thing as syphilis.

Strangely, however, the only person who was profoundly and irremediably shocked by The Balcony *seems to have been Jean Genet himself:*

JEAN GENET IN A TEMPER

GENET TO INTERVIEWER

Last Tuesday, Jean Genet, aged forty-six, watching the production of his latest play, *The Balcony*, at a London theater club, was possessed with the wrath of the gods. He climbed up on to the stage, demanding that the show be stopped. He offered to remain in London for ten days, so as to reshape the entire production; but when the English director turned down this proposal he sent for sandwiches, declaring that he would not budge from the theater, and that he would use all the vocal powers at his disposal to prevent the curtain being raised again.

On the following day, police barred his way into the theater.

From an anonymous interview in *L'Express*, no. 305 (26 April 1957). Reprinted by permission. Translated by R.N.C.

Whereupon Jean Genet returned to Paris and calmly explained the reasons for his bad temper:

> *My play,* The Balcony, *takes place in a brothel, but the characters are as little rooted in the reality of whorehouses as those of* Hamlet *are rooted in the world of courts and courtiers.*
>
> *The universe of the cottage, of the factory, or of the palace each comprises its own ethical significance. The description of a "whorehouse" can have an immoral significance; and this is what is essential to transpose.*
>
> *The real theme of the play is the theme of illusion.*
>
> *Everything is spurious: the General, the Archbishop, the Chief of Police—and everything needed to be treated with infinite delicacy.*
>
> *And what happened? Instead of giving the play a touch of nobility, it was cheaply vulgarized.*
>
> *The characters were transformed into grotesque and disgusting puppets, whom even I could not recognize. The director, Peter Zadek, even brought on a pack of whores all got up in lace, who swayed nauseatingly across the stage and whose presence I had never so much as suggested. I intended my characters to be larger than life; they were reduced to caricatures straight out of* Hellzapoppin.
>
> *A bad production of* The Maids *or of* Deathwatch, *by this time, no longer worries me because I know that these plays have been well performed, and I know that they can come off. But this was the very first time that* The Balcony *had ever been seen on the stage and it drove me crazy to think that it was I who had engendered this abortion.*[1]

---

1. For a German version of the same incident, see *Der Spiegel*, 1 May 1957. [Ed.]

"I HAVE BEEN THE VICTIM OF AN ATTEMPTED MURDER!"

GENET TO MICHEL BREITMAN

Not fair play![2]—that is the least I can say about the way the English treated me after the staging of *The Balcony* in London. I am referring, of course, to the producer. At the dress rehearsal, the audience heard nothing but a bit of shouting behind the curtain. As for the audience on the first night, all it saw was two empty seats in the stalls, while the rest of the theater was bursting at the seams.

If I'd had my way, I'd have sent for sandwiches, and I'd have installed myself then and there in the middle of the stage, and stayed there as long as necessary.

I had taken no precautions, I was caught completely by surprise. Peter Zadek had already produced *The Maids*, I don't know whether he made a decent job of it, I suppose he did. But the mess he made of *The Balcony* was indescribable. Where I had imagined a tragedy, he took scenes straight out of the Folies-Bergère.

As for the text, if one character says: "You are beautiful," and if another replies: "Not so beautiful as you, my dear"—is it "respecting the text" to have both lines spoken by the same actress?

Besides, Bernard Frechtman's English translation was generally rehashed, squeezed through a wringer, stuffed with howlers. And, if this production messed about with the script, it was nothing to what it did with the spirit of the play!

Imagine that my stage directions required a dumb-show in front of the Arc de Triomphe . . . does the producer have the right to bring on a full chorus from the Paris Opéra? The

---

2. The opening three words of the interview are in English in the original. [Ed.]

Record of an interview with Jean Genet, taken down by Michel Breitman. *Arts*, no. 617 (1–7 May 1957), p. 1. Translated by R.N.C.

dramatist has a duty to see that his play is treated with proper respect. This is not a question of divergences in interpretation; it's downright attempted murder! When Chantal was executed on the stage, I had the feeling that it was me the firing squad was aiming at!

If I had been allowed to get up on the stage, I would all but have gone down on my knees to Peter Zadek, to try to get him to *understand*. I had begged him to put off the opening night for ten days, but he had refused. The very least he could have done would have been to keep the audience waiting for an hour; or else let me produce the play as *I* saw it: "Well, now, here is M. Genet, who is going to show you how *he* puts a play on!" It might have amused them, it would certainly have been interesting, and if I really failed, if I made a complete fool of myself in the process—so much the worse for me! But not a hope! From the word go, it was all lawyers and threats: "Keep him out of it! I've got the law on my side!" The law, indeed! What law? The producer, it seems, can act like a little Hitler. He can play around with the text—and with simple common sense, too—as much as he sees fit. My play, to all intents and purposes, was turned into a satire against Buckingham Palace . . . a caricature! But caricature will never move an audience.

I am not denying that my play *does* contain a court, a ceremonial, a queen . . . but that is a far cry from making one of my characters turn up in the Order of the Garter! In any case, my starting point was Spain, Franco's Spain; and the revolutionary who castrated himself was the symbol of all Republicans who have acknowledged their defeat. From that point onward, however, my play went one way, while Spain went another. All my characters wear masks, so how do you expect me to say whether they are true or false? Even *I* can't tell any more. But what I hold against Zadek is that he *vulgarized* them. Just because my play is set in a brothel, that is no reason why it should be vulgar. Realism is much farther from truth than is my house of illusions. Besides, the ultimate sublimation of any commonplace event is through poetry. It is through poetry that any work of literature attains its highest realization. What is one humdrum event picked out at random among a thousand others? Unless it is transformed, transmuted into poetry, it is nothing. This, without question, is why I so frequently go to sleep in the theater. The whole apparatus needs to be put full steam into reverse. For instance, the majority of dramatists might make a start by taking up another trade altogether (I am not referring to Ionesco, of course, or to Beckett). . . . No one has the right to play fast and loose with language. I would cheerfully swindle a publisher rather than betray my thought in a book. In other words, in this matter, I am on the side of morality. Or rather, I was never anywhere else. I am not just "interested" in the guilty, I slip inside their skin. One *must* be guilty. A moralist is not just a man who moralizes.

The artist resembles his own characters: he is working toward immobility. Reality, in him, is frozen into permanence. Yet whatever this reality may be, no one has the right to betray it. In my view, what Zadek really needs is for somebody to invent a machine for kicking people in the ass.

ACTS OF VIOLENCE

PETER ZADEK

"If you want Genet's genius," I was told by his translator in the midst of the conflagration, "you'll have to take his violence." At that precise moment Jean Genet was standing on the stage of the Arts Theatre, haranguing actors, stage staff, management, director, using some pretty choice adjectives and leaving us all wondering whether there would ever be a first night of *The Balcony*.

From *New Statesman*, 4 May 1957, pp. 568–569. Reprinted by permission.

The violence of castration, rebellion, flagellation on the stage; he violence of the collision between author and director, beween author and management; the violence of popular revulion, of the sensation surrounding the opening night—all were ubordinated to the violent clash, in real life, between fantasy nd reality, both in the author's mind and, during every perormance of the play, in the minds of the audience. For this backstage row" (as the press dubbed it) had far deeper roots han disagreement over interpretation. Some critics complained hat the production had "made the play obscene," others that t had "softened it." Whatever the truth of these comments, ne thing is clear: Genet, whose main preoccupation is with he ambiguous boundary between fantasy and reality, had been isillusioned when he realized the distance separating his vision f the play from its realization. Genet's whole life seems to epeat the pattern of the visionary who tries to make "his antasy penetrate into the reality" of the world. But the world as always crucified visionaries, and "St. Genet" is no excepion. Once again Genet had found the world lacking beside he purity of his own imagination. For him, his own perfect ream of *The Balcony* was reality, and in an effort to make this oncrete, our reality, the production of the play on a stage, ith actors, had to be sacrificed.

It is this complete inability to compromise with his vision hat makes of Genet one of the few great poet-dramatists of ur century. It may be uncomfortable to work with such a nan, where normal standards of theater suddenly cease to pply. And yet, when he demands five months' rehearsal, he eems quite reasonable when he tells one that no actor can earn to walk beautifully on ten-inch lifts (as they have to do n *The Balcony*) in four weeks. He is right too, when he states ategorically that the movement of the play requires a Grock n every role. One can also understand when Genet carries the aint-Criminal, good-evil paradox into the real world of the heater and asks that "the play be performed with the solemnity f a Mass in a cathedral" and, at the same time, "that it be vulgar and in bad taste." It is on the theatrical realization o this paradox that the difference over the production of *Th Balcony* centered. Confronted by an interpretation not wholl his own, a violent outburst ensued. Its effect on production actors, on the success or failure of the play was something Gene never considered. But this violence is inseparable from Genet' genius. Violence in his personal relationships, in the creation o beauty, in his attack on conventions. We have no choice bu to accept it, if we believe that Genet the artist has enough t offer.

Genet's great importance in the theater is his theatricality He does not "use" the theater to imitate the externals of ou world; he shows us that our world is as fake as grease pain itself, and that therefore the theater can be the perfect mirro held up to the *danse macabre* which is life as Genet sees it. I other words, Genet's theater at its best, abstract, stylized, de liberately stagy, comes closer to penetrating reality than th illusionist theater ever did. In *The Balcony* and, to a lesse extent, in *The Maids*, Genet gives back to the theater a vita quality that it has not had since the religious drama of th Middle Ages. He gives back the quality of ritual, of ceremony He does not do this externally, as some twentieth-centur verse-drama has attempted to do, but by putting on the stag the very ceremonies, be they sexual or religious, that he see being performed in real life. I have been asked on sever occasions to explain what *The Balcony* says. It is not a pla that says; it is a play that sees.

Genet's vision is never cozy—it never allows the audience t sit back and pass the time of day. The ceremony has the beaut and the terror of a Black Mass. We recognize our own predic ment in the pathetic figure of the meter collector who drean of being a bishop, and, whether or not we like to admit it, h sexual frustrations are too near the knuckle to leave us ve comfortable. The horrible face of the Chief of Police wh dreams of his statue in the form of a phallus is never very f from the legend of Hitler eating carpets—a farce combined i eality with the sadism of the concentration camp. In *The alcony* we see acted out a legend, a ritual—but there can be o doubt that it is *our* legend, the ritual of *our* world.

I am not claiming that the play is faultless. Parts of the vast anvas are not completely integrated and M. Genet has told ıe that he will reconsider some of the second act for the Paris roduction. Nor do I wish to suggest that the present producon at the Arts Theatre has succeeded in solving all the play's roblems. It is certainly possible that in trying to stand beveen author and audience, the direction has been too greatly oncerned in trying to make the play comprehensible to the tter. But *The Balcony* seems to me to point toward a more rofitable line of development for *new* and adventurous develpment in the theater than the pseudo-avant-garde writing of ostwar English dramatists. *Cards of Identity,* which unfornately lost itself in intellectual tomfoolery, was the only play roduced by the English Stage Company that tried, imaginavely, to find new form for new content. Whereas our "angry oung man" lacks precisely that quality which he spends so uch time in publicizing: anger, violence. He has quickly beome respectable and therefore—a little boring? Or is it true say that he has always been surreptitiously respectable? fter all, he has confined himself mainly to social and to ocial-psychological protest, and even there has tended to reuce himself to the chairman of a private club whose insignia the roll-neck sweater. Jimmy Porter's protest appeals only to ıose members of the audience who agreed with him before ıey ever saw *Look Back in Anger.* As for the opposition, Ir. Osborne's attack on society is sufficiently cozy for society settle back in the stalls for a couple of hours of quiet asochistic pleasure. But, above all, theatrically speaking, Mr. sborne has accepted Ibsen's realism and no amount of omposite setting and broken walls will hide the fact.

Genet is as startling in his retention of some theatrical conntions as he is ruthless in his rejection of many others. His introduction of the cothurni of the Greek theater, for instance, is powerful and completely successful. Above all whatever he does, he does wholeheartedly, violently, uncom promisingly. It is his courage that should inspire other drama tists and once the dust from the explosion of *The Balcony* ha settled, it remains to be seen whether it will find an echo i English playwriting.

In spite of Genet's misgivings, the success of The Balcony *i London was such that plans were immediately set afoot t have the play produced in Paris, at the Théâtre Antoine, the under the direction of Simone Berriau; and—unexpectedl given his uncompromising views on the original English pr duction—Genet chose another English producer, this tim Peter Brook. But now, for the first time, Genet ran into seriou trouble with censorship. By early November 1957, Mm Berriau had been discreetly but unmistakably informed by th Préfecture de Police that "certain pressures" would oblige th authorities to close down the theater if she went ahead with th production. Mme Berriau weakened before the prospect of head-on collision with the Préfecture, and at the last minu withdrew the play (See* Combat, *7 November 1957).* Th Balcony *was effectively banned in France. As a consolatio Peter Brook was invited instead to produce Arthur Miller* A View from the Bridge *at the Théâtre Antoine. Unhesita ingly, Brook took Genet's part, and not only refused to produ the Miller play, but threatened never to produce another pl in Paris until such time as the ban was lifted:*

INTERVIEW

PETER BROOK

It was I who produced Miller's play in London. But if were to agree to produce it in Paris under the present circu stances, I should make myself an accomplice to the underha ntrigue which has been worked up against *The Balcony*—a play which I consider to be a masterpiece—and this would be antamount to betraying Genet.[3]

Meanwhile, on 18 March 1959, the play was produced in German at the Schlosspark-Theater in Berlin, and created a considerable sensation.[4] In Paris, however, it was not until after the production of Les Nègres *at the Théâtre de Lutèce on 28 October 1959 that plans were resumed for the French première of* Le Balcon. The Blacks *is a far more violent and provocative play than* The Balcony: *yet it had given rise neither to rioting nor to police intervention. Consequently, the way seemed clear; and once again, it was Peter Brook who was invited to undertake the production:*

THE MAN OF THE WEEK

AN INTERVIEW WITH PETER BROOK

Peter Brook: . . . Two years ago, when I decided for the first time to produce *The Balcony*, the *Préfet de Police* told us straight out that if we were to put the play on (it was in the days of Lars Schmidt and Simone Berriau) there would cer-

---

3. Reported in *Le Figaro*, 23–24 November 1957. Reprinted by permission. Translated by R.N.C. For further details of the "plot" against *The Balcony*, see *Le Figaro*, 1, 13, 14, 20, 21, and 31 November 1957; *Combat*, 13 and 23/24 November 1957. [Ed.]

4. See, for instance, Ilse Urbach in *Der Kurier* (19 March 1959); "Mando" in *Berliner Zeitung* (20 March 1959); Manfred Barthel in *Der Abend* (20 March 1959); Georg Zivier in *Berliner Morgenblatt* (20 March 1959); Rudolf Brendemühl in *Nachtdepesche* (20 March 1959); Werner Fiedler in *Der Tag* (20 March 1959); Dora Fehling in *Telegraf* (20 March 1959); Hermann Wanderscheck in *Hamburger Abendblatt* (21 March 1959). [Ed.]

From *L'Express*, no. 466 (19 May 1960), pp. 44–45. Reprinted by permission. Translated by R.N.C.

tainly be disturbances, to such an extent that he would be
forced to ban further performances.

—: Do you believe that *The Balcony* is really a "scandalous"
work?

Peter Brook: As soon as the curtain goes up, and as soon a
the audience hears the opening speech, it will realize straigh
away that it is not going to see a "realist" drama. Undoubtedl
the play, through its poetic vision, is devastatingly violent. Bu
I am convinced that anyone who has enough sensitivity an
enough imagination to understand this essential violence is no
the sort of person to stand up and cause disturbances in
theater.

—: Given the current political climate, it was already slightl
surprising to observe, when *The Blacks* was produced, that th
audience remained untouched by the hidden yet intrinsic an
flinty violence of the play. . . .

Peter Brook: On the first occasion that I proposed to produc
The Balcony, I was still in London when I received a lette
from the director of one of the leading Paris theaters, tippin
me off, as between friends, and advising me to drop my projec
"*since the time was not propitious.*" . . . I replied that if he wa
right—and indeed, I was convinced that he was right—the
this was in itself incontrovertible proof that *The Balcony* wa
crying out to be produced. Conversely, as soon as one begin
to sense that a play is likely to upset people less than befor
then perhaps the time for putting it on has already gone by.

—: For these last two years, then, you have been determine
to produce *The Balcony,* whatever the odds? From the pr
ducer's point of view—which is your own—why this obstinac

Peter Brook: . . . As soon as I laid my hands on the text
The Balcony, I discovered that I was confronted by a poet wh
as Cocteau used to say, wrote true "poetry for the stag
[*poésie de scène*]. A poet who, with rigorous self-discipline ar
from the outset rejecting all facile naturalism, was forcin
himself to invent new forms to express what he felt and wh
he believed. The final outcome, with Genet, is a drama whi

s purely traditional and perfectly classical, but conceived in he intensest atmosphere of passion and violence.

—: Did you have difficulties in casting *The Balcony?*

Peter Brook: Almost insoluble ones. For each and every part required first-class actors who knew how to bring out the full 'alue of a poetic text. At the same time they needed a classical raining; on the other hand, almost all actors who have spent heir lives performing the [French] classics become inevitably anting and utterly useless in parts written by Genet. Now, look t the Elizabethan theater—take Shakespeare. Shakespeare reates a "natural" climate, a "true" climate; then, all of a udden, he shoots off into declamation and high rhetoric, only o fall back again, equally suddenly—just as Charlie Chaplin n his films used to tumble to the floor at the end of a dance—rashing to the ground with a vulgar word or a phrase of slang. 'here you have the whole of Shakespeare: marvelous flights f poetry, the word "shit" suddenly introduced, and then on vith great speech. But this broken style is extremely hard for n actor to achieve, if he is constantly tempted to let himself et carried away by the high-flown sweep of classicism. However, here, precisely, you have *The Balcony*. A classical actor is ompletely at sea. But a film actor, or an actor from the comercial theater, is no less at sea, only for opposite reasons. Vhile I was trying to cast *The Balcony*, I was confronted—or the first time in my life—by the sight of first-class actors urning down first-rate parts....

'he French première of Le Balcon *finally took place on 18 Iay 1960 at the Théâtre du Gymnase. Peter Brook not only roduced the play, but designed the sets and costumes as well. rma was played by Marie Bell (a famous Racinian tragic ctress), Carmen by Loleh Bellon, Arthur by Tony Taffin, and he Envoy by Roger Blin. The incidental music took the form*

of "structures sonores" by Jacques Lasry and François Bachet To avoid conflict with the Préfecture, the Théâtre du Gymnas was transformed into a sort of ad hoc theater club: the norma seat prices were doubled and the play was put on for a limite run (fifty performances) only. After all this excitement, th reviews by the average French drama critics seem dull and ar hardly worth reproducing. The really striking exception was th Marxian-sociological interpretation of the play by Lucien Gold mann.[5] The following may also be noted: Jean Fayard, in L Figaro (19 May 1960: an amusing collection of remarks over heard in the foyer); Jean-Jacques Gautier, in Le Figaro (2 May: "delirious, nightmarish, lunatic, morbid, scandal-provok ing"); Paul Gordeaux in France Soir (20 May: "a philosophi farce . . . in which De Sade rubs shoulders with Lautréamont") Paul Morelle, in Libération (21/22 May: "a play of despai combined with a nostalgia for something better"); Jacque Lemarchand, in Le Figaro Littéraire (21 May: "overflowin with all the naked power symbols of childhood"); Marcel Capron in Combat (21/22 May: "a degree of irony rarely befor expressed in the theater"); Gabriel Marcel in Les Nouvelle Littéraires (26 May: "disgusting . . . turgescent and feverish, a evil influence"); Bernard Dort, in Les Temps Modernes (Ju 1960: a comparison of the function of dramatic illusion i Genet, Shakespeare, and Calderón); and Michel Zéraffa, i Europe (July-Aug. 1960: "a Pirandello working with social typ instead of with individuals").

THE BROTHEL AND THE WESTERN WORL

ROBERT BRUSTEIN

Jean Genet is at once the most brilliant, the most gifte and the most depraved of the new French dramatists; and whi

5. "Une pièce réaliste: *Le Balcon* de Genet," *Les Temps Modern* 15 (June 1960), pp. 1885–1896. Omitted from this *Casebook* only make room for the same critic's later and more general interpretation Genet's drama. [Ed.]

From *Seasons of Discontent* (New York: Simon & Schuste London: Jonathan Cape, 1965). Reprinted by permission.

The Balcony is probably the most subversive work of literature to be created since the writings of the famous Marquis, it is a major dramatic achievement. Fashioned by a genius of criminality and revolt, the play is absolutely stunning in its twists and turns of thought, and (despite occasional thefts from Betti, Cocteau, and the surrealists) highly original in its use of the stage. In its interpretation of history, it is both provocative and scandalous; in its assault on what we take to be "the real," both inexorable and intolerable; in its violent demolition of established authority, both appealing and appalling. It is extremely difficult, in short, to speak of Genet without employing the *both . . . and* construction. If you consider yourself a good citizen concerned with preserving the social contract, you might feel inclined to stone the author and picket the Circle in the Square;[6] but if you are curious to know what the theater can be like when a perversely honest immoralist writes for it, empty your pockets of missiles and doff your picket boards, for *The Balcony* is one of the richest and most fascinating philosophical plays of the decade.

Genet's most important ideological influence, aside from de Sade, is the tradition of French pornography, and the opening scenes of *The Balcony* contain some ritual echoes of the Black Mass. A bishop confesses and feels up a half-naked penitent; a judge, aided by a whip-happy executioner, judges, condemns, and kisses the foot of a fleshly thief; a general is taken on an imaginary tour of his battlefield by a pulchritudinous horse—all as a prelude to sexual relations. For The Grand Balcony is a brothel—a house of illusions where ordinary men, by identifying with the Great Figures of the Christian state, may engage in blasphemous revels. These revels are stage-managed by Madame Irma, the severe proprietress of the establishment, who provides the "props of a display that they have to drag in the mud of the real and the commonplace": the studios in which the mas-

---

6. This essay appeared as a review in *The New Republic*, 28 March 1960, pp. 21–22, of the production by José Quintero at The Circle in the Square, New York, with Nancy Marchand (Madame Irma), Roy Poole (Chief of Police), and Betty Miller (Carmen). [Ed.]

querade takes place, the ladies who perform the supporting roles, and the proper costumes and cothurni, padded to give the impersonators a sense of their historical importance.

But Genet is less interested in the titillations of pornography than in its philosophical implications; and the erotic scenes are merely a prologue to his theatricalized vision of society, of life, and of history. For the various sacred offices are not only being desecrated in the brothel; they are also being *preserved* there, since to imitate these functions even blasphemously is to assume their authority. The real threat to the System lies not in whorehouse imposture but in a puritan rebellion that is being waged outside, dedicated to "reality" on the destruction of the whole artifice of Government, Clergy, Magistracy, and Army. The rebellion is successful in that individual functionaries, including the Queen, are killed, but a failure because the hieratic sanctions of two thousand years cannot be destroyed. Led by Madame Irma, who assumes the robes of Queen, the brothel Bishop, Judge, and General begin to play their imposture in earnest, and—exploiting the people's love of illusion and their need to worship images they can be unworthy of—immediately establish their authority. For Genet in other words, all functions are the manufacture of fakery and sham, and the artifice of the brothel is identical with the make-believe of the world. If the whorehouse is a mirror of society, society, in turn, reflects the whorehouse.

Yet, the play goes even deeper than this mordant social comment, becoming at last a rebellious assault upon the very heavens. The agent of this revolt is the Chief of Police (Irma's failing lover and the leader of the Government forces). Although, having quelled the rebellion, he is hailed as the Hero and has a colossal mausoleum constructed in his honor, his real ambition is to be impersonated in the brothel and thus to become a part of the Nomenclature. In his longing after classical *gloire*, in his desire to be the "One and Only," in his lust for power even over God's functionaries, he actually aspires toward godhead—and his godhead finally is achieved. Simulated by an impersonator who castrates himself in the process (mutilation is the destiny of the Man-God, whether he be Dionysus, Osiris, or Christ), the Chief orders "grub for two thousand years" and descends into his tomb, while the rat-a-tat-tat of machine guns announces that religion, revolution, and the cycles of civilization have been completely redefined as purely erotic phenomena, and a new rebellion is beginning outside. The Grand Balcony has become, in the short course of the evening, society, the universe, and the entire stage of history, as conceived by a cunning and diabolical mind. . . .

THE TRIUMPH OF POLITICS

PHILIP THODY

. . . On a political level, the plot of *The Balcony* is extremely clear: a working-class revolution is defeated by a chief of police efficient enough to maintain his authority over his men, and intelligent enough to exploit the traditional establishment until his own power is recognized as absolute. Genet himself,[7] protesting against what he considered was Peter Zadek's distortion of his play into a satire of the British monarchy, stated in an interview that he had originally set the action in Franco's Spain and added that the revolutionary who castrated himself represented "all Republicans when they acknowledge their defeat." Roger's action is, indeed, as blatant a piece of symbolism as any in *Deathwatch*, for the establishment of a police state by Hitler in Germany, by Franco in Spain, and by Stalin in Russia was either preceded or accompanied by a destruction of the power of the revolutionary working class. In *The Balcony*, the Chief of Police adds a further element to this account of how

---

7. Interview in *Arts*, 3 May 1957.

From *Jean Genet: A Critical Appraisal* (London: Hamish Hamilton, 1968; New York: Stein and Day, 1968), pp. 182–195. Reprinted by permission.

a revolution can be made to fail when he speaks of the "wild hope" that the people have had: "In losing all hope they will lose everything," he declares, until they finally come to lose themselves in him. Camus' *L'Homme Révolté* argues that the dictatorships of the mid-twentieth century proved acceptable because men were exhausted by an absolute revolt and disillusioned by its failure, and this remark by the Chief of Police suggests a very similar idea. It is not, of course, a particularly original one. Alexis de Tocqueville expressed it by quoting a phrase that was already four hundred years old when he wrote *L'Ancien Régime et la Révolution:* "Par requierre de trop grande franchise et libertés chet-on en trop grand serviage" ("By demanding too great and too extensive a liberty, men fall into too great a slavery"). There is also a parallel between the ending of *The Balcony* and that of Flaubert's *L'Education Sentimentale,* where the ex-socialist Sénécal becomes a policeman and shoots the idealistic Dussardier. What is curious is to find an author as unconventional as Genet suggesting ideas so closely associated with conservative and even reactionary thinkers.

Lucien Goldmann, arguing in *Les Temps Modernes*[8] in favor of a sociological interpretation of Genet's play, pointed to a fundamental difference between modern dictatorships and the absolute monarchies of the past when he compared the fame of a Himmler or a Beria with the obscurity of Louis XIV's minister for police, La Reynie. What *The Balcony* expressed, in his view, was a phenomenon that modern writers had so far tended to ignore: *"l'accroissement de prestige des techniciens de la répression dans la conscience de la grande masse"* ("the growth in prestige, among the masses, of technicians of repression"). It was quite possible, he suggested, that this aspect of social reality had found its way into Genet's text *"implicitement et en dehors de toute volonté consciente"* ("implicitly, and independently of any conscious intention"), and both *Querelle*

8. Lucien Goldmann, "Une pièce réaliste: *Le Balcon de Genet,*" *Les Temps Modernes,* June 1960, pp. 1885–1896.

of Brest and *The Thief's Journal* bear witness to a personal attitude of Genet toward policemen that may alone have inspired this aspect of *The Balcony*. Yet whatever Genet's original inspiration may have been, it is certainly true that this play deals more directly and more perceptively with the fundamental structure of modern society than any of his other works. This is visible even in relatively minor details, for another supposedly powerful figure whom no one coming to the brothel wishes to imitate is a colonial administrator. Empire-building never really caught the popular imagination either in France or in Great Britain, and it seems unlikely that this gap in what the English translation of *The Balcony* calls The Nomenclature will ever now be filled. In contrast, the position which the Chief of Police finally obtains still seems relatively secure.

Lucien Goldmann also pointed to a number of other features that, in his view, enable *The Balcony* to be interpreted as an allegory of the power relationships existing within modern capitalist society. Thus the Bishop, Judge, and General have no authority of their own. They can play at being powerful only when provided with a ready-made scenario by Madame Irma, or with a ready-made situation by the Chief of Police. They represent what Anthony Sampson called "the divorce between prestige and power" which characterizes much of modern British life, or what Marx would have seen as an example of imbalance between economic infrastructure and ideological superstructure. Genet also provides a fascinating vision of the pretensions which outmoded social institutions can still sometimes legitimately entertain when he shows the Bishop, Judge, and General, after their triumphant procession through the streets, trying to assert their independence of the Chief of Police. They know that until someone comes to the brothel with a request to impersonate him, the social institutions which they represent will still be able to use their prestige as a bargaining counter in their relationship with the holders of real economic or military power. Genet's view of society in *The Balcony* is a curious mixture of Marx and Pascal. Like the first, he seems to be arguing that real power lies not in the official institutions of society but with those who have the financial or physical means to enforce their will: Madame Irma counting her money and organizing the imaginary lives of her clients, the Chief of Police who goes as automatically to her in a moment of national crisis as reactionary dictators are reputed to run to Wall Street. But like Pascal, Genet also suggests that human nature is so in need of illusions that no social order can ever be based on reality. Madame Irma is afraid that if the revolutionaries win, they will bring the reign of her *maison d'illusions* to an end. The workers, she says, are "without imagination. Prudish and probably chaste," and her words are an apt commentary on the puritanism that seems to have characterized all revolutionaries from Cromwell to Castro, and from Robespierre to Mao Tse Tung. However, the revolutionaries are not so far above the common run of humanity as she imagines, since they too need their emblem. They find it in Chantal, a girl only recently rescued from the brothel by Roger, and whose ability to inspire the troops with her songs is reminiscent of the role played by La Passionaria in the Spanish Civil War. Chantal is shot dead at the very moment when Madame Irma, the Bishop, Judge, and General appear on the Balcony itself, which, as the stage directions indicate, "projects beyond the façade of the brothel," and the audience is later told that this killing had been arranged by the Bishop. From that point onward, the revolution is doomed to failure as much by its inability to offer a rival image to those of the Church, Monarchy, or Law, as by the superior fighting power of the police. It is almost as though Genet were agreeing with Pascal that men can act politically only if led by illusions, and the Chief of Police himself is inspired less by a desire for real power than by the hope of attaining the prestige symbolized by a place in the Nomenclature. By its associations with Pascal's ideas, *The Balcony* puts forward an essentially reactionary view of mankind, which seems to contradict the wider implication of Lucien Goldmann's contention that Genet had written "the first great Brechtian play in French literature."[9] Moreover, the insistence throughout *The Balcony* that nothing whatsoever is real constitutes a major obstacle to interpreting it as a left-wing play in the full sense of the word. True, it deals critically with the failure of a left-wing rebellion; Roger, Genet implied in his remark about Spain, was wrong to act as he did. But nowhere is there any suggestion that right action in politics is possible. If everything is illusion, nothing really deserves to be taken seriously.

The theme of illusion reaches its climax at the very end of the action, when Madame Irma comes to the front of the stage to remind the audience that they have, after all, only been watching a play. "You must now go home," she tells them, "where everything—you can be quite sure—will be falser than here." The insistence upon the unreality of what happens on stage is a truism in modern drama, but Genet gives it an extra twist by introducing it at the end of a play which itself shows people attempting to realize their identity through acting a series of roles. In *The Maids*, Solange and Claire were perpetually condemned to playing a part in order to be what they were, and in *The Balcony* it is only when the Chief of Police can play at being himself in the Nomenclature that he really feels himself becoming the Chief of Police. This idea has analogies with some of the views which Sartre expresses in *L'Etre et le néant*, but the importance of play-acting is too frequent a theme in the novels which Genet wrote before he met Sartre for there to be any serious question of a direct influence. In *Our Lady of the Flowers*, the criminals and homosexuals are all playing at being criminals and homosexuals, and the convicts in *Miracle of the Rose* draw their prestige less from what they are than from the success which they have in projecting a certain image of themselves. The characters in *The Balcony* are all intensely aware of the motives which inspire their actions, and the Bishop gives a lucid account of how

9. *Ibid.*, p. 1896.

superior to reality illusions are when he recalls how happy he and his fellows were when they pursued "the quest of an absolute dignity" in the privacy of their rooms. "In peace, in comfort, behind shutters, behind padded curtains, protected by a police force that protects brothels, we were able to be a general, judge and bishop to the point of perfection and to the point of rapture!" Reality does, it is true, offer other pleasures, but these are "the bitter delight of responsibility." The ideal, suggests the Bishop, is to dream and not to do.

When the Chief of Police first suggests that they should help him, the clients incarnating the Notables show considerable reluctance to be dragged from their dream world into the harshness and dangers of reality, and their misgivings are shown to have been justified by what happens to them. It is not that they suffer physically by going out among the people, for the crowds greet them with quite extraordinary enthusiasm. It is that once they have become, for the outside world, what formerly they only pretend to be in private, they are deprived of the solace afforded by imagination. The Bishop complains that he no longer looks forward to putting on his lace ornaments because they have "become himself," the Judge laments that he is "just a dignity represented by a skirt," while the General sums up their whole problem by saying that he no longer dreams. Were they to remain in reality what they had so enjoyed pretending to be in the past, they would have to go to another brothel, where the General would be, for example, a judge or a stonemason, and the Bishop a plumber or a soldier in the Foreign Legion. "Human kind," wrote T. S. Eliot, "cannot bear very much reality," and *The Balcony* provides quite unexpected support for his view. It is partly to compensate themselves for the loss of their dreams that the Bishop, General, and Judge make their attempt to exercise real power, and it is significant that everyone in the play is much more anxious to *be* than to *do*. While this may reflect something of Genet's own experience in trying to *be* evil, he greatly enlarges the appeal of *The Balcony* by making his characters want to be bishops, generals, judges, or policemen and not merely famous criminals. Its treatment of the contrast between illusion and reality undoubtedly benefits from being placed in a wider context than a prison cell, and the jokes about sex and religion make it the most relevant of all Genet's works to the ideas and experience of the average reader or theatergoer.

A central theme in Genet's novels was undoubtedly the gap between criminals as he had imagined them and criminals as he found them to be. This gap is even wider if the almost idyllic atmosphere of his poetry is compared to the much more disillusioned account of crime provided by his novels, but the humor which arises from the contrast in his fiction is almost certainly unintentional. The middle-class reader, secure in his own values, may find Mignon very funny, but there is little evidence in *Our Lady of the Flowers* to suggest that Genet is presenting him with deliberate comic intent. In *The Balcony*, on the other hand, there is no doubt that when he suddenly allows reality to intrude into the general atmosphere of illusion, he is doing so to raise a laugh. At one point, for example, Madame Irma is so carried away by the splendor of the illusions which she can offer that she launches into a magnificently rhetorical speech where she quite loses contact with reality. Carmen, the girl to whom she is speaking—and for whom, in what is apparently an established tradition, she nourishes markedly Lesbian feelings—suddenly interrupts her to say how well she speaks. "J'ai poussé jusqu'au brevet" ("I went through elementary school"), replies Madame Irma, and the audience is brought quickly back to earth. Her remark also echoes a detail in *Our Lady of the Flowers*, since Divine, Genet remarks, "*porte toujours sur elle le diplôme graisseux et gris de son certificat d'études supérieures*" ("always carries in her pocket her oily gray diploma for advanced study") and it may well be that this was yet another way in which Louis Culafroy repeated one of Genet's own habits. The interesting point is that Genet should have been able to take up this minor feature of his first fictional character and use it to such excellent and apparently impersonal dramatic effect. According to Jean Fayard's review of the play in *Le Figaro*,[10] Marie Bell said the line in a voice worthy of Bérénice, and in a way it epitomizes the complexity of the dramatic illusion in *The Balcony*: the characters cease to play one part only to begin another, and the humor lies in the different degrees of unreality that this fact suggests. Like all Genet's works, it expresses that side of his personality which Sartre emphasized when he called him a *comédien*. The difference is that the play-acting is now controlled and exploited to provide both laughter and social comment.

The play is indeed constructed around the contrast between reality and illusion, and a number of other incidents emphasize this in a humorous and perceptive way. The General, for example, hears a woman cry out for help in an adjoining room, and prepares to leap to her defense. However, Madame Irma tells him not to bother since he is now in civilian clothes. The Bishop also takes the greatest pleasure in forgiving the sins committed by his pretty penitent, but insists that she should really confess to them. "Our holiness," he tells the girl, "lies only in our being able to forgive you your sins," and he obviously could not do this unless he could persuade himself that she has sinned. When, however, she suddenly asks him what he would do if her sins were real, his mask immediately drops. "You're mad," he exclaims, "I hope you didn't really do all that! . . . If your sins were real, they would be crimes, and I'd be in a fine mess." Like the man who said that he was a masochist until it started to hurt, the Bishop can extend his fantasy world only up to a certain point. Once reality breaks in, the fantasies become unbearable. While he is playing his role, however, the Bishop makes a remark which again emphasizes how many of Genet's own preoccupations are still dodging about only slightly below the surface of this play. In the brothel, the Bishop maintains, "There's no possibility of doing evil." "You live in evil," he tells the girl. "In the absence of

---

10. Jean Fayard, in *Le Figaro*, 19 May 1960.

remorse. How could you do evil?" The brothel not only reflects the real world because people spend all their time there playing social roles; there too, as in life as we know it, absolute evil is impossible. The insistence upon pretense is also linked to another theme in Genet's novels, since like them, *The Balcony* stresses the elusiveness of satisfactory experience in the realm of sexual abnormality.

In an article published in *Encounter* in May 1959, Wayland Young argued that *The Balcony* expressed more of the nature and atmosphere of prostitution than any social survey could hope to reproduce. Although there is a reference in the play to "*les passes simples*," it is clear that very few of Madame Irma's "vi-si-tors, I don't allow myself . . . even to refer to them as clients" come to the brothel for straight sex. The emphasis throughout is on perversions, and this very much reflects the general picture which Wayland Young gave of prostitution in London. All the sexual deviations which Genet mentions in *The Balcony*, from the Judge or General with their major power fantasies to "the one you tie up, spank, whip and soothe, and then he snores," also have the same feature in common: they are attempts to use sex in order to obtain a particular psychological mode of being. The men who indulge in them are, apparently, referred to by prostitutes as "*cérébraux*"—people concerned with ideas rather than physical reality. Because such people are, to use a phrase coined by Gilbert Ryle to express a different kind of mistake, "trying to gaff a salmon with an ace of spades," they will always remain unsuccessful and unsatisfied. One of the characteristics of de Sade's novels, and of sado-masochistic literature in general, is the accumulation of more and more complicated tortures in a frenzied attempt to attain a particular mental state: that of the person who feels either that he has absolute power or that he is a helpless victim. But since this psychological state has to be achieved through dwelling on physical events, there is a constantly frustrating discrepancy between the means employed and the results pursued. In the presence of genuine suffering, the reaction of the sadist or masochist who had not sublimated his sexual urges into other channels would be like that of the Bishop with a real sin: horrified indignation. When, at the very end of the play, the Chief of Police goes down into his tomb to wait two thousand years for his apotheosis, he adopts the only permanent solution which there is to the problem of aberrant sex: he goes mad. The Bishop, Judge, and General will simply have to come back for more. They are not only incapable of transforming their illusions into reality; they do not even want this to happen.

The Balcony differs from Genet's novels by presenting sexual deviations with no shade of compassion or complicity. In *Our Lady of the Flowers*, Divine is pitiful as well as comic, and in *Querelle of Brest* there is Madame Lysiane's comforting: "Heureusement qui y a les vicieux, Mesdemoiselles, ça permet aux mal foutus de connaître l'amour." ("Good thing there are perverts, girls. It lets the ugly know what love is like.") In showing Madame Irma's clients as funny, Genet is endorsing the conventional attitude in a way quite unique in his whole work. Discuss sexual perversions in any saloon bar, and the reaction will be the same: kinkies are comic. Perhaps Genet adopts this attitude toward his characters because they are all, for all their peculiarities, heterosexual. He may thus be replying to the implications of the English term "queer" by pointing to a corresponding queerness in heterosexual behavior, and there is no doubt that Genet carefully directs the laughter away from his own characteristics. Nevertheless, it is possible to see links between the experience of homosexuality described in Genet's novels and his account of heterosexual perversions in *The Balcony*. In the same way that Divine gradually infected Mignon and Notre-Dame with her own wild, feminine ways, or Mario and Querelle became more feminine through their sexual relationship with each other, so Madame Irma's visitors gradually impart their own taste for illusions to her girls. Carmen, for example, has so enjoyed being the Immaculate Conception of Lourdes for "a bank-clerk from the National Provincial" that she implores Madame Irma to allow her to play the part again. The world of homosexuality, as *Our Lady of the Flowers* showed, is also one of illusions, where men are attractive through a masculinity that has to be false if they are to have sexual relations with their male admirers. In transposing the need for illusions into the heterosexual world of Madame Irma's "Grand Balcon," Genet is by no means taking an unjust revenge. It would be a brave heterosexual indeed who claimed that fantasy was totally absent from his own sex life, and the following conversation is an indication of the extent to which Genet makes *The Balcony* into a fairly serious discussion of this particular problem.

CARMEN: *He's married, isn't he?*

IRMA: *As a rule, I don't like to talk about the private life of my visitors. The Grand Balcony has a world-wide reputation. It's the most artful, yet the most decent house of illusions. . . .*

CARMEN: *Decent?*

IRMA: *Discreet. But I might as well be frank with you, you inquisitive girl. Most of them are married.* (*A pause.*)

CARMEN: *When they're with their wives, whom they love, do they keep a tiny, small-scale version of their revels in a brothel. . . .*

IRMA (reprimanding her): *Carmen!*

CARMEN: *Excuse me, Madame . . . in a house of illusions. I was saying: do they keep their revels in a house of illusions tucked away in the back of their heads in miniature form, far off? But present?*

When *The Balcony* was virtually banned in Paris in 1957,[11] it was suggested in *Combat* that the reason lay in Genet's audacity in showing a General and a Bishop in a brothel. This

11. See *Combat*, 7 November 1957.

may well have been the case, and the Fourth Republic was, by that time, so ill-assured that it could afford to offend no possible pillar of the establishment. The ban must have given Genet great pleasure, for it showed him that blasphemy was still possible because the official view which society had of itself still coincided with his vision of it. He had spoken in *The Thief's Journal* of "the supposedly rational disposition of our epoch," and it could certainly be argued that a truly rational society would not have been offended by *The Balcony*. For such a society, judges and generals would be no different from other civil servants. No sacred aura of the Law or of Military Glory would hang around them, and a Bishop would be merely a person paid and disguised to run a particular organization and perpetuate alternately comforting and frightening myths. For the Genet who was still, even in *The Balcony*, living out what Sartre calls his "original crisis," such figures were very different, and the reaction which he evoked from the French authorities in 1957 showed how acute an analysis of the irrationality of modern society his private obsessions could still enable him to make.

The banning of his play also indicated, however, not only that the France of the Fourth Republic was still trying to give its social myths a semi-sacred function, but also that its censors could not understand fairly conventional works of avant-garde literature. Genet was not showing a bishop going into a brothel, but a gas man[12] going into a brothel in order to play at being a bishop. An ingenious advocate could even have pointed out that this was less of an insult to the Church than a compliment to the prestige which it still enjoyed, and Genet's treatment of religion in *The Balcony* is not without certain perception. Perhaps by accident, the Bishop puts his finger on the contradictory situation of those clerics who seek preferment but also wish to observe the Christian virtues when he says: "Never—I affirm it before God Who sees me—I never desired the epis-

12. Cf. *Picture Post*, 11 May 1957.

copal throne. To become bishop, to work my way up—by means of virtues and vices—would have been to turn away from the ultimate dignity of bishop. I shall explain: in order to become a bishop, I should have had to make a zealous effort not to be one, but to do what would have resulted in my being one." From the context, he appears to be talking about the impossibility of anyone coinciding absolutely with his function, for he continues: "Having become a bishop, in order to be one I should have had—in order to be one for myself, of course!—I should have had to be constantly aware of being one so as to perform my function." But whatever ideas Genet may have intended to suggest, it is the paradox of the ambitious cleric which he underlines most clearly, and this particular incident embodies his whole achievement in *The Balcony:* he talks about his own permanent concern with illusions, and does so in terms of ceremonies; but he also sheds light on a much wider variety of general topics than he evokes in any other work.

For a number of reasons, however, none of the productions which *The Balcony* has so far received has given equal importance to all the different themes which it presents. Invariably, the opening tableaux representing the Bishop, Judge, and General have gone over very well, while the second half, with its insistence upon the failure of the revolution, has been less convincingly performed. T. C. Worsley,[13] reviewing the 1957 London production, summed up a fairly general reaction when he wrote: "A plunge into the visionary comedy of the first act is warmly recommended. But at the interval you may well reach for your respectable hat and coat and you would not miss much by obeying the prompting." Kenneth Tynan,[14] commenting on the same production, also showed how fully the political theme had been underplayed when he stated that "a stranger asks permission to dress up as the Chief of Police." This was

13. T. C. Worsley, *New Statesman*, 27 April 1957.
14. Kenneth Tynan, *Curtains* (New York: Atheneum Press, 1963), p. 171.

not altogether Peter Zadek's fault, for his production was still based to a large extent upon the early version of the play which Genet had published in 1956. In this, Roger's self-castration takes place off-stage and is reported to the audience by Carmen. Moreover, since she refers to him merely as "*l'ancien plombier de Madame Irma*" ("Madame Irma's former plumber"), the wider significance of his gesture inevitably disappears. Even in the revised version which Peter Brook finally managed to put on in Paris in May 1960, a number of cuts[15] were made in the scenes dealing with the defeat of revolution, though these prevented neither Lucien Goldmann from writing his brilliant analysis of the play nor Bernard Dort[16] from underlining how relevant it was to the immediate political atmosphere in France. "For us who live under the Fifth Republic," he wrote, "in this republic with no republicans, in a régime which borrows its appearance and language from History in order better to deny it, the games at which Genet invites us to be present are far from gratuitous."

Relatively few critics, however, have discussed the very obvious political ideas which the final text of *The Balcony* presents when read in its entirety in the study, and this lack of comment throws an interesting light upon the way in which an author's general reputation may, especially in the theater, affect the interpretation given to one of his works. Because Genet has, for the most part, been associated with the essentially apolitical "theater of the absurd," and because he has almost always chosen to emphasize this aspect of his work in his writings on the theater, directors have fought shy of bringing out the full political significance which his work undoubtedly contains. They may have been right to do so, and there is also a strong temptation even for the sociologically minded critic to share David Grossvogel's interpretation of

---

15. See *Libération*, 21 May 1960; also Jacques Lemarchand, in *Figaro Littéraire*, 21 May 1960.

16. "Le Jeu de Genet," *Les Temps Modernes*, June 1960, pp. 1875–1884.

Genet's plays in terms of his homosexuality.[17] "The patterns of this drama," Mr. Grossvogel wrote of *The Maids*, "are like the sterile turgescence and detumescence of the homosexual act, conceived in loneliness and fraud and ending in deception. This is also the way in which each of Genet's plays is constructed." For it is true that, with the exception of *The Blacks*, each of Genet's plays tells the story of a defeat, since even in *The Screens* there is no hope of an individual salvation for Saïd in the revolution which he has helped to make possible. The fact that Genet is so unremittingly pessimistic in things political should not, however, necessarily prevent his plays from being presented as comments on how modern society is evolving.

17. David I. Grossvogel, *Four Playwrights and a Postscript* (New York: Cornell University Press, 1962), p. 149.

The Blacks

Les Nègres was performed for the first time at the Théâtre de Lutèce in Paris on 28 October 1959, in a brilliant production by Roger Blin, with sets and costumes by André Acquart. On 16 December 1960, this production was transferred to the Théâtre de la Renaissance, where it finished its remarkable first run of 169 performances. It was awarded the Grand Prix de la Critique for the year 1959.

The critics and the authorities were expecting the usual Genet "scandal": instead, they were greeted with a furor which seems to have taken them completely by surprise. To begin with, the actors—a Negro troupe called "Les Griots"—were completely unknown. Originally consisting only of three professional players: Toto Bissainthe (Bobo), Robert Liensol (Ville de Saint-Nazaire), and Judith Aucagos (Neige), the group had been encouraged by Blin since about 1956; it had grown gradually in size, but mainly by the addition of amateur or semi-amateur actors, not all of whom were always fully audible under the conditions of the professional stage. Furthermore, the company included a wide variety of nationalities (various West Indians, two Senegalese, two Haitians, and one each from Guinea, Guyana, and the Cameroons), of colors—and of accents. But Blin rehearsed this mixed party with such incomparable skill and thoroughness that Les Nègres proved to be one of the finest pieces of theater seen on the French stage for years.

As usual, the press and the literary reviews were sharply divided in their reactions, the clan of the outraged being led by Gabriel Marcel in Les Nouvelles Littéraires (17 Dec. 1959: "the rejection, the spitting forth, the vomiting of everything that has constituted the honor and the dignity of the Christian

West"), while the enthusiasts were headed by Pierre Marcabru in Arts (11/17 Nov. 1959: "a rare and precious achievement... brilliant and somber beauty"). In between came a whole range of qualified distaste or approbation: Jean Duvignaud in Les Lettres Nouvelles (28 Oct.: "Roger Blin at grips with 'The Blacks' "); Bernard Poirot-Delpech in Le Monde ("an exceptional work which defies all the rules"); Jean-Jacques Gautier in Le Figaro (4 Nov.: "the author's caricatural, degrading, and defiling intentions"); Marcelle Capron in Combat (4 Nov.: "an iconoclast smashing true and false gods indifferently"); Jean Cau in L'Express (5 Nov.: "A Portrait of Jean Genet"); Jacques Lemarchand in Le Figaro Littéraire (7 Nov.: "a true poet has taken the stage and a hundred books on dramatic theory have been made useless"); Maurice Regnaut in Théâtre Populaire (No. 36, 1959/IV: "a bourgeois betrayal of socialism . . . traces of racism and apocalyptic manichaeism"); Claude Olivier in Les Lettres Françaises (12/18 Nov.: "a courageous work . . . a vibrant denunciation of racism"); André Camp in L'Avant-Scène (11/17 Nov.: "I know of nothing more tragic, more 'sick,' more desperate, or more sinister"); Michel Zéraffa in Europe (Jan. 1960: "a work of grandeur"); Robert Abirached in Etudes (Jan./Mar. 1960: "stars of purity amid the mud"); and Guy Dumur in Spectacles (30 Oct. 1960: "Jean Genet's dramas are by themselves enough to replace the whole classical theater").

In spite of this wide range of opinion, however, few critics attempted any serious analysis of the themes or implications of the play. The following review is typical:

THE GOSPEL ACCORDING TO SAINT GENET

ROBERT KANTERS

Moving from Giraudoux [*Electre*] to Jean Genet is like going from the drawing room to the . . . to the whorehouse. From

From *L'Express*, no. 438 (5 Nov. 1959), pp. 36–37. Reprinted by permission. Translated by R.N.C.

blossom to dungheap, from an art of ironical understatement to an art of lewd and filthy imprecation. But a change of air is good for the health of the mind, and when lewd and filthy imprecation is exalted to the status of an art. . . .

It is impossible to give a valid summary of *The Blacks*. Genet himself calls it a "clown show"—it is drama-as-ambush, in which the innocent who least expects it gets a custard-pie slap in the face. . . .

If you enjoy getting bashed on the head, then you *must* go to see *The Blacks*.

Having said that much, however, the question remains: what *is* the Gospel according to Saint Genet which is propagated at this curious Mass? A gospel of derision rather than a gospel of hatred. The degradation of the White Man, the degradation of Woman, the degradation of the Priest—these are the three chief articles of the anti-credo which is intoned at us *ad nauseam*. The Queen, the Judge, the Missionary, the Governor are *guignol* figures, or rather simple Aunt Sallies which are to be knocked down with immense hilarity . . . which often becomes hilarious obscenity. Blasphemies fall like huge turds on the altars of Faith and Fatherland. . . .

The play is provocative, a crying scandal to the pious-minded; but, after all, it is sometimes necessary to shout too loud in order to be heard at all, and there is courage in smashing idols in the very faces of the worshipers. But having said that, it is important, in these troubled times of ours, that everyone realize that in the matter of provocation it is as well to beware of *agents provocateurs*. The Chief Constable and the Archbishop would be ill advised to take offense too hastily at the scandal; but then M. Sekou Touré [President of the Republic of Guinea], for example, would be no less ill advised to celebrate too quickly. Jean Genet's work in general, and *The Blacks* in particular, does not constitute a revolution: it is nothing but a revolt.

It is one long cry of revolt, the revolt of a man who is alone. Of a "Black." And when that cry of revolt and of suffering reaches our consciousness, then at last, in spite of the hall-of-mirrors that makes up the action, in spite of the tom-tom throbbing of bawdy language, there is something that speaks straight to our hearts. Then the voice of the poet exalts, and we discover within our grasp a substratum of Truth.

M. Jean Genet's fire and brimstone fall from the skies on all manner of men and on all manner of institutions, because all men and all institutions alike have striven to prevent him from becoming what he has now become. But he is not in favor of anything—even if it seems that he is in favor of freedom, it is a dismal sort of freedom, this ideal of his, and he cherishes it with bitter delectation, for the wrong reasons. Thus, for instance, the excellent Negro actors at the Théâtre de Lutèce are required to make themselves up blacker than nature in order to perform the play of our white author . . . the savage! A crankish and crazy play, now nauseating and now sophisticated; and the performance lasts two hours on end, without an interval—and yet this savage, this outlaw, this Byron of the bawdy-house . . . he is *our* Byron for all that, our brother. . . .

In spite of the success of The Blacks *in Paris, however, its repercussions were limited compared with the splendor of the triumph that followed in New York. The play opened on 4 May 1961 at the St. Mark's Playhouse, in a production by Gene Frankel, with sets by Kim Swados and costumes by Patricia Zipprodt; the cast included James Earl Jones (Village), Roscoe Lee Browne (Archibald), and Godfrey Cambridge (Diouf); and it ran for over three years, closing finally on 27 September 1964. Clearly, the relevance of the theme to that most pressing of American social and political problems—racism—accounts in part for its extraordinary effect, and it was undoubtedly through* The Blacks *that America discovered Genet's stature as a writer; but there is also the fact that the average intellectual level of literary and dramatic reviewing in America had been rising steadily ever since 1945; and there is no more striking evidence of this than a comparison between the French and American reviews of this same play.*

BEING BLACK IS A TRAGEDY

HENRY HEWES

There are those who would interpret *The Blacks* as simply a burning indictment of white society and white inhumanity. But isn't the virtue of this play the fact that it is unrelated to political or sociological policy? Of course, the whites have behaved immorally toward the blacks, but Genet's concern is not with making them behave better. Rather, he is writing pure description of the qualities he finds in the whites and the blacks of organized society as he views them through his prismatic eye. It appears to be Genet's point of view, that being black in our times is itself a tragedy. Thus the dilemma of the various-shaded clowns in this play is that they can never be black enough. Conversely, he suggests that the comedy of their situation may be that they can never be white enough. If M. Genet is plumping for anything in this play, it is perhaps for a destruction of a sentimental and hypocritical society that happens to be white, in favor of a more cruel and realistic society that happens to be black. He also indicates, however, that such a shift in power is more likely to come from white exhaustion than black militancy and that it might result in a society just as squeamish and ignoble as he feels the present one to be. Thus *The Blacks* is a porcupine with quills of sharp paradox aimed at anyone who would embrace it. . . .

From "It's Your Funeral," *Saturday Review*, 3 June 1961, p. 29. Reprinted by permission.

THE REACTION OF A CRITIC IN HIS FIFTIES

JOHN GASSNER

. . . Do I think well of *The Blacks?* I would be evading the question if I were to reply that Genet strikes me as the most gifted member of the avant-garde and a genius, if the term is allowable for minor figures in the theater, as I think it must be, let us say, in describing the dramatic work of Büchner, Musset, and Montherlant. It would also be evasion on my part if I merely suggested that everyone should see this rancorous play for its tonic acidity, its expressive use of mimetic and choreographic elements, and its example of a creative recession of conceptual thinking in dramatic writing. I have in mind here a "direct," non-Aristotelian, pit-of-the-stomach mode of communication (we seem to owe this to the *surréaliste* mutiny of the nineteen-twenties), requiring from the playgoer a "sitting back in a sort of wise passiveness, a state of negative capability, to let the play work on one as a total theatrical experience." I believe that this is an important "new" approach to dramatic art and an approvable one, if kept within bounds to make sure that play-writing does not degenerate into echolalia or into sign language and smoke-writing. Personally I prefer it to the explicitness of banal sentiment and blatant rhetoric that afflicts most Broadway and West End plays, including those on racial conflict, that carry a message via the theater that, as someone (was it Humphrey Bogart) said, should be given instead to Western Union.

Would it still be hedging, if I said that I found *The Blacks* loathsome as well as fascinating? That it is altogether too arrogantly convoluted, that its author is also too self-consciously ingenious, that his playing with the audience is as cute as it is sadistic may explain a good deal of my resentment. Some of my resentment—nay, a good deal of it—is also produced by its

From "Broadway in Review," *Educational Theatre Journal,* October 1961, pp. 214–221. Reprinted by permission.

unconscionable capitalization on race hatred. Friends of the play will call this "truth-telling." Just so! and I, for one, would rather see it *repressed* than *exploited*; and I would certainly prefer to have it under control rather than have it invading the theater and *crawling* all over it. (I use the word "crawling" because the hate has a Genet way of insinuating itself into the soul with a mordant mockery that is both sheer genius and sheer meanness.) Finally, I must confess that some of my irritation derives from the complacency with which a younger generation of playgoers than mine appeared to be receiving this play and other negativistic pieces as though the Bible consisted of only portions of Ecclesiastes, or, to change the figure, as if a fistful of gunpowder had the aroma of the finest perfume. Admittedly, this is the reaction of a critic in his fifties. It is the kind of reaction that middle-aged critics registered when expressionism was young and ran riot for about a decade in Germany and, before that, when Naturalism had its brief vogue on the European stage. And were they so very wrong, I wonder! Still, I am not at all sure that my negative reaction, only partly canceled out by my fascination, is not excessive. Indeed, it may be to the credit of the author to be able to evoke strong reactions. Of one thing, however, I am confident. It is that this alternately ironic and snarling work, which makes innocents of Ibsen, Shaw, and even Brecht, is no pretense but a genuine eruption of hostile feelings that becomes, in the end, *self-destructive*.

"I think," said the actor Godfrey Cambridge, "that they [the playgoers] are mesmerized by the surface excitements"—and, one might add, by the surface ingenuity and overcomplication of the work. It is not a play that achieves penetration and illumination as its final result, for the mind stops understanding the work under mesmerization even when it is not already distracted by confusion or irritation. And the same thing can be said about the emotional end result; I would put it this way—the work is so drastically cathartic that it is not actually purging, for it produces new tensions and leaves one groggy from the assault on the nervous system. The result may well be that a work of tremendous honesty of emotion that makes short shrift of traffic with social bromides becomes in effect sensational and self-defeating. . . .

THE BLACKS *AND RITUAL THEATER*

GEORGE B. MACDONALD

Of the current playwrights on the avant-garde scene, few have been more influential in effecting a single, lasting change on the naturalistic theater than France's Jean Genet. A man whose dramatic achievements are still being quite heatedly debated, Genet is fiercely concerned—if not obsessed—with the obligation of contemporary theater to parallel rival arts by examining closely man's most elemental fears, drives, and values. And despite some approbation from both casual theatergoer and perceptive critic, one finds that even his harshest detractors cannot avoid a certain perverse fascination with Genet's concept of ritualistic drama, the blackness he is trying if not to purge, at least to illumine for our edification, and the unending depth of his vision of illusion and reality. . . .

What Genet is attempting, not only in *The Blacks*, but in *The Maids* and *The Balcony*, is a shift from the naturalistic theater—an institution whose longevity easily outranks corresponding developments in rival arts—to a ritualistic, "theatrical" theater, one which embodies all the spontaneous and natural expressions of man and which includes music and dance as well as poetry and acting. By using a ceremonial approach to convey immediate ideas, Genet is returning to the deepest roots of theatrical endeavor; for primitive drama, like its creators, was eminently practical in its concern for the basic needs of the race. To prepare for battle or insure a prosperous

From *Humanities*, Spring 1962, pp. 32–44.

hunt, man would act and dance out his desires with unshaken belief that willing a thing would make it so. Like Genet's plays, these rites assumed "greater complexity, dance, rhythms, subtler symbolization, and more lyric representation."[1] In a similar manner, developments found in Genet are paralleled in the earliest evolution of ritual theater. When it was realized that some of man's ceremonies—such as dancing for a fruitful harvest in autumn—had an unfailing correspondence with the nature of things, a certain fusion of theatricalism and scientific predictability arose. Half-aware that some of the acts he effected were independent of his rituals, man nevertheless retained the rituals; they satisfied his creative and dramatic impulses and somehow made life's mysteries easier to bear. In like manner, just as there grew in primitive drama this combination of action and ritual to accomplish an act, the spectator discovers the Negroes in *The Blacks* performing a drama—the violation and downfall of the Whites—which would seem to have definite repercussions in a world outside the theater. It is because Genet believes the irrational, ritualistic, theatrical instincts of man are as basic to him as they were in his cave-dwelling ancestors that he has the frustrated denizens of Madame Irma's bordello in *The Balcony* achieve a most palpable reality in their mighty illusions, and the ferocious, but cunning and carefully disciplined Negroes in *The Blacks* actually attaining supremacy over the Whites partially through the sheer dynamism of their worked-up hatred—a fury which would seem to prompt some positive action on the "outside," some transformation of desire and ritual into act. As Gassner writes on the dramatic impulses of primitive man:

> *Like children and mentally diseased adults, he thought he could influence events by willing them. If only he could describe something he needed or if only he could think wishfully enough, he believed he might get his heart's desire.*

---

1. John Gassner, *Masters of the Drama* (New York: Dover Publications, 1954), p. 5.

In fact, we still make this assumption more often than we care to admit. And since primitive man was not adept at uttering his thoughts (Genet's ideas on incommunicability enter here) he resorted to actions.[2]

Thus, the playwright never allows his audiences to understand, or have their attention restricted by, a comprehensible plot or the development of conventional characters or theme. Constantly being diverted and distracted, charmed and terrified, the spectator finds any rapport on a literal level denied him; rather, he is supposed to be moved not by isolated incidents and individual character relations (the true meaning of which may be unknowable for Genet), but by the ceremony itself—the very ritual in whose theatricality and often magnificent illusion Genet seems to find a profoundly real answer to man's most primal needs. Holding that Genet's basic assumption is that "man is a theatrical animal, and his theatricality explains his greatness and his folly," translator Bernard Frechtman, in his preface to the Showbill of *The Blacks*, writes:

> *Genet is endeavoring to create a theater which is ceremony. In* The Blacks *and* The Balcony, *ceremony is achieved through the behavior of characters who enact a ritual. . . . Genet seems to be presenting an action. . . . At the end, when the elaborate structure seems to be completed, we discover that there has been no plot at all, that the magician has been diverting us with* ceremony itself.[3]

In *The Balcony* this ritual, performed dark within the plush secrecy of a perversely sacred brothel, consists in the assumption of identities which life never granted an archetypal group of misfits; in *The Maids* it is a similar masquerade, this time maids of their mistresses; and in *The Blacks* it is, to use Mr. Frechtman's summation, "a lyrical and symbolic murder of

2. Ibid., p. 4.
3. Bernard Frechtman, Showbill for *The Blacks* (New York, 1961), p. 5.

the oppressor": a ceremony of incommunicability which paradoxically carries more meaning and strikes home more deeply than words and other traditional conveyances of human expression which have become sterile, almost useless, in their nonrelation to reality.

With man depicted as little more than a self-interested animal whose only ascendancy to achievement lies in the knowing degree to which he is able to deceive himself and his fellows, we find nothing in *The Blacks* discussed in terms of concrete imagery. Genet is much more fond of intricate networks of abstractions and illusions, all of which are cloaked in deceptively earthy, sometimes grossly obscene, and often wildly funny terms. Rich in its symbolism and almost hypnotic in the grandeur of its lyricism, the sardonic fury of its irony, and the symphonic quality it assumes in the musical voices of an all-Negro cast, Genet's dialogue is the ideal foil for the elusiveness of his theme, the seemingly absurd contradictions of his play. For none of the work's ideas—in direct contrast to the often vulgar concreteness of its individual images—could be described in such a way that a purely rational intellect would understand them. Since *The Blacks* in its totality is a play, the entertainment of the Negroes a play within a play, the White girl's murder a play within a play within a play, Diouf's ascension into Heaven a play within a play within a play within a play and so on, a true paraphrasing of the entire work becomes not the labor of a lifetime, but of an eternity. Its levels are continually being shuffled, its juxtapositions become identities, its opposing forces fight on either side.

From the initial sequences of *The Blacks*, it would seem that Genet is wholly concerned with the tormenting repression and the near paranoic schizophrenia which Western culture has imposed upon the African—that exotic breed the White man once hunted with the antelope, but now, owing more to a general lack of interest than anything else, is treated with a peculiar blend of vague resentment and polite tolerance. In a world which has watched, feared, patronized, and despised him the Negro is beginning to realize that unless his split image of half-assimilation is rejected, unless he lives up to his color, Black, and finds a comforting identity in the falseness of the darkly mysterious and evil connotations the Whites have given it, he is doomed to a life of meaningless, subjugated grayness. His rebellion is facilitated by the lethargy of his masters, men of a superior race whose time for acting out *their* color—and with it self-righteously treating anything dark or obscure, such as a black race, with the proper superiority that Whiteness, or the forces of goodness, should naturally maintain over the forces of evil—is running out. As the Missionary says, "God is white." Otherwise, "would he have allowed the Miracle of Greece? For two thousand years God has been white. He eats on a white tablecloth. He wipes his white mouth with a white napkin. He picks at white meat with a white fork. He watches the snow fall." Because their power is now taken for granted, because they have forgotten that they are no more than actors using their color as a criterion and as a sanction for their thoughts and their behavior, the Whites no longer realize that those who have had to pay for the purity of their supremacy are the Negroes and anything else suspiciously unfathomable in its non-Whiteness. The self-destructive sterility symbolized in the foppery of an apparently homosexual valet, the ineffectual pomposity of the Judge, the Governor, and the Missionary—not to mention the pampered fatigue of Her Majesty—are indicative of the wasted endurance of the White race. Felicity, in her magnificent dance of death with the Queen, realizes this: "Before long you'll see what's hidden beneath our display . . . You're exhausted, all of you . . . Your journey has worn you out. You're dropping with sleep . . . You're dreaming!"

The Negroes' faith in the efficacy of ritual, the power of their brutality, and their knowledge that words and conventional means of communication have lost all relevance, lead them to perform their grotesque little entertainment—a macabre harlequinade which becomes increasingly horrifying as the hidden sufferings of the Negro subconscious, like suppuration from a festering wound, begin to ooze forth. The ceremony itself reveals no inconsistency between Genet's dramatic principles and those of ancient ritual theater. For although from its totality a great deal may be learned not only of the basic selfishness of the unrestrained human animal, but of the nature of the eternally vacillating master-slave relationship, the ritual's individual elements, like all the illusion springing from man's instinctive theatricality, defy rational interpretation. The very springboard for Genet's ideas is a play within a play. Marie, the white woman, is played by a Negro wearing a hideously smiling mask, the members of the Court are shot with a bullet-less revolver, and the work's philosophy is discussed in the most illusory terms conceivable—color, a phenomenon, a mere sensation having no reality except when embodied in an object. And just as man's first drama might have been a pantomime in which an enterprising cave-dweller conveyed, "I came across a lion, killed and ate him, and am now strong," Genet's play itself is the most basic type of ritual presentation: the ruthless sacrifice of one race by another.[4] The ancient custom of portraying the victor eating the flesh of his vanquished enemy is suggested, sexually, in the gross atrocities performed on Marie during the microcosmic ritual within the play itself, and by Archibald, who alludes to the race's "cannibal tastes" while telling his Negroes not even "to be content with eating Whites" in the glorification of the color Black.

Thus, staying within the confines of ritual theater, the playwright has rooted all his dialogue and component situation—except, perhaps, the final, possibly optimistic, scene in which Virtue and Village *seem* on the brink of establishing some true contact—in theatricality. For ritual theater is nothing more (nothing less, Genet would say) than a lapse into irrationality or, perhaps going one step further, falseness in the traditional

4. Gassner, pp. 8, 11.

sense. Working with the abstractions of reality and illusion through the colors black and white, Genet, in reality turning inside out, discovers that the two are interchangeable and usually mistaken for one another. Accordingly, the Negroes will now assume all the godlike qualities of the Whites (Felicity tells us that all that is tender and kind in the new world will be black: "sugar, rice, the sky, doves, hope, will be black") and in all probability will eventually mistake the illusion of their grandeur for their rightful place in the universe and be overthrown by a new race—another theatrical people willing to live up to the code of their predecessors and take on the attributes as well as the reputation of evil and savagery. The finest irony in Genet, however, is that just as we do not know whether the slaves are the real rulers because they have the insight and the fury to recognize power and seize it from what is probably a continually weakening ruling class; just as we are led to believe that reality exists insofar as the individual mind of man somehow makes nature conform to the subjective code of his hungers, so too *The Blacks*, because it could be nothing more than a mere performance, may be utterly without meaning. It is only the brief final exchange between Virtue and Village—which may itself be nothing more than the beginning of new illusions—that gives the spectator any hope at all in a way of life built on human communication rather than ritual participation.

BLACK POWER AND WHITE POETRY

RICHARD N. COE

The Blacks—certainly the best play that Genet has written to date—came something like ten years ahead of its time. In 1959, the term "Black Power" was one that few people had

---

Adapted from *The Vision of Jean Genet* (London: Peter Owen, and New York: Grove Press, 1968).

heard of; violence was the official prerogative of statesmen and soldiers rather than the common weapon, defensive and offensive, of the student, the striker, and the man-in-the-street; and "racial issues," even in the context of apartheid and the Algerian War, were problems that could still be discussed objectively . . . more or less. In 1959, a "political play" was a play which *discussed* politics; it was not (save in the marginal case of Brecht) a political act in itself.

In 1969, this atmosphere of traditional liberal humanism, these behavior patterns of a society still based fundamentally on deference and on debate, are difficult to recapture. And this makes it ever more difficult to see exactly what Genet was intending when he wrote *The Blacks*. Even when it was first presented, the critics were sharply divided between those who thought it was a political play and those who swore that it was not. If it was a political play, then why did Genet refuse to treat the theme as seriously as it obviously deserved? As Norman Mailer argued, in his brilliant review of the New York production:

> *White and Black in mortal confrontation are far more interesting than the play of shadows Genet brings to it. If he insists with avant-garde pride that he will not be bullied by the major topicalities of his theme, and instead will search out the murmurs, the shivers, the nuances, one does not necessarily have to applaud. Certain themes, simple on their face, complex in their depths, insist on returning to the surface and remaining simple. The murder of Lumumba is thus simple. It is simple and it is overbearing. It is inescapable. One cannot treat it as a pantomime for ballet without making an aesthetic misjudgment of the first rank.*

On the other hand, if Genet did *not* intend that the play should have political repercussions, if he thought that a white

The Village Voice, May 18, 1961, p. 14. This notable review may also be found, in an abbreviated version, in *The Presidential Papers*.

audience could sit through *The Blacks* without a stirring of commitment one way or the other, then clearly he was making an equally serious misjudgment in his choice of subject.

The answer is probably to be looked for on a different plane altogether. Jean Genet is a supremely competent dramatist; and no dramatist who deserves the title, even if his competence is no more than mediocre, makes this sort of misjudgment. All the evidence suggests rather that he took a calculated risk: that his intention was perfectly clear and precise, and that he was prepared to accept a whole range of unwanted (but not necessarily undesirable) side effects, provided that he could realize it.

That the world should see him, regardless of his most explicit statements to the contrary, as a politically committed, left-wing dramatist was clearly something that he had had to envisage—and if he had forgotten it, there was always the experience of *The Balcony* in London to remind him. What he pardonably could not foresee was the speed with which events would overtake him. In this sense, but in this sense only, he miscalculated. A play which could be considered marginally and debatably *engagé* in 1959 was destined to appear as a most emphatic and indisputable *événement* less than a decade later. And so history, rather than Genet's own misjudgments, has provided the Sorcerer's-Apprentice element in the sequence of events. Genet's deliberate and calculated intention was to use certain themes of politics, violence, intolerance, and hatred for his own private and esoteric ends; but the hatred and the violence have got out of hand, and his poetic fantasies have become—through no precise fault of his own—a reality more alarming than he had ever envisaged. An aesthete's dream was transformed into a political Happening; and the decadent poet, with his paradoxes, his Wildean imagery, and his art-nouveau symbolism, suddenly found himself speaking with the voice of LeRoi Jones.

Jean Genet is, and always has been, first and foremost a poet. And, as a poet, he is a symbolist rather than an absurdist. Far from denying the significance of human experience, he has been constantly concerned to discover new dimensions of meaning. Admittedly the profane world, taken in isolation, tends to reveal itself as gratuitous, while the domain of mystic or sacred experience is inhuman, unfathomable, and all in all beyond the range of our mortal faculties to comprehend. But it is precisely at the point where the two meet that "poetry" is created—the point at which dream is simultaneously reality, where the invisible coincides with the visible, where the object is both itself and the revelation of something not-itself, where the meaninglessness of the unique act in time is identical with the timeless, archetypal gesture. It is not that Genet has a Blake-like vision of a profounder reality beyond, and detached from, apparent reality: it is the revelation of two coexistent and inseparable realities, each simultaneously made manifest in the other, of meaning discovered in unmeaning at the same time, and in the same instant of perception, that unmeaning is apprehended in meaning, that holds him fascinated. In other words, the essence of his imagination lies, not in the symbol conceived as the key, the open-sesame, to a transcendental reality, but in the dualistic nature of the symbol itself.

And the drama itself is a symbolic act. The drama is both true and not true simultaneously—it commands, or should command, absolute belief, but only in a context of absolute unbelief; and the absolute belief (or suspension of disbelief) is only valid if it knows itself to exist in a context of unrealities—that is, if it is unceasingly aware of itself as an illusion. The actor is like the priest officiating at the ritual of the Mass: he must not only *know* himself to be at the same time both an individual and a symbol, but he must also have an equal faith in the significance of both—and so must the audience. "Any performance," writes Genet, "is a failure unless I believe in what I see—which will cease to be, which will never have been, as soon as the curtain falls." In terms of a naturalistic theater this is an impossibility, for, where the essence of drama is illusion, we either believe in it, or we do not. We cannot do both simultaneously. But as soon as illusion is transformed into symbol, then the impossible becomes possible. The officiating priest at communion is *both* Father*** handling a bit of wafer *and* the Vicar of Christ offering the Body of Christ. His faith, or belief, in both is simultaneous. He *is* both actor and the part acted. In *Deathwatch* and *The Maids*, in spite of the dramatic and symbolic intensities of these plays, the problem remains unsolved; for Genet's private mysticism cannot command the faith, either among his actors or, still less, among his audience, with which the Demoiselles de Saint-Cyr performed *Athalie* to a congregation still under the sway of a Bossuet. It is the weakness of all modern dramatists who have tried to return to the classical concept of the drama as a religious ritual that religion no longer exercises sufficient influence on the life of the average person to make the symbolism seem more important than the play itself—and this alone would solve Genet's dilemma.

One cannot believe (religious sense) in what one knows to be a pure illusion. To become the object of a Faith, the illusion must be transformed into a symbol—that is, it must owe its transmutation, not to anything in itself (disguise, etc.), but entirely to the *wish to believe* in the mind of the believer. There is no *illusion* in the Communion wafer; it is neither disguised nor modeled nor painted; it does not even try to look like a lump of bread. If it is felt to be the Body of Christ, this is exclusively because the believer desires that it should be so.

But obviously this transmutation by Faith can take place only in a context of extreme, violent, and irrational emotion—intense love, intense fear, or intense hatred: and of these three, in Genet's analysis, the last is by far the strongest, the most effective. While Christianity continued to be more a religion of hate than of love, as it was during the sixteenth and seventeenth centuries, then it was the perfect medium for inspiring the intensity of irrational belief in a symbol that the drama requires. But now, outside Ireland, doctrinal disputes have become rather marginal. Religious heresy no longer shocks us—only deliberate sacrilege still produces a few faint stirrings of the old subconscious resentments. But these hidden reserves of violence and hatred are by no means exhausted: it is merely that, in our minds, they are released by a different set of stimuli. And, according to Genet, the three most powerful of these stimuli, whose function is to release vast nuclear forces of hatred—and therefore of potential mystic-dramatic experience—are sex, racial antagonism, and politics. To produce a maximum of intensity, all three should act concurrently. In extremely simplified form, what Genet proposes is that the stage should present, ideally to a white audience of Episcopalian Goldwaterites from Arkansas, the spectacle of a Communist Negro raping the wife of the State Governor. Given this context, Genet argues, the degree of *illusion* created by the acting becomes irrelevant; the audience will provide all the hatred, and consequently all the belief, that is necessary. The actor will become a *symbol*.

This, then, is the essential pattern of ideas which underlies *The Blacks*. It is a play designed to exploit the emotional violence, the hatred, and the tensions generated between whites and Negroes in confrontation with each other, in such a way as to raise the status of the drama from illusion to symbol—thus offering the spectator the occasion to participate in the supreme experience: the experience that Jean Genet calls "poetic." And to this end, Genet exploits every technique which can contribute to the intensification of this atmosphere of hatred and mass hysteria. The structure of *The Blacks* is that of total theater—that is, of a theater employing *all* media which can contribute to the dramatic impact of the spectacle: it uses music, dance, rhythm, and ritual; it contrasts masks and faces, illusion and reality. It borrows its techniques from the jazz band and the jam session, from the church service, from the music hall, and from the circus. In such a context, the chief function and the dramatic value of language are as a medium of incantation; the words sway and pulsate like African dancers and their very sound is hypnotic, hallucinatory, and cruel. Their meaning is rarely more than a contributory factor to their physical impact: it is the simple *motif*—perhaps only three or four notes of a scale—on which a Miles Davis, a Bix Beiderbecke, would weave his patterns of primitive color and sophisticated violence.

This comparison between *The Blacks* and the improvisations of a Negro jazz band is not merely suggested by the common racial origins of the performers. Genet has rejected the whole traditional structure, intellectual, logical, and conceptual, of the European theater—the time-honored techniques that Artaud refers to as "a theater of idiots, madmen, inverts, grammarians, grocers, anti-poets, and positivists—in short, Westerners!" Instead, he has constructed a play which has much more in common with music than with normal drama, where representation has given way to abstraction, and the aim of convincing an audience assumed to be intellectual has been replaced by that of rousing it to a state of mystical or hysterical delirium by means which the High Priest shares with the Maoist, and the pop group with the snake-charmer. Yet the final effectiveness of the play lies in the fact that it is not by any means devoid of ideas. The dialectic is there, as ingenious as in everything else that Genet has written, but it is conveyed by implication rather than by statement: it can be thought about, argued about after the performance is over; but not while it is in progress.

Given such a concept of the play as a whole, it is obviously not to be expected that *The Blacks* should tell a coherent story in the manner of *Deathwatch* or *The Maids*. It has a theme, the theme of Black and White, and this theme is worked out in an intricate series of variations, constantly changing in tone and tempo, but never in mood, for the mood is hatred. But it has no plot. Instead, it possesses a structure; and this structure, as it gradually reveals layer after layer of significance and symbolism on a multiplicity of different and unsuspected levels, provides all the dramatic tension necessary to sustain the play.

The actors, of course, are basically Negro actors. With Archibald as compère, they are introduced as a group of Negroes with ordinary, everyday backgrounds, but now come together to produce an entertainment—*une clownerie:*

> *When we leave this stage, we are involved in your life. I am a cook, this lady is a sewing-maid, this gentleman is a medical student, this gentleman is a curate at St. Anne's, this lady . . . skip it. Tonight, our sole concern will be to entertain you. So we have killed this white woman.*

The murdered White Woman lies entombed on the stage in a white-draped, flower-covered catafalque, and around this, the third dimension of illusion is developed: the rhythms, rituals, and ceremonies of hatred and murder. Meanwhile, high up in their gallery, five Negroes masked as Whites—the Queen, the Missionary, the Valet, the Governor, and the Judge —provide a fourth dimension: an audience for the *clownerie* of the others. But what, precisely, *is* this audience? For those below them on the stage, Archibald, Village, and Virtue, Snow and Bobo and Diouf, the Court both is and is not an audience: it watches them, listens to them, applauds them, yet it is composed of actors *acting* an audience. It is also a chorus. It is also, in symbolic form, the Enemy. And so the play develops for over half its length, working out permutations and combinations with the elusive material of dimensions, of plays-within-plays and audiences-within-audiences, until suddenly, with the dramatic entry of Ville de Saint-Nazaire, the whole delicate structure collapses with the revelation of a new dimension still: this time, a play-*outside*-the-play. Ville de Saint-Nazaire is not concerned with any dream of love or murdered Whites; he is a *real* political agitator (but what in Heaven's name, by this time, *is* real?) who has been attending a secret meeting just up the street, at which, not a White, but another Negro has been condemned to be liquidated for having betrayed a clandestine Black Power organization. And meanwhile all the rest—actors, audience true or false, dimensions one to four—disintegrate into dreams: for the whole evening's *clownerie* was merely a deliberate diversion (as Archibald warned us at the beginning), a smoke screen to keep our attention fixed while the Executive Committee got on with the job. The White Court strips off its masks, the rest strip off their personalities, and for an instant, they are any group of real Negroes having an urgent political discussion, with the ex-Valet, that erstwhile masked caricature of the bourgeois intellectual or artist in capitalist society, now revealed as the cell leader, whose orders are obeyed instantaneously and without question. Eventually he commands the members of his cell or combat section to take up their parts again, and to resume the *clownerie*—and we are back in the dimensions of illusion. But of course, the victory lies with Genet. For in the closing scenes, when we know that all that we are watching is merely an illusion, we forget, or half-forget, that the hard, political play-outside-the-play is even further from reality than the actors-acting-actors of the play itself. Or . . . is it? For in yet another dimension, there is more reality—immediate political reality this time—in the idea of an armed and organized Direct Action Committee of a Black Power group than there is in ritualistic dances about the imaginary catafalque of an imaginary murdered White. Which is real and which is illusion? Compared with *The Blacks*, Pirandello's experiments with the same problem seem almost childish. Heaven forbid, though, that we should take all this too seriously. After all, the idea that Black might conquer White is simply . . . ludicrous. It is, as Genet assures us so consolingly, only a *clownerie*. Perhaps. Or perhaps not. Not by accident does Genet arrange his fairy tale so that the symbolic murder of the White Woman takes place to the strains of *Dies Irae*.

Genet's sympathy for Negroes, as the scapegoats of *les salauds*—the dominant white bourgeoisie—goes back to *Our Lady of the Flowers*. On the one hand, he sees them as bearing the sacred stigma of all "expiatory victims whether goat, ox, or child, and which kings and Jews still have today"; on the other, he explains the traditional antisocial behavior of the Negro in a White society as being, not innate, nor even an expression of resentment, but rather as an imitation of the Whites. The characteristic of the Black, however, is not his social status (there are at least two bourgeois occupations named among Archibald's troupe: preacher and medical student), but precisely his *blackness*. As Genet's thought develops, he comes more and more to visualize blackness and whiteness as contending absolutes: individual Blacks may be coffee-colored—*café nature, café turc, café au lait* or even *Nescafé*: "But what exactly *is* a black? First of all, what's his color?"—but The Black is black with an unqualified, undiluted, uncompromising blackness. His blackness is his function, just as the Bishop's mitre is his function in *The Balcony*. It is his symbol, his reality as it is designated by the Others. "A Jew," maintains Sartre, dealing with a similar problem, "is a man whom other men think of as a Jew."

And just as the Jew, in an anti-Semitic society, may insist upon and emphasize his Jewishness, as his only defense, his ultimate guarantee of authenticity, so Genet's Negroes blacken their already black faces with black boot polish, thus raising their status from the particular to the universal. "My color!" exclaims Snow. "Why you're my very self!" "When I beheld you," says Village of his first meeting with Virtue, "you were wearing a black silk dress, black stockings, patent-leather pumps and were carrying a black umbrella." "The tragedy will lie in the color black," proclaims Archibald, thus summarizing the whole drama; and gradually the theme develops. Blackness becomes not merely one symbol among others; it determines the whole polarity of the play. "I order you to be black," intones Archibald, gravely, to Village. "I order you to be black to your very veins. Pump black blood through them. Let Africa circulate in them." And with their color, the Blacks, in their incantations, summon up and claim eternally as their own all that goes with it: their savagery, their cruelty, their "smells" and their "yellow eyes," their past of slavery, their heritage of Africa, culminating in a superb and terrifying tirade by Felicity, the goddess, the fertility symbol, the Earth-Mother that has been and again shall be when all the earth is Black:

> *Dahomey! Dahomey! To my rescue, Negroes, all of you! Gentlemen of Timbuctoo, come in, under your white parasols! Stand over there. Tribes covered with gold and mud, rise up from my body, emerge! . . . Are you there, Africa with the bulging chest and oblong thigh? Sulking Africa, wrought of iron, in the fire, Africa of the millions of royal slaves, deported Africa, drifting continent, are you there?*

The corollary of this is the absolute, total, and uncompromising rejection of all that is White. Whiteness, for Genet, is never associated with light. In *The Blacks*, light, with all that it implies, aesthetically and mystically, is the product of darkness; for the dark precedes the light and contains its possibility, just as the darkness of Chaos covered the Waters and preceded the Creation, just as the night sky contains and makes visible the stars. "We were Darkness in person," declaims Felicity. "Not the darkness which is absence of light, but the kindly and terrible Mother who contains light and deeds." The opposite of Black, therefore, is not just White, but White-without-radiance: pallor, absence; the colorlessness of Death and of the Void. Black is virility, white is effeminacy—a symbolism which probably enables Genet for the first time to dissociate the effeminate from the feminine, and to create such unforgettable female characters as Snow and Felicity, Bobo and Virtue.

White, then, is Death; and into the category of Death fall all the virtues of the Whites: civilization, politeness, culture, beauty, objectivity, humanitarianism . . . all the "*bonté des blancs.*" Archibald even refuses to allow Village to use the words "my father," on the grounds that the very act of pronouncing the word veiled the cutting edge of his voice with "a shade of tenderness." When Felicity summons up her cruel hordes of Africa, the White Queen replies with an invocation to all the Arts—all the products, past and present, of a pale-faced civilization:

> *To the rescue, angel of the flaming sword, virgins of the Parthenon, stained-glass of Chartres, Lord Byron, Chopin, French cooking, the Unknown Soldier, Tyrolean songs, heroic couplets, poppies, sunflowers, Aristotelian principles, a touch of coquetry, vicarage gardens. . . .*

Obviously, however, this clear-cut distinction, which pushes all beauty and all culture, all poetry even, resolutely into the arms of Death, poses something of a problem. Above all, the lovers, Village and Virtue, find in each other's beauty an inescapable temptation. In every other respect, the Blacks reject the very concept of Beauty as an alien convention, a gift as cruel as all other charity, condescendingly granted from above: a pretty disguise to hide the iron reality of economic slavery and exploitation. When Village describes the blackness of Virtue in poetic terms, Bobo objects; he is betraying his race, she argues, he has heard the siren call of a White culture, he is the fifth columnist by whose agency all will be lost. Not beauty, but vulgarity—a deliberate, defiant, and hate-inspired vulgarity—is the symbol of the Blacks; lilies and roses belong to the colonial oppressor; for themselves, "soot and blacking, coal and tar" are more appropriate emblems.

And yet . . . the fact, the *force* of love is there. "I'm handsome, you're beautiful, and we love each other," says Village to Virtue. This is perhaps the most poignant contradiction in *The Blacks:* that it was the White man who invented love and the Black man who now feels it; and consequently, that every stirring of the Black man's heart must either remain silent or else allow itself to be contaminated at source with a White vocabulary, a White imagery. This is the cruelest domination of all, far crueler than an overt slavery. The White man has not only stolen the Black man's land and his liberty; he has stolen his poetry, stolen his power to love. Village at first is afraid even to look at Virtue, in case she should be beautiful. . . . But gradually he begins to see the glimmerings of a solution. If it were possible to replace a "White" beauty, by a specifically "Black" beauty—even a beauty which, in White eyes and in White words, was ugliness, even if it meant reversing the very order of a White-ordered universe—then the miracle might be achieved, and freedom regained. At the end of the play, Felicity takes up the same theme in her reproaches to the Queen. To the White man, all things white are beautiful; but to the Black "Whatever is gentle and kind and good and tender will be black. Milk will be black, sugar, rice, the sky, doves, hope, will be black." Meanwhile, as the theme develops, it is Virtue who takes the lead. If love is the very core and symbol of whiteness, she argues, then she and Village have only two alternatives: either to go away and lose themselves forever among the alien race; or else to "love blackly," inventing a new love, a new language and formula of love, in spite of all the power, poetry, and beauty of Europe. If they can achieve this, then not only will they realize themselves, but the secret power of the White world will be destroyed. Black victories, Black freedom, Black territorial gains are nothing while the key to the mysteries of the relationship between man and woman remains White. For it is not the missionaries who hold the key of Heaven, but those who have discovered the difference between *das ewig Weibliche* and a wife worth twenty head of cattle. Romeo, Tristan, Faust, Don Rodrigue, Swann . . . not a touch of the tar brush among the pack of them.

That the realization of a Black love would constitute a fatal threat to the White man's supremacy, the Court realizes only too well. "Damn it, they're going to gum up the works!" blusters the Governor; and the Missionary chimes in: "They've got to be prevented from continuing." But their fears, as yet, are premature. To create a Black love is not easy. Virtue tries, and fails—word by word, as she whispers her love to Village, a change comes over her: it is not love which is growing Black, but she who is growing White: "Oh noble pallor, color my temples, my fingers, my belly! . . . I am white, it's milk that denotes me, it's the lily, the dove, quicklime and the clear conscience, it's Poland with its eagle and snow! Snow. . . ." Village struggles on, but all in vain. Syllable by syllable he builds up his language of a Black beauty, and Felicity helps him with her "Dahomey! . . . Dahomey! . . ." —but the pull of the other world is too great. As Village hesitates, Archibald and Snow come to him with a challenge: to overcome love with hate "for the last time." And, on condition that it is "this evening, for the last time," Village agrees. The White world must *first* be destroyed with hate; then, and then only, Black Village can love Black Virtue. Which is what happens at the play's end. One by one the Whites descend toward obliteration; and as they die, the great lyric of Black Love rises into the air, its incantations haunting the theater as this ferocious *clownerie* closes:

VIRTUE: *I, too, for a long time, didn't dare love you . . .*

VILLAGE: *You love me?*

VIRTUE: *I would listen. I would hear you striding along. I would run to the window and from behind the curtain would watch you go by . . .*

VILLAGE (*bantering tenderly*): *You were wasting your time. I strolled by like an indifferent male, without a glance . . . but at night I would come and capture a beam of light from between your shutters. I would carry it off between my shirt and skin.*

The moral to be drawn from the tale of Village and Virtue is the same as that which emerges from every other episode in the play: that Black and White are irreconcilable. There is no middle way. And to make the moral clear in different terms, there wanders in and out among the other figures of the action the strangest being of them all: Samba Graham Diouf. Diouf is the halfway house: a Negro by blood, a Christian by faith (he is variously referred to as Curate at St. Anne's, as His Reverence the Canon, as my dear Curate, as Mr. Vicar General, for whom Christ died on the Cross, and as Our Grand Vicar; moreover, the Graham allusion in his name is unmistakable), he is the humanist, the compromiser, the arbiter, the half-and-half. When a symbolic White Woman is required for the ritual murder, it is Diouf who dons a White mask and flaxen curls and plays the part. It is he who preaches "meekness" and aspires to Heaven. When the Missionary objects that the Holy Eucharist must be either white or black, it is Diouf who proposes the most sweetly reasonable compromise: "White on one side, black on the other." And it is Diouf whose doctrine of tempering hate with love, antagonisms by diplomacy, is sharply criticized by Archibald, and its author called to order: "Sir, if you have any intention of presenting even the most trivial of their ideas without caricaturing it, then get out! Beat it!"

If there is something of the Reverend Billy Graham in Diouf's doggedly optimistic cross-breeding of God and politics, there is a great deal more of the late Dr. Albert Schweitzer—a far more dangerous individual, from Genet's point of view. In one sense, one might argue that the whole of *The Blacks* was a direct warning to the black populations of the world to reject the temptation of the Schweitzerian solution. Schweitzer at Lambarene; Schweitzer building hospitals, dedicating his life and his knowledge to the regeneration of a Black community; Schweitzer bringing his organ to the swamps of the Gabon, playing Bach fugues under the tropical stars; Schweitzer the humanist, the theologian, the musicologist, the scholar, the doctor, the intellectual Christian: and Schweitzer, the man who, more than any other, has contributed to blur the political issues in Africa, and to damage the cause of the Blacks. Or so Genet believes, and in this he is not alone. Many of the more enlightened Africans believe it also.

For, while the enemy was the trader or the big capitalist combine, the governor with his whip, his ceremonies, and his squad of Senegalese or Gurkha troops, the Bible-bashing missionary, the objective was unmistakable. The White man was the oppressor, and must be evicted or destroyed. But when the White Man comes with university education in one hand and penicillin in the other, when he comes veiled in disinterested generosity, then the simple-minded Black Man may be deceived into thinking that he is not the enemy after all. Or even the not-so-simple-minded Black Man, like Diouf. Diouf is as well aware as any of his fellows of the poison that is called charity. Nevertheless, in Christ's words, "He that is not with me, is against me"—and Genet provides the echo and the application. He who is not with the Blacks, sharing the totality of their hatred of all things White, is against them. And although Diouf is not taken in by the charity of the alien race, he is infected with their rationalism no less than Village is infected with their love. Perhaps, in the end, the natives of Dahomey or of Gabon will give the world a Black Descartes . . . why not? But this is still in the future. As yet, there is no specifically Black rationalism, there is only White rationalism adapted—and disastrously adapted, since it saps the very foundations of an African liberation: the cult of unadulterated hatred. When Diouf calls Bobo "a technician of hatred," he pays her the greatest compliment that Genet can imagine; and if *The Blacks* belongs technically to a Theater of Hatred, the practical political need for this emotion informs the content of the play just as clearly as it dictates its form. And so poor Diouf, for all his good intentions, is the villain. Dramatically speaking, he is doomed. After a welter of high-flown humanistic phrases, in which he almost loses himself, he senses the weakness of his cause, and begins to apologize: ". . . but I'm old, and I think. . . ." Bobo, however, cuts brutally across the end of his excuses with yet another restatement of the central theme of the play: "Who's asking you to? What we need is hatred. Our ideas will spring from hatred."

And beyond the dramatic statement that the day of compromise is over in racial conflict, and that the only conclusion that could have been drawn from Dr. Albert Schweitzer's patriarchal age was that his ideas had been out of date for even longer than one would have suspected, there lies another assumption which is fundamental to *The Blacks:* namely that in spite of the metaphysical and linguistic struggles of Virtue and Village, the outcome of the battle is already known. The supremacy of White over Black is already a thing of the past; and indeed, the reactions of the Court to the insults aimed at them from below are more of nostalgia for a vanished age than fury or even mild anger. Moreover, if the Blacks have no pity for the vanquished Whites, the reason, paradoxically, is that there is no need for it. Romantic chivalry is not part of Genet's creed—nor of Archibald's. The Whites are finished anyway; and so the Blacks propose to finish them off, scientifically and objectively, yet without either fear or malice, as though they were simply rather unpleasant insects. Not scorpions, which are still dangerous; merely silverfish. The only possible victory left to the Whites, as the Queen observes, is to anticipate by suicide the inevitable execution.

It is these basic assumptions which account, in part at least, for the power and originality of the play. Different in this from almost every other play or novel on a similar subject, the Blacks are shown entirely without fear. They have already won. They are even now the equals, if not the superiors, of the Whites. Such fear as there is (mainly concealed) is on the side of the Whites. It is a measure of Genet's stature as a dramatist that he was able, in *The Blacks,* to show a conflict of equal contempt on both sides of an argument, and yet to have distinguished, by infinitely subtle gradations, between the contempt that is based on fear in the Gallery, and the contempt that has conquered fear in the center of the stage. And it is also his supreme boldness as a political commentator to have put the case for the oppressed by showing the oppressed triumphant and utterly remorseless in their victory.

The Screens

Published in French in February 1961, Les Paravents received its first performance in an unsatisfactory German translation (by H. G. Brenner) and in an incomplete form at the Schlosspark-Theater, West Berlin, on 19 May of the same year. On 4 May 1964 the first twelve scenes were performed in London, at the Donmar Rehearsal Rooms (a converted warehouse), by members of the Royal Shakespeare Company Experimental Theatre Group, produced by Peter Brook and Charles Marowitz. However, the first full performance of the text—and hence the true world première—appears to have been given in Swedish, in the summer of 1964, at the Alléteatern, Stockholm, produced by Per Verner Carlssen.

In France, the play was deemed unperformable, owing to the political passions that it was certain to arouse, until, in 1966, Jean-Louis Barrault (presumably with the authorization of the Minister of Culture, M. Malraux, who himself attended the final performance) decided to give it a limited run at the state-subsidized Odéon–Théâtre de France. The play opened on 16 April 1966, and twenty performances were cautiously given between that date and 7 May, followed by a further twenty in September and October of the same year. The director was Roger Blin; costumes and décor were by André Acquart; Saïd was played by a young Algerian actor named Amidou, the Mother by Maria Casarès, Warda by Madeleine Renaud, and Si Slimane by Jean-Louis Barrault.

Genet himself appears to have been very uncertain whether he wanted the play to be produced or not. He refused to authorize Mme Simone Benmussa to issue the special "Genet

Number" of the Cahiers Renaud-Barrault, which would normally have been sold with the programs in the theater, in consequence of which No. 54 of this valuable review is misleadingly entitled "Répertoire Contemporain," and the articles in it refer only deviously and obliquely to The Screens; and later, when trouble did start, he is reported to have begged Jean-Louis Barrault to remove the play from the repertory immediately . . . since he could not bear the idea that some of the actors might get hurt, and that he would be responsible.

In this production, certain cuts were made (such as the episode of the "dummy covered with medals" in scene xii), but these were done, not with the intention of "toning down" the impact of the play on the audience, but simply of reducing it to a reasonable length; on the contrary, certain other episodes, such as the death of the Lieutenant, which Genet had directed to take place off-stage (scene xv), were at first produced by Blin in full view of the audience, and only withdrawn out of sight later, under a storm of protest. For, this time, the long-expected protest did materialize:

PROTEST

I. THE INCIDENTS

For the second time running there were a number of incidents on Saturday night during the performance of Jean Genet's play *The Screens*, at the Théâtre de France. A woman in the audience received slight injuries from a Bengal light.

The performance was interrupted on two occasions. The incidents were caused by a group of some fifteen or so first-year cadets from the Military Academy of Saint-Cyr.

On the first occasion, toward half-past ten, in the middle of Act II, they threw eggs, tomatoes, and pieces of glass in the direction of the stage.

From *Combat*, 2 May 1966, p. 9. Translated by R.N.C.

The actors were obliged to break off. A few minutes later, when calm was restored, the performance was taken up again, but before long new projectiles began to hurtle in the direction of the stage.

One of the actors was hit by a bolt, and the stage was covered with Bengal lights. One of these, as it went off, hit a woman in the front row of the orchestra and burned her on the leg.

The police intervened and removed sixteen young men from the auditorium. Three of them were later taken to the police station.

Before going on with the performance, Jean-Louis Barrault called all his company together on the stage and, while the audience loudly applauded, apologized for the interruptions and requested the troublemakers to restrain their demonstrations of disapproval until the play was over.

Members of the audience encouraged Jean-Louis Barrault, with shouts of "We're for you!" The performance continued without further incident until the final curtain.

A short while afterward, the theater management was informed by an anonymous telephone-caller that a bomb had been hidden in the auditorium. Police searched all the different levels of the Théâtre de France but nothing was discovered.

On the preceding evening, the performance had similarly been disturbed by a number of violent incidents, which degenerated into a general riot. One actor and one stagehand suffered light bruises. Later, the Public Relations Committee of the Indochinese and Algerian Ex-Servicemen's League issued a proclamation calling on the people of Paris to stage a demonstration this coming Wednesday in front of the Odéon-Théâtre de France and to demand that *The Screens* be banned.

The French Actors' Union, referring to these incidents, has issued the following statement:

"Once again, freedom of expression is under fire. In addition to this, actors and other theater employees have been exposed to serious bodily injury and assault. The French Actors' Union expresses in terms of the strongest indignation its protest against such criminal acts. It insists that the proper authorities take steps, both to enforce respect for those fundamental freedoms without which no true flowering of expression in any of the various media available is to be dreamed of, and at the same time to guarantee the personal safety of workers who are simply engaged in the legitimate and proper exercise of their trade.

"The French Actors' Union declares that it proposes to support, by all means at its disposal, any legal proceedings which may in the event be brought by any actor who has suffered bodily harm against the person or persons responsible."

II. THE CRITICS

Irrefutable fact number one: the author of *The Screens* is a vile individual. . . .

What is assaulted, crushed, and battered to death, in the intolerable episodes of *The Screens*, is something much more than Honor, Flag, Country, and Nation—all concepts which are so foreign to Genet that it never even occurs to him to jeer at them as such. It is rather that essential and virile pride, that fundamental human dignity, in the name of which Genet's enthusiastic supporters conjure us, by the craziest of paradoxes imaginable, to accept and acknowledge those very insults which contradict it most flatly. I know what I am talking about. I know what humiliation means. I too am familiar with prisons, their promiscuities and their stench. And these very prison memories explain how it happened that, during those intolerable scenes, the shamelessness of the spectacle hit me like a personal insult. I jeered. And all around me, other spectators were jeering too. . . .

. . . It is conceivable that M. Jean Genet proposed to demon-

---

From Georges Portal, "Une Descente aux Enfers," in *Ecrits de Paris*, July-August 1966, pp. 122–128. Translated by R.N.C.

From Jean-Jacques Gautier in *Le Figaro*, 23–24 April 1966. Reprinted by permission. Translated by R.N.C.

strate the absurdity of such warfare, to show how hatreds are engendered, to illustrate the evils of colonialism, the fatal mistakes of those who represent our nation overseas, the Arab mentality, the universal madness, and finally the affliction of one and all—that affliction which will not cease to prevail and which is, in the last analysis, the destiny of the human condition.

It is conceivable.

I wouldn't know where to take hold of the argument.

The author's manner of expression leaves me absolutely impervious to his intentions.

Every fiber of my being rebels, rears up in revolt. Genet's ideas, the working of his mind, the instincts which impel him onward, the constant choice of his imagery, his manifest predilection for everything that is ugliest, filthiest, and crudest, this barrow-load of muck that he pushes around with a little thrill of pleasure, the smug self-satisfaction with which he piles insulting incongruities one on top of the other, the delight he feels in concocting his witches'-brew of indecencies, in wallowing in the language of the urinals, in hugging obscenities, and in spitting in the face of the audience for the pleasure of seeing it spin into a dizzying ecstasy of adoration—all this stinks to high heaven, and reflects a longing, an intention, an ambition, a firm resolve to smirch everything, to debase everything, to cover everything in degradation.

And to some extent he has succeeded, since his play is popular, since a whole theaterful of people receives his slap full in the face without taking the least offense, or for an instant demanding that its dignity be respected.

In a word, this crowd accepts a playwright and a company of actors addressing it in the most disgusting language, and performing under its very eyes the vilest of actions.

In this second half of the twentieth century, here in France, in Paris, is there any limit to what will be acclaimed and admired and applauded by thousands of well-bred people, who have forgotten how to distinguish between the repugnant and the sublime, between the pearl and the dunghill, the generous and the unspeakable, insults and talent, obsessions and genius—inspired thereto by the sole and simple "destructive taste of intellect" (as Genet himself would put it).

III. THE PUBLIC

General Vanuxem voices his indignation at the deliberate insult which is offered to the Army and to the dead in that geniusful play by that geniusful genius Jean Genet, *The Screens*, which the hexagon-subsidized state theater No. Two has been presenting for the last ten days or so. M. Jean-Louis Barrault has his own notions, which are very far from being shared by us, but he is a plain man of the theater; and it is inconceivable that without express injunction from the Highest Quarters (M. Malraux?) he would have agreed to put on this bag of shit which is drearily bad theater, and whose popularity is but the crudest *succès de scandale*.

General Vanuxem tells us what *he* thinks about it in *Carrefour*, 27 April 1966:

> *In spite of all that is said in praise of the mixture of burlesque and pathos, it seems to me utterly intolerable even to think of reliving this terrible drama—not the stage version, but the real one—in such distorting terms of degradation, obscenity, and ignominy. That life afforded its share of exaltation; it also brought forth its quota of miseries and meannesses. But the men who lived through it were at once lamentable and admirable; they drudged and they suffered; in the heart of their dignity they believed—even while they sneered and joked about it—that they were soldiers in the service of a great human cause, a cause which was infinitely greater than they were themselves, and when they died for it, it seemed to them only to grow the greater.*

Pierre Chaumeil, "Revue de la Presse," *Aspects de la France*, no. 919 (5 May 1966), p. 12. Reprinted by permission. Translated by R.N.C.

The protagonists of *The Screens,* invoking on the one hand the doctrine of Freedom of Expression and the Great Ancestors, on the other the light of dawn flooding forth from the USSR, are oddly illogical.

The strangest, the oddest, the most ironical fact is to find in that very same daily paper which gives review space to Genet's play a report of the onslaught waged by the *Red Army Gazette* against certain so-called "modernist" writers accused of libeling the nation's heroes.

A letter signed by some of the greatest names in the Red Army delivers a broadside against the review *Novy Mir,* which had attempted to deromanticize certain deeds of valor and certain military encounters which are considered legendary—"our dearest, our most precious heritage"—and in particular comes down on a novel by Valeriy Bykov which this review had published: *The Dead No Longer Suffer,* in which certain officers of the Stalinist epoch are shown up as cowardly and ambitious. But then, of course, the Red Army is the Army-that-moves-in-the-direction-of-History.

However, these great gobs of spit (*officially inspired* gobs, let's face the fact!) aimed at the French Army are already bearing their poisoned fruits; since the end of the Algerian drama, the contempt and mistrust with which the Army is regarded in High Places are having catastrophic consequences.

In France, in the years 1964 and 1965, 4,650 officers resigned their commissions in the land-based forces at their own request. In 1966, 2,580 have already applied for discharge. Our Friends in High Places didn't mean things to go *quite* so far. Today, attempts are being made to stop this hemorrhage. DISCIPLINE is a word whose letters of gold are inscribed on tablets of marble. And in the daily run of life, it signifies: Esteem and Confidence. A whole generation has been duped, mud has been slung at it, and now it has turned its back on the ideal of Service. . . .

Our colleague Patrice de Nussac interviewed one of the

"rioters" at *The Screens*, whose opinions can be read in *Paris-Presse* for Tuesday of this week, 3 May 1966:

> *Boileau himself argued that a spectator had the right to demonstrate once he had paid for his ticket, and that it was the author who must take the risks upon himself. All the same, what really makes it our duty to intervene is the fact that the Odéon is a state-subsidized theater. This is the real scandal. It is none of the state's business to subsidize the avant-garde, particularly if it is in doubtful taste. It is quite wrong to place state money and a national theater at the disposal of a highly debatable work.*

M. de Nussac then asked this disturber-of-the-peace whether the fact that he had been a serviceman in Algeria had anything to do with the degree to which he felt shocked. Here is the reply:

> *It stands to reason that our Army out there, in the magnificent fight it put up, had nothing in common with that of a Courteline, still less that of a Genet—a notorious deserter! But I am just as shocked, purely and simply as a human being. In the play, there is a French lieutenant who dies to the accompaniment of a chorus of filthy language from the other actors.*
>
> *I would have been just as shocked to see a Fellagha chieftain exposed to similar insults. It's the whole problem of death in wartime. It has to be respected. It shouldn't be held up to ridicule in the theater.*

Could it have been better put?

The full history of the "Scandal of The Screens*" can be traced in all its sensational details through the press, beginning with an article by Simon Glady in* Aux Ecoutes *(14 April 1966; see* *also 12 May); then see* Le Figaro, *16, 18, 20, 25, and 30 April,* 4 May, 17/18 Sept., 9 Oct., 7 and 8 Nov., and 12 Dec., France-Soir, 19 Apr. and 4 May; Le Monde, 4 and 6 May, 18/19 Sept., *1 and* 2/3 Oct.; Aspects de la France, *21 and* 28 Apr., 12, 19, *and 26 May; etc., etc. However, no one can, in this case, claim to have been taken by surprise, least of all the management of the* Théâtre de l'Odéon. No. 54 of the Cahiers of the Company, *sold in the theater with the program, actually contains two articles devoted to a general "Theory of Scandalization": "Brief Preliminary Notes on the Elaboration of a Metaphysics of Scandal" by Maurice de Gandillac; the second by the famous theater director himself:*

SCANDAL AND PROVOCATION

JEAN-LOUIS BARRAULT

There are, in art, two ways of provoking a scandal.

Firstly, there is the scandal that *other people* let loose upon the artist, that is to say, upon the created work of art; now, as often as not, this work of art is the product of an ingenuous and unreflecting sincerity, and of a notably original temperament.

Secondly, there is the scandal which is premeditated by the artist himself, when, purposefully and deliberately, he fashions a work that is precisely designed to shock these same *other people.* This second case is at bottom an imposture, since the artist is attempting to pass off as something unreflecting and original a work that is the outcome of careful calculation.

Never does the *true* artist seek to provoke a deliberate scandal. All of a sudden, to his considerable surprise, to his astonishment, to his stupefaction even, he discovers that he has "caused a scandal," whereas he was simply obeying evidence dictated by his own vision.

Extracts from "Scandale et Provocation," *Cahiers de la Compagnie Madeleine Renaud–Jean-Louis Barrault,* no. 54 (April 1966), pp. 14–29 [dated, Milan, 13 December 1965]. Reprinted by permission. Translated by R.N.C.

Neither Villon, nor Baudelaire, nor Mallarmé, nor Van Gogh, nor any one among countless others, was expressly aiming at a scandal. It was their very genius which was scandalous . . . in the eyes of *other people.*

None the less, it may happen that the artist, without ever deliberately seeking out a soil fertile in scandal, will *provoke.* . . .

Now provocation, contrary to whatever may appear to be the case, is not a straightforward attack. In the majority of cases, it is a riposte. A riposte which is expressed as a cry of indignation . . . of *provocative* indignation.

Primarily, it is existence itself—existence as distorted by society and, in particular, by the society of "right-thinking people"—which is a very hotbed of matter for provocation. Spurious moral codes, specious "rights," bad faith, hypocrisy, imposture, calculation, false charity and false sentiment, the great carnival of masks acted out by the *other people,* parts into which they pour their being, leaving themselves hollow and empty: the inflexibility of a narrow-minded soldiery, the humiliating compassion of a church-going piety, the unseeing incorruptibility of the law; the spider's web of Order, the traps and snares of charity, the comedy of remembrance, the masquerades of patriotism, the sticky mire of pseudo-solidarity, etc.

"Right-thinking people" never cease to provoke us, from the day of our birth to the day of our death.

Without deliberately seeking to cause a scandal, merely in the name of a conception of justice, or rather, of a kind of urge to set the world to rights, above all, perhaps, because there are limits to what a man can take, we react with a cry which is a defiant refusal of provocation; we hurl the provocation back into the faces of those who provoke.

Whereupon the sect of right-thinking people is thunderstruck, holds up its hands in sudden horror and, having long lost all awareness of its own ignominy, calls out in the name of order—its own order—for sentence and punishment.

Which of the two had started it all? The behavior of men who, in art, thus hurl back the provocation into the very faces of those who, day after day and in every sly and secret manner, provoke us, reveals the highest courage and deserves the highest respect; but it is also a very delicate business.

Forged in the fires of "righteous indignation," it needs to be sane and long-suffering.

Once tinged with self-indulgence or self-complacency, it becomes vulnerable.

The artist who, exasperated beyond bearing, turns to the art of provocation is like the beast defending its young, like a man fighting for his life.

He is justified on the grounds of legitimate self-defense. In his cry of anguish, he is denouncing the whole structure of social pretense, of lies and hypocrisy. It is this challenge which constitutes the nobility of the art of provocation, for it is a challenge which is based on love, and only on love.

On the other hand, as soon as we find a trace of self-indulgence, or satisfied spite, or personal enjoyment, or intimate delectation, or secret titillation, then both nobility and legitimacy vanish together into thin air, and instead of love, we discover that there was nothing but viciousness.

And so it seems that the same principles hold good for provocation as for scandal. There is a good variety, born of naïveté or of honest indignation; and there is a bad variety, engendered by calculation or by vice.

In reality, the problem is never quite so simple. Frequently, both varieties coexist in the same artist, since we are one and all creatures with a double existence, observing the lives that we ourselves are living.

. . . And, in the midst of all this, what about the audience?

Art is synonymous with freedom. In Art, all things are permissible, even scandal, even provocation.

Nevertheless, the situation changes from one art to another.

A painter, a sculptor, an architect, or a writer creates objects that become independent of their creator and make their own way in the world. Freedom, in these cases, is no problem.

A composer is dependent on his instrumentalists; but the audience does not make *them* responsible for the music they perform. The composer has his published score. And, in the shelter of his score, he continues to keep his freedom.

In the theater, however, the situation is a particular one, for without the participation of an audience the "phenomenon" of theatrical experience cannot exist. Outside the theater, the dramatist remains free *as a writer;* but not as a man of the theater.

In the cases we have so far considered, freedom remains within the artist's reach. He has only to stretch out his hand.

But for theater people—actors, producers, directors—the problem is very different. To begin with, their lives are public property. Secondly, since these lives have to be fashioned anew every night, they are never exactly identical with what they were before. And thirdly, these lives are meeting points.

In this case—but in this case only—there is perhaps a stage of consciousness which is even more sacred than the consciousness of liberty: it is that of respect for the Being-that-is-man.

How to preserve an unqualified liberty in the domain of his art without infringing the respect that he owes to the Being-that-is-man—here you have, in terms of human behavior, the ticklish problem that theater people have to solve.

Nevertheless, it is important not to overemphasize the respect which is owed to the audience. We owe it more than that. Our relationship with the audience is a love relationship. And everyone knows that, if it is right and proper that women be respected, there is a nobler attitude still, which is to *override* the bounds of this respect!

Our problem is to take the audience by the hand and to carry it along with us, sailing over the boundless ocean of dreams. The audience has come to us in search of forgetfulness of its daily life. It is asking us for catastrophes that wreck the lives of *others,* for a crystallization of existence, for a passport into the land of dreams, for passions that burst the bonds of

reason, for the cruelty of heroism and, in the last resort, fo
justice, that is, for the condemnation of imposture and o
everything that falsifies existence. And this is the exact poin
at which—if it consents—both scandal and provocation hav
their part to play. On the other hand, without this essentia
consent, nothing can be justified.

An audience, like all simple souls, hates vulgarity; but it wil
admit a savage scream of indignation, it will accept the fac
that this given character or that given situation may be scandal
ous, it will even, if necessary, take its part in the reflex o
provocation, it will vibrate to the discords of cruelty.

But there is one indispensable condition: that life, as a con
sequence, be set to rights, strengthened, reinforced. An audienc
has all the qualities of childhood . . . above all, its sincerity, it
sense of justice. It can be induced to accept the most darin
of inventions, the most scandalous and the most provocative
provided only that it is able to share with us the emotions tha
inspire them, namely unforced simplicity, indignation, and th
sense that our behavior is justified; and also with this on
further condition, that it share with us our suffering and ou
thirst for justice.

But if, by some mischance, it should detect on the stag
traces of a self-satisfaction which in no way concerns it, of
spiteful thrill in causing shocks regardless of concern for th
truth, of a delight in upsetting people for the mere pleasure c
watching their dismay, or worst of all, evidence of contemp
or even of a calculated and heartless intention to cause di
turbance—then it will be right to turn away its face, to becom
indignant, and to show its displeasure. For in this case, th
freedom of art has usurped a privilege not its own: it ha
failed in human respect. And the theater has no right to d
this.

It follows, then, that scandal and provocation are valid i
the theater only if the sincerity that fires them is intact, if th
subject excludes any other manner of treatment, and if th
suffering involved is felt to be genuine.

Delacroix used to say: "Never show yourself in public until you have wiped away the last trace of that carelessness which so passionately excites the artist."

The dramatist should follow a similar piece of advice: "Never offer the public a sight of that sheer, sensual enjoyment which is the private delight of the poet."

Then, but only then, will the audience follow us into the lyricism of scandal and accept our legitimate apologia for provocation. . . .

THE GREAT DISCOVERY OF THE PLAY

ROGER BLIN TO NICOLE ZAND

Roger Blin: As far as I can recall, the play grew out of a true story. Genet was staying with friends who were building on to their house. Some of the masons were Algerians, and one of them, who was due to go home in order to get married, had all his savings stolen. . . . And he was in despair because, now that he no longer had any money, he would not be able to buy anything except an ugly girl. That was the starting point: the humiliation of the man who could afford nothing but an ugly wife, so ugly that he would never dare show her around, but would have to hide her under a cowl.

But between this couple, a love would grow up. The great discovery of the play is the story of the love that springs up between Saïd and Leila: the love that uses words of hatred and words of contempt. This is the real subject, not colonialism or politics. Of course, when he was writing the play, Genet

---

From Nicole Zand, "Entretien avec Roger Blin à propos des *Paravents* de Jean Genet: 'C'est une tragédie avec le langage du burlesque,'" *Le Monde*, 16 April 1966. Translated by R.N.C. Many further details about *The Screens* will be found in *Letters to Roger Blin* by Jean Genet, trans. Richard Seaver (New York: Grove Press, 1969). [Ed.]

could not avoid integrating the piece into a social and historical context of decolonization; nor has he ever concealed his opinions. In 1954–1955, when he was asked: "Why are you on the side of the Algerians?" he replied: "Because I am always on the side of the strongest." . . .

CRUDE POLEMICS AND VISIONARY INSIGHTS

TOM MILNE

. . . What makes *The Screens* so extraordinary, and such an advance on Genet's previous essays along the same lines (enriched progressively through *Les Bonnes, Le Balcon,* and *Les Nègres*) is the extreme complexity of the levels of fantasy (or reality) spread out in the play. In one scene, for instance, the Arab men feel the stirrings of rebellion as they talk to the whores Warda and Malika; the whores scoffingly retaliate by telling of the legendary hero, Si Slimane. Here the stirrings of rebellion are a dream; Si Slimane, who appeared "on his horse in sixteen villages at the same time," is a dream; even the whores, empty shells with rotting teeth, gloriously painted and bejeweled, and robed in dresses which protect their fantasy with a massive weight of lead in the hems, are a dream; which leaves the Arab men themselves—are they a dream too, or are they the only reality? In one sense everything in the play is false: the valise of gifts which Saïd and his mother laboriously carry to his wedding turns out to be empty; Saïd's ugly wife—so ugly that she has to wear a mask all the time—whom he cherishes as a symbol of his abjectness and misery, may under her mask be beautiful; the clock which Leila steals is merely a painted image; and even death is simply an easy leap through

From "Reflections on *The Screens*," *Encore*, no. 50 (July–August 1964), pp. 21–25. Reprinted by permission.

a paper screen. But behind the falsity lies the naked impulse, and old words like hatred, fear, misery, oppression, even aspiration, take on a new, disturbing power in Genet's mirror images.

The play is not an easy one. On paper it tends to look like an inchoate mass of epic-Brechtian scenes, a mixture of crude polemics and visionary insights, vulgar humor and extraordinary beauty of language. The prime merit of the Brook-Marowitz experiment was to illuminate the breathtaking precision of Genet's conception, to make one realize that this is certainly Genet's best play to date, possibly one of the great plays of the century. . . .

GENET THE NETTLE

MAURICE SAILLET

S'il n'est ordure
ou boue dont la science
ne sache tirer profit
Je pense qu'il n'est point
d'être si vil et si infime
Qui ne soit nécessaire
à notre unanimité.

When Maria Casarès, some ten years ago, spoke these lines from the stage of the Théâtre National Populaire, we clearly never could have guessed that today she was destined to incarnate—with what eagerness and audacity!—that being who, among all others, is the vilest and the most degraded: the Mother in *The Screens*. Nor could we have prophesied that Jean Genet, a poet of exceptions if ever there was one, would fashion this admirable fresco which is something rather more than a dramatic masterpiece (for, in the domain of the New

---

"Genet l'Ortie," *La Quinzaine Littéraire*, 15 May 1966, pp. 28–29. Reprinted by permission. Translated by R.N.C.

Theater, "masterpieces" seem to crop up and disappear with singular frequency . . .); rather, it is a work which is, in the most profound, most absolute sense, "essential to our unanimity."

Before paying homage to the creator of this "unanimity" who, it is easy to guess, is in no way more dependent on any universal approbation than he is on the limited approval of the (fairly select) audience at the Théâtre de France, I would like to pause an instant and consider the two articles—"Scandal and Provocation," by Jean-Louis Barrault, and "Brief Preliminary Notes on the Elaboration of a Metaphysics of Scandal," by Maurice de Gandillac—which stand as lightning-conductors at the beginning of No. 54 of the *Cahiers de la Compagnie Renaud-Barrault*, which is sold together with the program for *The Screens*.

"Haven't you got beyond *that!*" exclaimed Antonin Artaud when, toward the end of his life, the most brilliant and fashionable of his disciples offered him the chance to put on a thoroughly "scandalous" production. The sad fact is that Barrault *hasn't* "got beyond that"—hasn't got beyond the *most scandalous revue in the world!* or docile group insults, or the stereotyped disturbances of election meetings—when he feels it incumbent upon himself to glorify (thereby doing the greatest disservice to the human background which forms its inseparable context) what is in fact the least of the virtues of *The Screens*.

Beyond the fact that provocation looks oddly comfortable when it is state-subsidized, and that it's an easy game to use Genet as an excuse for sticking out a schoolboy tongue at the Establishment,[1] it is time that the doyen of our avant-garde drama should learn finally that scandalizer and scandalized, or provoker and provoked, both in fact belong to the same clique and haunt the same clubs. Whereas the genius that radiates from *The Screens* far transcends the boundaries of any clique

1. An untranslatable pun: "et que cela lui va bien de faire le jeunet sur (révérence parlé) le dos de Genet." [Ed.]

or club, and therefore to exalt its "scandalousness" is not only o fashion a rod for one's own back, but also to do the play a great deal of gratuitous harm.

To tell the truth, here in our parish of Mrs. Grundy literature, candalmongers and scandal-seekers form a pair of rival guilds which, however, resemble each other to the point of being nterchangeable, for there is no real difference at bottom between a literature that provokes and a literature that edifies. If evidence of this is needed—and since he so reverently quotes hat cheap and flashy aphorism that Aragon hatched out in his *Treatise on Style:* "faire en français signifie chier"[2]—Barrault might do well to lend an ear to that modest, but infinitely ensible comment that Valéry Larbaud wrote actually in the margin of this same *Treatise on Style:*

> *All this noisy vulgarity strikes me, who never appreciated anything in a book except what was human, as the exact equivalent of those high-flown speeches of official praise in honor of Important Persons, or of those idiotic panegyrics of Established Institutions and Constituted Authorities, which conclude, invariably, with a set of patriotic verses.*

As for Maurice de Gandillac and his highly instructive views on the metaphysics of scandal, I would rather leave them to hat pretty little clothes-moth of drama criticism, which has promised to deal with the matter as soon as it gets back from Japan, where (in Spring, as we well know, clothes-moths get the wanderbug), at this very instant, it is busy scattering the benefits of Christian Existentialism.[3] Whatever may be the outcome of this quarrel between journeymen goldsmiths, it is unlikely that it will have any effect one way or another on a work which is so amply self-sufficient that it can afford the

---

2. Literally: " 'to do,' in French, means 'to shit.' " [Ed.]

3. The reference is to Gabriel Marcel. The reader will find specimens of his "clothes-moth criticism" elsewhere in this volume. Marcel's journey to America and Japan is announced in *Les Nouvelles Littéraires,* 21 April 1966. [Ed.]

luxury of offering itself as a jousting ring for rival Professors-Errant of Philosophy.

It follows that I, for one, refuse point-blank to discuss *The Screens* from the sterile angle of scandal and provocation. I am rather inclined to believe that it was precisely in order to put an end to a certain scandal that this play was originally written in 1960, that is to say at a period when, like some monstrous spring-tide at the height of the flood, the scandal was threatening to drown everything within reach. For if "the scandal must come"—and it goes without saying that the interminable and complex scandal represented by the war in Algeria came and, having come, endured, without Genet being in any way responsible for its coming—it is even more essential that it should cease. And in order to induce this appalling tidal wave to withdraw into the depths of the ocean whence it came, it was not enough to let oneself be carried along by the foam on its crest—which is what most people did, their susceptibilities hypersensitized by one particular aspect of the scandal or another—but it was necessary to get down to the very heart of the scandalous thing in itself, there to cope with the very root and origin of those mysterious and often monstrous forces from which it drew its life-blood. And in fact *The Screens* does precisely this: it reaches to the very heart of the matter, and thus proves that there is no living dramatist today *who has higher moral qualifications* (to use the same sort of language as our clothes-moth referred to above) to exorcise the ghosts of the Franco-Algerian drama.

For the moral bases of Jean Genet's world are as solid and as rigorously structured as are those of the world of Joseph de Maistre; and they are similarly irreversible and providential. (For anyone who has read both *Pompes Funèbres* and the *Eclaircissement sur les Sacrifices*, the blood relationship that links these two men of genius will be unmistakable.) There is only one difference, but it is of the highest significance: Genet implores of the powers of Evil what De Maistre implores of the powers of Good—namely, *Salvation:*

Evil, wonderful evil, you who remain when all goes to pot, miraculous evil, you're going to help us. I beg of you, evil, and I beg you standing upright, impregnate my people. And let them not be idle!

This incantation of Kadidja's, who is a mourner by profession (and who is mourning the very first casualty of the insurrection), bursts like a thunderclap over Scene Twelve of *The Screens*, and gives the signal for the atrocious War of Liberation. But it has been prepared from afar by that poverty-stricken and hangdog trio, the Mother, her son Saïd, and her daughter-in-law Leila, who have been outlawed by their own race because they constitute a separate species, that of the *Nettle*. And it is in the name of the Nettle, proudly and as it were with a flood of joy, that this family takes upon its shoulders the entire sum of hideousness, thieving, and betrayal that exists in the world, and which is condemned, without exception, by every morality the world has ever known.

It is in no way astonishing that the rough stinging-nettle of the wastelands and ruined buildings should be dear to the heart of Genet. Rejecting all the orange groves and rose gardens of Algeria "the Blessèd," he prefers the little patch of nettles which is the sole heritage of the Mother and of the wife of Saïd. Not only do they themselves return there, to soak up new strength in order *to injure the world;* but in similar fashion, it is in *the night full of Nettles* that the Revolution is born, and that it prospers. For the Revolution is in truth the daughter of this same Nettle which, in broad daylight, it scorns and renounces and, in the long run, sacrifices to the glory of those who sing aloud of the *Parade of Glory* and of the *New Order.*

Hence the destiny, shameful and yet splendid-glittering as a black sun, that awaits Saïd, son of the Nettle, spouse of the Nettle, and who, point by point, corresponds to that being invoked by Leila:

I want you to stop looking backward. I want you to lead me without flinching to the land of shadow and of the monster.

I want you to plunge into irrevocable grief. I want you—it's my ugliness, earned minute by minute, that speaks—to be without hope. I want you to choose evil and always evil. I want you to know only hatred and never love.

And while Saïd and his family sink ever deeper into the depths of abjection, we watch the procession of the screens—that is, of the various décors placed and hastily painted by the actors in the drama themselves, in order to furnish their own justification. With a liberal-minded impartiality which is never altered—for he leaves one and all in full possession of their individual illusions of "truth"—Genet makes us halt in front of each screen in turn, albeit with a marked preference for those which bear a liturgical character, and with an unmistakable tenderness toward those great artists, Warda the Whore and the Lieutenant of the Legionnaires, who both remain faithful to their "style" until death do ensue.

Plainly, Genet himself would adopt the ethics of a Warda, the *Queen of Showers*, her petticoats ballasted with lead, who, at the conclusion of twenty-four years of service in the brothel, can proclaim: "To whom are we to offer our lives, and our progress in our art, to whom, if not to God? Just like the cops, in fact. We perfect ourselves for God. . . ." In similar fashion, he shares the aesthetic concern of the Lieutenant, ever on the watch to insure that *each man be a mirror for every other man*; and that the multiplication of such human mirrors produces that generalized narcissism whose power nothing can resist ("Oh, beauty, beauty, the cement of armies . . .") and whose reward may, with indifferent consequence, be either glory or death. Thus the death agonies of the Lieutenant provide us with the notorious "fart-offering" scene, which already occupies an eminent place of honor among the finest funeral hymns in the national repertory—an elevation which is due, as we all know to the squeals of the hysterical and of the simple-minded, who thought it their bounden duty to come in crowds and to deride this singularly original ceremony in which high chivalry and barrack-room humor, the grandiose and the ludicrous, all coincide in so miraculous and so perfectly balanced a composition.

O immense and delicate-fingered Genet! His *Screens* swarms with profound and ingeniously original inventions, ranging from a rabid lyricism to a supremely good-humored farcicality. And yet, whenever the situation, as one might say, demands desperate remedies, whenever straightforward ingenuity gets out of its depth and calls for genius to come to its rescue—then Genet keeps his (and our) invariable, unwavering balance on the tautest of tightropes, where the sublime provides the exact counterweight to the abject and then gradually, imperceptibly, and as it were ineluctably overtakes it and absorbs it into itself. In this respect, there is no finer achievement than the scene, worthy of Melville, in which the old miser woman, Mother of the Nettles, gently, langorously, and tenderly—as though she were rocking a child to sleep—strangles the young French soldier.

In the closing scenes of the play, the dead on both sides burst through the screens, and, with all hatred now evaporated, are reconciled (*and they make such a fuss about it. . . !*) without even having to discuss the question. It reaches the same degree of intensity as we meet with in Shakespearean drama when, in the evening following the battle, peace appears on earth as it is in Heaven. Yet take care: for two terrible figures among the dead are absent from this somber roll call. Nor is there any point in waiting for them, for, as Claudel summed it up referring to Gide, "Evil knows no compromise," and the Seed of the Nettle cannot compromise with Heaven.

This is why all men of good will owe a debt of gratitude and of respect to Jean Genet, Warden of all that will not compromise and Poet of that Nettle which, more than all our Good Apostles with their moth-eaten humanism, is *essential to our unanimity*.

DON'T SING YOUR CRAP

LIONEL ABEL

Genet's new play is objectionable—but it is not morally objectionable. To be sure, the play smells; but it does not smell of badness, crime, or evil, which, because of their metaphysical connotations, may be thought of as having pure or elegant odors. Did not Baudelaire call his poems of evil "flowers"?

In his new work, though, Genet seems to have dropped his past aim of justifying aesthetically the morally unjustifiable. His present hero is not heroic in crime; in fact, he has no virtues of any kind. In glorifying criminals, Genet was led until now into presenting them as more energetic, more physically attractive, more powerful, decisive, and interested in what they do than most people are. Thus his glorification of criminals made them seem virtuous—his justification of crime and the criminal was unvaryingly changed into praise of the good: of the criminal as good. For it is good to be attractive, energetic, powerful, decisive, and interested in what one is about.

All this Sartre pointed out brilliantly in the book he devoted to Genet, *Saint-Genet comédien et martyr*. Sartre showed very clearly that anyone who wants to do evil, or who wants to praise evil for its own sake, is bound to fail; and he showed that to make a career of these aims one must consent to fail: to fail first of all in doing evil, and then to fail in praising evil simply for being evil. The love of evil and evildoers is vowed to a contradiction; this contradiction, according to Sartre, Genet has incarnated.

But now Genet has tried, perhaps in order to answer Sartre, a new shift: the glorification of the character who is simply low, and who is lacking in energy, sexual attractiveness, power, will, and even in any interest in what he does. The protagonist

---

From *The New York Review of Books*, Winter 1963. Reprinted with permission from *The New York Review of Books*.

of *The Screens* is Saïd, a miserable Arab from the lowest class of Algerian Arabs, who is without money, sex, scruples, force, will, or character. He marries Leila, the ugliest girl of his village, simply because he cannot afford a better wife. Leila's ugliness prompts him to steal, and to steal not from the French, but from his Arab neighbors, who revile him and cast him out. He is arrested. So is Leila, who, to be as low as her husband, becomes a thief also. Finally, Saïd betrays the Arab combatants against France to his French jailers. It must be noted that there is no particular sense of progress in his passing from a bad marriage to theft and treason. Did not Gide write of one of his characters: he went from bad to worse; first he committed a murder, then he began to tell lies? But Saïd does not go from bad to worse, or from bad to better. He cannot fall. When the play begins he has already fallen; he has fallen like a turd. The only thing he can do from then on is smell, physically and morally, and this he does—*à l'outrance*—from the beginning to the end of *The Screens*. What else is he capable of? Saïd is human crap, socially and morally. And Genet wants us to have a good whiff of him whenever he is on stage.

Here is an example of how Saïd expresses his feeling for Leila: "It's dark in my cell, too. The only light I get comes from your decayed teeth, your dirty eyes, your dull skin. . . . Are there still any places in you that could be bowed to? . . ." Leila replies: "There must be, but the one who bows to them—boyohboy!—has to have a strong stomach. . . . You've never beaten me, Saïd." And Saïd replies: "I spend all my nights training. As soon as I get out, you'll get it in the puss."

Here is another of his love declarations to Leila: "There's not much you lack now: you were ugly, idiotic, a thief, a beggar, and now you're crippled."

What a man! But Genet wants us to see him as a thorough stinker. At the end of the play, after Saïd has put out one of Leila's eyes—à la Edmund in *Lear*—everyone wants to glorify him, not only the living Algerian combatants whom he has betrayed, but also the dead Arabs who, having died in the struggle with France, want Saïd to deny the meaning of any kind of honor. Both sides solicit him, and at the culminating point of his life, solicited by both the living and the dead, Saïd expresses what he himself is, and what the whole play is about: ". . . to all of you, I say shit." What else could he have said?

2.

When the protagonist of a play lacks interest—as Saïd does—the playwright is likely to concentrate on the décor or setting. In *The Screens* Genet's hero is nothing, but Genet's décor is original and interesting. Saïd smells; the décor Genet has invented for his story is subtle and delicate. Certainly the one real theatrical invention of this play is the substitution of screens—sometimes brought onto the stage already painted, sometimes painted on during the action by the characters—for conventional props. But the screens in *The Screens* do not really hide the quality of the protagonist or that of the action in which he is caught. We may think of screens as interposing their delicate structures between us and what we would not like to see, hear, or smell. In this play, though, Genet is determined to make smells triumph over even what is one of the best human ruses against ugliness: screens. When the old and dead Arab woman, Kadidja, calls on the Arabs to shout with pride the crimes they have committed against their French masters, one of the Arabs, Abdesselem, claims to have cut off feet. Kadidja says, "Set them down," and Abdesselem draws four feet on a screen. But Kadidja is not satisfied. She asks, "What about the smell? Let's see the smell. . . ." And Abdesselem draws above the four feet a few spirals. In *The Screens* we are meant not only to smell what smells, but even to see it, and on the very screens interposed between it and us. . . .

3.

In order to make the ignoble Saïd acceptable, Genet has apparently chosen to regard all persons—humanity, if you like

—as crappers of two kinds: crappers in uniform or costume, and crappers *tout court*, crappers without uniforms, costumes, medals, or decorations, which might disguise what they are and what they do: they are crap and what they do is to crap. In *The Screens* there is a sergeant, a fine soldier, who shoots his own lieutenant. Why? The sergeant is taking a crap. He is unbuttoned, hence not really in uniform, and thus can kill his superior officer, for whom he would die if his pants were on, his fly buttoned. The sergeant's final words are: "My beauty grew with my cruelty, one heightening the other. And the rays of their love, when I took off my pants, gilded my behind!"

Napoleon once said, "Hide your crap" ("Cache ta merde"). One wonders why the remark was repeated, though it was certainly not meant literally. No doubt Napoleon was implying that we are not crap fundamentally, even if we are not all emperors or generals. Hence we have a right to hide what we eliminate. But what about the contrary injunction, suggested by this new play of Genet's: show your crap, expose it, promote it, exalt it? Finally, Genet seems to be saying—but I think he says it in a bad, forced lyricism, which is not song at all: sing your crap. My answer is: it can't be done.

Even Genet, if this new play of his may be taken as evidence, can't do it.

POET OF THE IMAGINARY

MARC PIERRET

In Jean Genet's *The Screens* the revolt of the Algerian Arabs against their French colonizers is not characterized by the emancipation of human beings. Although the colonizers are described as oppressors inflated with their own power, the

---

"Genet's New Play: *The Screens*," trans. Rima D. Reck, *Tulane Drama Review* (T19), Spring 1963, pp. 93–97. Reprinted by permission.

misery and the intolerable condition of the oppressed are not denounced in order to promote the liberation of the colonized people. On the contrary, these misfortunes are exalted so that the humiliated individual has the opportunity to make his misery the occasion for an inner experience based on the absolute contrast and conflict between his values and those of the Other—an unceasing contestation through which Saïd achieves a sovereignty which no action founded on the hope of a more just world could yield. For hope can take root in this world, and the hope of claiming one's rights is lost in the desire to become the Other. The subjective, ascetic, and tragic experience of Saïd has indeed no political value. Genet has not written a historical play.

We must doubly guard ourselves against being fooled by the dramatic illusions of this extremely complex work. Like all great poets Genet succeeds in making the very unreality of the theatrical situation one of the dimensions of the poetic reality he wishes to show us. Thus during the performance of *The Screens* the spectator will be constantly mystified; he will think he is watching an action, whereas what is happening to the Arabs is always fictional. Fictional because they are dominated by colonial laws and power; any real grasp of the world is forbidden them; their very being is lived by their masters who use them as the instrument of colonization. What attracts Genet first of all is this impossible situation of the excluded one. This is Saïd's situation, and also Genet's. He wants to live it to the end, right to death, which contaminates and transfigures all reality. The radical criticism which Genet levels against society is strictly apolitical, but profoundly disturbing and subversive. It strips bare the foundation of existence. After having undergone this revelation, it is up to each man to give a meaning to this, his own, experience.

When we say that Genet has identified himself with the Arabs we fall into the trap, we run up against the screens of fiction. On the contrary, it would be more appropriate to recognize that the dramatist has traced certain special aspects of the decolonization process, of the "objective historical" scale, back to his own personal destiny. Although we expect a work about the Algerian war, we must be prepared to read a play in which the Algerian war merely serves a rhetoric itself dependent on a predetermined poetic universe.

It is particularly striking that the author of *The Blacks* and *The Balcony* seems here to have deliberately devoted himself to frustrating all possibilities of an ideological validation of his own work. Some critics, on the other hand, had believed that by including history (to which, in fact, he had given only a purely theatrical role) his work would develop toward a representation of the world—a representation pointing the way to the future and drawing its support from those objective forces which govern historical evolution.

Genet's refusal to write politically engaged theater is here so evident that one can almost see in this refusal *the subject* of *The Screens*, in Henry James' sense of the word.

"If we had the misfortune to take the country's misfortunes seriously, then farewell our misfortune and farewell our pleasures." Thus speaks Warda, the prostitute in the brothel. This is the stake of the primordial question which Genet has in mind when he asks: what kind of liberty does one lose in becoming involved in the revolutionary project? "Revolutionary project" is, however, too vague a term to define the war of liberation waged by the Arabs against the French Algerian bourgeoisie. We can too easily interpret as we wish the circumspect use made by the rebel leaders of the Marxist ideology. This vagueness immediately restricts the "philosophical" scope of the question and prevents us from considering Genet a counterrevolutionary author. In my opinion, if Genet answers this question negatively by making Saïd, whom he favors, a traitor to the national cause, it is for the purpose of demonstrating the impossibility of reducing consciousness to any role whatsoever. Even the most humble, the most theatrical, or the most abject role—such as that which Saïd plays at the end of the drama when he is executed—does not finally fix consciousness. To call a French author a reactionary because he makes the radical assertion that the Algerians tend today to borrow modes of thought and blind patriotism from the colonials they fought yesterday is only a typical reaction on the part of our leftist do-gooders who will feed their sanctimonious depression by dreaming that the Africans will accomplish their work for them.

Of course I hasten to add that *The Screens* could not for long withstand this kind of near-sighted analysis. Nothing is further from a thesis play than this burning work with its constrained and ironic lyricism, whose perfect verbal coherence never for an instant ceases to haunt our consciousness right down to its most well-guarded ramparts. The play breaks through our alienation as spectators and reveals itself to us as an extreme, poetic experience—an alienation comparable to that of Saïd caught in the trap of his own ever moving negativity which is worshiped by the crowd.

Here we touch upon the central theme of this play which, if it were to be related to a current mode of thought, would most certainly better reveal itself to us by evoking the atheistic mysticism of Georges Bataille or the metaphysical interrogation of Heidegger than the demonstrative and already didactic anarchism of the young Brecht.

To be nothing, less than nothing. . . . The fleshy, bloated, ridiculous, and terrible fullness of colonial power is possible only when the native is reduced to nothingness. Thereafter the native has no other way out—if he wishes to live—except *to be* this negativity which he is for his masters, or to revolt against them. But as I pointed out earlier, by revolting, the native paradoxically begins little by little to resemble his masters. Slowly he passes from negativity to positivity, and along the way he loses the reasons for his revolt. He becomes courageous and intelligent; he is possessed and rehabilitated by the seriousness of a project which gives him a certain virtue. He is looked at with fear—he is a fighter.

Within this framework—or rather in this relation of the self to the world—Genet is once again unwilling to take into account the historical evolution resulting from the conflict between the opposing forces. And these forces are themselves economically determined by all kinds of material interests, ideological superstructures, ethnographic conditions, etc. . . . He leaves these reflections to the historians and the dialecticians, materialist or otherwise. The poet remains on the individual level, which is more static. On this level there exists a fixity in the structure of sensibility and imagination. But there is much more real movement here as well, the movement in which the need for the absolute exerts itself in the evanescent, fluid, obscure, and scarcely identifiable immediacy of everyday life. The danger for Saïd, whatever his choice, is that he may become someone—a hero or a beggar-thief; for even the humiliation into which others transform your flight or your refusal can fill you with being and distill in you honorable thoughts. These thoughts push you over the brink and you topple into the Good, along with cathedrals, uniforms, and vamps. This is why Saïd becomes a traitor in whose skin, however, he does not agree to immobilize himself. Perhaps "why" is too strong a word. Saïd does not reason; reason arises from the Good. It is better to understand Saïd's behavior (he seeks the lowest depth of abjection; his very search for it is itself abject) as a mystical renunciation, an attempt to escape the grotesque and afflicting positivity of symbols. But, unfortunately, he is bound to these symbols by his own stubbornness.

"Certain truths are not applicable, otherwise they'd die.... They mustn't die but must live through the song they've become," cries Ommu at the end of the play. These are the inapplicable truths which Genet tries to communicate to us throughout the entire length of *The Screens*. Saïd dies for them because he demands absolute communion with his own legend (the negation of all legends). Saïd wants a communion so perfect that it will not permit the Other's look to seize him and bring him into the world. Because of his speed Saïd overtakes everyone and, arriving at the end of the race, he finds himself confronted by the same death he fled from. His life is changed into a song: the corrupting song, corroding all the limits and all the impossibilities in the midst of which, deadened, sleepy, reality rests—the reality which "lives you" even before you make a gesture.

The fact remains that this play—and I have only sketched some of its intellectual problems—so absolutely without ideological, and therefore political bias, vigorously expresses those deepest conflicts which pit the individual against himself and against others in our society—a society which is hierarchical, sadomasochistic, and dominated by patriarchal myths. The contingent truths found in *The Screens* attest to the authenticity of a thought which wants to be unique and whose uniqueness, although provocative and violent, is never gratuitous.

Poet of the imaginary, Genet is also a realistic author. All his power springs from the fact that he is able to make us forget that he is a writer so that he may then drag us to the outermost limits of knowing and not-knowing. Detaching himself from the bitterness and hate he feels for the bourgeois world, Genet uses these very emotions as instruments of meditation on the being and non-being of the Word. But the Word can become meaningful only after it has been stripped of all the feeling society has heaped on it in order to possess it. For Genet poetry is an act of stripping away. He creates death. When the human landscape surrounding Saïd is touched by the falseness of his acts, it crumbles and collapses.

Genet is the only dramatist who consciously uses theatrical illusion to betray the spectator during the performance and deliberately makes him feel ill at ease. What you see is a lie; but you remain suspended like some Damocles over his sword which has been stuck between his bedpillows. The chicken yard is a fake. Saïd's suitcase is empty. Only the bitterness of his despair counts. He is the one who is not.

Genet's writing touches the very source of conflict. His work, especially *The Screens,* illustrates the vocation of men—which is to refuse the fate others impose on them and to deny the cultural conspiracy which maintains the illusion of their freedom.

General Interpretations

THE PSYCHOLOGICAL UNIVERSE OF JEAN GENET

THOMAS B. MARKUS

Genet's dominant concern is for Being. His plays are a manifestation of his personal inquiry into the nature of Being, and the nature of its counterpart, Nothingness. It follows that Sartre, author of *Being and Nothingness*, would be vitally interested in Genet's work, and his exhaustive study *Saint-Genet comédien et martyr* is an attempt to explicate Genet's life and art in terms of his (Sartre's) philosophic dialectic.

Genet's dramas deal with the problem of man's identity. This is most succinctly discussed in the terms of existential analysis, for the basic human predicament, a concern common to both this school of psychology and Genet's dramas, may be seen as existential anxiety. Existentialism, as a philosophy, asserts that the individual is whole only if he accepts himself as such. Existential analysis deals with those who (like Genet's characters) cannot accept their existence as real. They are thus suffering neuroses of the types discussed by the British psychiatrist R. D. Laing, who describes three major neuroses: *Engulfment* (the individual fears contact with anyone or anything. He even fears himself, for he is so uncertain about his own identity and autonomy that he believes any contact will cause him to lose them.); *Implosion* (the individual believes himself to be like a vacuum: completely void. He may, however, find some repose in knowing himself nothing, and thus he is in constant fear of a contact which might fill the emptiness or Nothingness which he accepts as himself.); *Petrification*

From *Drama Survey* 3 (1964), pp. 386–392. Reprinted by permission.

(the individual depersonalizes everyone and everything. If others are *its*, then they present no danger to one's identity. The neurotic, since he knows he has meaning only as he relates to the Other, cuts off his source of Being for fear of Nonbeing. That is, he refuses to recognize the very source from which his Being might gain significance. Thus he himself becomes objectified. Laing cites cases in which patients have literally become unable to move.).

The individual who is not neurotic, who is "normal," is ontologically secure. Self-knowledge, existentially, is gained through acceptance of the responsibilities for one's acts. Thus both the philosophy and its corresponding psychoanalysis are concerned with the nature of the act. If I understand Sartre, he asserts that the act is tautologically described. The act defines itself in terms of itself, the act is essentially an object.

The problem that immediately arises is how to recognize an act. What, in essence, is an act? How is it defined? How is it experienced? The American psychiatrist W. Van Dusen believes that Sartre's conception of the act is that which is devoid of images. He explains:

> *When Sartre plunges into critical experience he is throwing off false pretenses, all artificial dogmas, all that makes us feel safe, secure, and conventional. To Sartre, if a man truly seeks what is real he throws off his clothes, disdains appetite and faces the cold of the night in fear and trembling. Whatever saving grace of positive religious feeling comes to him, he also throws it off as a mere comforting illusion. He reaches his greatness by this naked, deliberate facing of death (Nonbeing).*

Man defies death, which is the antithesis of Being, and thereby gains assurance of his existence. Man's self-awareness, Sartre asserts, is his true and authentic experience. Immediately, the problem of the Other is raised. The existentialist recognizes that he can never see himself as the Other sees him. This is because he cannot truly know the Other, and consequently cannot know the entirety of the Other's impression of him.

To Genet, knowledge of the image of another may or may not be knowledge of the image of the reality; it might only be knowledge of the image of a reflection. The Other cannot, Genet believes, know the individual. Similarly, Genet suggests that *the individual cannot know himself*—and it is here that he splits seriously with Sartre—because all the individual sees is the reflection of himself. Man cannot both experience and observe, Genet maintains. Man's self-consciousness, his ability to perceive his own actions, is the primary essence of man, that by which he becomes man. But this very quality negates conclusively his ability to know himself. Man is defined as indefinable. (He is ineffable; he is as God. Thus he is logically the core of his universe, and the psychological or man-oriented and man-limited view of the universe replaces the religious or god-oriented.) Genet would not argue that the individual does not act authentically, but that knowledge of these actions cannot be verified. It is entirely possible that man observes only some reflection of his authenticity. This reflection, being two times removed from the "real," becomes an imprecise and consequently unreliable source for verification. Man cannot observe his own authentic acts because his very perception of them proves their artificiality. If existence does indeed precede essence, then we are doomed to the eternal cognizance of Becoming. Aestheticization of life creates only the obscurance of essential identity. Thus, man is condemned to remain removed from himself. He can never verify his Being, and Genet concludes that man's proper condition is ontological insecurity.

What existential analysts would assert as neurotic, Genet proclaims as normal. It is not to refute him to assert that he is a neurotic, suffering from a fear of engulfment, implosion, or petrification. Genet does not present his vision of man's condition without demonic logic, and to refute him, one would have to disprove his assertions. As long as Genet can validly maintain that man's self-awareness negates his ability to verify his authenticity, Genet remains a sane man.

In the psychological universe of Jean Genet's dramas there exists no central, fixed, or verifiable experience. I title his universe a psychological one, because it deals specifically with man's relation to himself: his vain quest for identity. Genet denies the existence of an exterior power above that of the characters themselves. This is evidenced in the plays. In *The Balcony* the Chief of Police, about to undergo a metamorphosis which will permanently alter his Being, suffers intense anguish: the *angst* of ontological insecurity. He does not cry out to any deity, superior force, or external order or fate. "Who am I," he questions, "without the image I must become to be anybody at all?" He finds himself to be no one, for he is unable to prove his existence, and so he accepts a role as the only escape from his insecurity. His quest for identity differs from that of Oedipus or Hamlet, for they sought theirs in relation to their deity. The Chief of Police seeks his in a universe which has significance only within the framework of the selected individual. And that individual is denied authentic knowledge of his significance and meaning. He is condemned to live a life of sham. Man, desiring to overcome his fear of Nothingness, accepts a role. A role is that chimera of existence which society has established over a period of time. It is also defined as a *function*. It has meaning in so far as the Other accepts the meaning. The entire hierarchy of our society is mutually interdependent. The role is a sublimation for authenticity, but it does alleviate man's serious *angst*.

Within Genet's logic, various opposites become fused as a result of the seemingly impossible situation in which man exists. Man's inability to become authentic, coupled with his acceptance of authenticity's antithesis (illusion), suggests that previous values and terminology become defunct in Genet's works. This concept of fusion of opposites is a key to understanding the plays. For Genet, living and dying become synonymous. To live, truly, means to be authentic—for while it is not recognizable, it remains theoretically attainable. Thus the opposite of authenticity is to die. Now, what we call living is the acceptance of illusion or role as real, and to Genet this is a kind of suicide: death becomes the denial of the possibility of authenticity. One who accepts a role becomes *petrified*, to use Laing's terminology, for he becomes fixed as a function within the nomenclature; any role with an established function is both eternal (eternally accepted as real by man's illusion of reality) and *petrifying* or killing. Life is then seen to be death, and opposites have fused.

Life cannot be lived, and we only pursue our death in life. The Envoy, in *The Balcony*, lives only in the realm of his symbolic role as Master of Protocol, and he can experience no anguish. He is limited to the nonvital emotions of amusement and indifference. In *The Blacks*, as the court is about to be killed, whiteness (which is a metaphor for death) is equated to weakness, frailty. Earlier, the Queen after her first exchange with Felicity, says, "I'm weary, and their odor is choking me. . . . And we're still too lively, aren't we? Yet all my blood's ebbing away." Later the Governor declaims, "First, you'll turn pale, then you'll fall, and you'll be dead." The whiter one becomes, the closer one approaches petrification. The role provides only an illusion of Being, and therefore only an illusion of vitality. However, an individual who accepts a role, who has been petrified, cannot act, and is therefore nonvital: dead.

Genet's use of a constantly metamorphosing illusion (or reality) is another manifestation of his psychological universe. What has been traditionally accepted as real is shown to be false. Similarly, what has traditionally been recognized as false is real—and hence false. Thus, illusion and reality become the same. They do not merely invert positions, they truly merge. Falsity is the only truth, and negation the only proof. A poet can establish new types of illusion, and these may be called beauty, but they remain illusion. The poet, being a man, shares man's condemnation. Genet admits his compliance, for in his autobiography he has written:

> *Without thinking myself magnificently born, the uncertainty of my origin allowed me to interpret it. I added to it the peculiarity of my misfortunes. Abandoned by my family, I felt it was natural to aggravate this condition by a preference for boys, and this preference by theft, and theft by crime or a complacent attitude in regard to crime. Hence, I resolutely rejected a world which had rejected me.*

Genet created his own world and his own role in it. It was a new role, or at least an uncommon one. But it was still a role, consciously adopted in order to make life bearable. In *The Balcony* the character Roger strives to lead a revolution that will finally destroy the need for illusion. He fails and ends by creating a new role, that of the Chief of Police. He augments the very nomenclature he hoped to abolish. This is the logical and inevitable development. In *Deathwatch* Lefranc tries to assume the role of murderer by strangling the boy Maurice. But Green Eyes, a true murderer, can't accept Lefranc as an authentic criminal because Lefranc chose his role. The very self-consciousness which permitted Lefranc to see the role he wanted precluded his attaining a genuine Being. Green Eyes murdered in a fit of passion that could not be controlled. Thus he murdered—*acted authentically*—out of intuitive, irrational, emotional motivation. He says that his crime chose him, and that he is truly a criminal, while Lefranc is doomed to play at his role. Lefranc cannot create himself in his own image, because his awareness of the image precludes his authenticity.

Genet proves the impossibility of authenticity in two other ways. One way around the dilemma which Genet establishes would seem to be the overlap of role and reality. That is, if the role coincides with the truth of the person, then he *is* himself on *both* levels. Genet denies this. Arthur, in *The Balcony*, attains a sort of immortality as his role as "corpse" is coincidental with his authentic death. He is a corpse playing at being a corpse. But his reality is subordinate to the role, and even duplication of authenticity and role does not allow the role to be denied. The pure self cannot be seen because the Others recognize only the role, which is enduring in their eyes. Arthur's recognition of his own truth is precluded by his authentic, physical death, and while he might have seen himself if he were alive, he is not. The only authentic action he could perform was his own death, and subsequently he could perceive neither authenticity nor role.

If the individual endeavors to see himself as other than the image he is, he is a schizophrenic. The Envoy, in *The Balcony*, states that the rebels want "each individual to be both himself and a shining specimen of himself." The example of Roger proves Genet's negation of this second attempt to circumnavigate the issue. The individual is either lost, or found in a role. He cannot be both, for then he is neither. Then he is no longer sane, claims Genet, who is sane himself; he is *ontologically insecure.*

There are two basic human emotions which might be considered authentic: love and hate. Genet investigates both of these, for he probably senses that most nonbelievers will use one of these two as proof either of his failure or of his inconsistency. Love, Genet shows, fails completely to allow man an authentic action. Village and Virtue, in *The Blacks*, experiment with love, to determine if it will aid them in breaking from the rituals which the Blacks pursue, while allowing them some belief in themselves and each other. Village comments:

> *. . . We—you and I—were moving along the edges of the world, out of bounds. We were the shadow, or the dark interior, of luminous creatures . . . When I beheld you, suddenly—for perhaps a second—I had the strength to reject everything that wasn't you, and to laugh at the illusion. But my shoulders are very frail. I was unable to bear the weight of the world's condemnation.*

It seems that Genet is saying that love is the borderline at which truth can almost—perhaps for a second—be attained. Perhaps at the moment of mutual sexual consummation acceptance of the Other in his authentic, essential self can be experienced. It is interesting to observe that at the end of the play Village and Virtue try to teach each other the naïve gestures of love. But what we are seeing is not Virtue and Village walking slowly from us. We dare not accept the reality of the illusion in a Genet play. At the conclusion of *The Balcony* Madame Irma tells us "it's morning already," which we know is a lie; so, too, *The Blacks* ends with a lie. We are seeing two actors, tired after a night's performance, about to take their curtain call, take off their theatrical costumes, and presumably go home. Yes, they turn their backs on our world of illusion—for perhaps a second—but who are they? Virtue and Village don't turn their backs, for they don't exist. No; two actors, in Genet's final lie, delude us into thinking that there is some resolution. But Village said earlier that he could not bear the weight of the world's condemnation. Genet is a liar, a cheat, and a thief. He lies, and tells us there may be some solution through love. He cheats us out of this belief, for as we leave the theater we realize that the actors who portrayed Village and Virtue are about to do the same. He robs us of our sense of repose—the repose into which he brutally lulled us, only moments before: a repose which can last, perhaps, only for a second.

The alternative to love, hatred, is also a central theme in *The Blacks*. Genet seems to suggest that hatred is the one authentic action which can be accomplished. Love, strong as it may be, is not as strong as hatred, for love is a positive emotion, desiring something which gratifies, and something which is, consequently, unattainable and illusory. Hate, by nature of its totality (the hatred even of hatred—total negation), is not a pretense. It is itself, totally. It is our one possible authentic act. Genet recognizes, however, that true hate is manifested only through total destruction, death. Murder is the one act, if executed without consciousness, which is authentic. Green Eyes truly exists as a murderer and a man precisely *because* he murdered out of passion. His lack of reason or rationality authenticated the primitive, elemental authenticity of the deed. Solange emerges finally as Solange when Claire drinks the poisoned tea (even though Claire also lives, since it is Madame who dies). Genet has admitted his own inability to murder. He admits to living a role made of illusory action. The act of murder, however, stops life. It is therefore not a creative act. True, it does negate the illusory creativeness of those accepting roles instead of their true selves, but it also negates itself, for it implies, by extension, total nihilism, the destruction of mankind. It does not imply mass suicide, for that is a conscious action. But it revels in such holocausts as atomic explosions which inflict gratuitous deaths. It thus negates itself as a creative action, and Genet leaves us completely aware of the impossibility of action coexistent with creativity or life.

Communication is only possible, he asserts, on the level of the role. Authentic action is not a shared happening. Relation of it makes it second-hand, a symbol of reality, and thus not the reality. Acceptance of the stage illusion as reality is the theatrical norm, and it follows that the theatrical norm is the purest expression of our illusions. This is why Genet has chosen to write plays rather than novels now that he has reached his literary maturity. The distance between the stage and man's internal ambiguity leads Genet to remark, through Archibald in *The Blacks*, "We shall increase the distance that separates us—a distance that is basic—by our pomp, our manners, our insolence—for we are also actors. When my speech is over, everything here—here!—will take place in the delicate world of reprobation." The very nature of a theatrical performance expresses Genet's vision of our world. The lie must be accepted as the truth cannot be perceived. The more we attempt to distinguish the truth—about a theatrical performance or about our own identities—the more deluded we become. As definition through denotation is impossible, Genet has turned to poetic metaphor in an attempt to reflect the essence of his vision. He has made his plays one whirling shifting metaphor, to which the action, diction, characters, and spectacle are contributing symbols. All elements of conventional dramaturgy merge into one consummate theatrical expression, an expression that is never fixed and without describable form: a *metamorphosis.*

GENET AND THE SADISTIC SOCIETY

JOHN ELSOM

In England, we assume that sadism is a form of sexual perversion, marked by the love of cruelty; but in France, the existentialists have given the word an altogether wider meaning which includes sex, but isn't circumscribed by it. Sartre, in his play, *Altona,* describes a relationship between two similar people: Franz von Gerlach, whose cruelty during the war earned him the title of the Butcher of Smolensk, and Johanna, his sister-in-law, who had been a film star before her beauty began to wane. Why are they similar? Because they both imagine themselves as placed above the rest of mankind, he through his strength and defiance, she through her beauty, and when the real world fails to recognize their pretensions, they create a fantasy world in which their nobility can have full sway. Franz's cruelty, which is what we in England would call sadism, is just one attitude in a far-reaching complex, which also affects Johanna, who is not cruel, the von Gerlach family, and indeed the whole Nazi society which they represent.

The existentialist definition of "sadism" briefly is this. It is the process by which one man tries to transform another into a mere object of his will. The masochist is delighted by the spectacle of himself as the object of another's will. The two attitudes are, of course, linked. When Johanna fails to dominate the cinema audiences, she submits tamely and masochistically

---

From *The London Magazine,* August 1963, pp. 61–67. Reprinted by permission.

to the will of her husband, Werner: and she is only tempted to take control again when Werner himself submits to the will of his father. The sadistic process can't be completed, because a man can't become an object without ceasing to be human. A man becomes an object only in death, and so the sadist may feel drawn to kill his victim. But this satisfaction is an illusion, for the sadist is haunted by the presence of an independent life. It is the *life* he wants to control. But to dominate an independent life lies beyond the boundaries of human capacity. It is the one thing that we can't do. Or rather, if we can, it is proof that we are more than human. And so, behind Franz's cruelty, is pride, but not simply "folie de grandeur," but that primordial pride in which men aspire to be god.

Thus, the sadist lives in a fantasy world, lured on by what he cannot attain. He beats his mistress, not because she is the object of his will, but because she isn't and never can be. Whether his sadism manifests itself in the cruelty of a Franz or the narcissism of Johanna, the central cause remains the same. He is trying to convince himself of his "divinity" by committing "godlike" acts, and because he's never quite certain that his acts are godlike, he stands aside from what he does to examine his image anxiously for traces of superhumanity. He is Caligula, if we want to find a prototype, rather than de Sade.

Sartre believes that the sadist is the victim of his own fear and bad faith. Franz feels guilty because a Polish rabbi whom he helped to escape was betrayed by his father to save his son's life. The murder of the rabbi by SS men, which Franz witnessed, has made him loathe and distrust human weakness, and this, coupled with his guilt, has made him determined to be strong, strong at the expense of his humanity. This is a logical, almost classical view of sadism. Because Franz loathes human weakness, he denies this weakness in himself and asserts his superhumanity. He beats his prisoners and bullies his subordinates always in an attempt to prove that he is not one of them. Because he feels that his will is tarnished with guilt, he attempts to assert his will on every possible occasion: to reassure himself perhaps that his will, though corroded, still exists.

But does this easy cause-and-effect logic exist between what we do and what we become? Is it true that we only long to be god when we have become ashamed to be human? And is it true that our shame is based on our personal fear and guilt? We must remember that it is almost an existential article of faith that we are individually responsible for what we become: and it is an article with which many people do not agree, and which is impossible to prove. Jean Genet, for example, believes that men are born with a sense of personal shame, and are also innately god-inclined. In *Le Journal du Voleur*, Genet describes how, at the Crucifixion, Christ delivered men from their sins, but punishes and humiliates them through the body. We can't escape this pain and shame. Indeed, we should embrace it. But we must try to transform our degradation into "ritual," either of behavior or art, which satisfies our "divine" aspirations. My body, Genet writes, is only a pretext, a pretext in his case, for poetry: "ma victoire est verbale." The man who has successfully transformed his bodily shame in this way has attained what Genet terms "sanctity." Sanctity means "union with God," but God is not a Christian god, or a humanist "first cause." God is the god-in-man, "*mon tribunal intime*."

In other words, Genet has described what the existentialist would regard as the essential preconditions for sadism: a loathing for human weakness, "divine" aspirations, and a continual self-examination which attempts to discover in the weakness the seeds of the hoped-for strength. Whatever definition of sadism one accepts, I don't believe that the constant preoccupation with sadism in Genet's work can be ignored. Three of his five plays are concerned with the right and wrong ways of committing murder: all the brothel scenes in *The Balcony* show sadomasochistic rituals. But if one adopts the existentialist definition of sadism, and remember what the implications of this definition had for Sartre in *Altona*, the preoccupation becomes infinitely clearer. Nearly all of Genet's characters can be caught in the same giant web. They are ashamed to be men. They act "divine" roles to themselves, like Caligula, heightening what they believe themselves to be until they have transformed their human characteristics into totems. A Negro can't simply be black: he must "negrify" himself by rubbing shoe polish into his skin. When the banker visits the brothel, when the maids amuse themselves while their mistress is away, or when the blacks act out the downfall of the whites, their humanity is buried under ritual. They don masks, cothurni, or elaborate clothes. They speak rhetorically in high supercharged voices. They keep to a predetermined script. They watch the ritual anxiously lest something go wrong . . . and when it does—when the maid's alarm clock rings, or the banker hears the sound of a machine gun—the wave of illusion breaks and the actors are left, stranded and panting on the sands of their own unavoidable humanity. The rhetoric which we associate with French tragic drama is for Genet a psychological necessity. No man can resign himself to being human.

Therefore Genet, unlike Sartre, tends to assume that sadism is innate. This difference between them is of great importance. Sartre believes that sadism, in spite of its overwhelming presence in society and the individual, is a complex that we can avoid. *Altona* is an explanation as well as a portrait of the sadistic society, and there is no point in explaining anything unless it alters in some way our understanding and behavior. But Genet doesn't explain. He takes sadism for granted. All that a moralist can do, for Genet like Sartre is a moralist, is to distinguish between types of sadism: between the successful and the unsuccessful, the sanctified and the abject. This is the theme of *Deathwatch*, Genet's first play. Both Green Eyes and Lefranc are murderers, but Green Eyes kills in obedience to an inner necessity, a wave of necessity which drowns his conscious, resisting will, but which lifts him up to a higher plane of being. "Destiny takes control of his hands." Time moves faster. He murders elegantly with a flower between his teeth. The murder is like dancing. But when Lefranc, who envies the strength and detachment of Green Eyes, tries to imitate him by murdering Maurice, a fellow prisoner, he is pulled back by sheer human frailty. He killed in anger and to be admired. Green Eyes is naturally disgusted. Killing by itself means nothing. Only submission to superhuman destiny counts.

But neither Sartre nor Genet thinks of sadism primarily in terms of individual behavior. Above all, it is a complex which society expresses and exploits. As the individual sadist is not simply a killer, so the sadistic society is characterized not just by cruelty, but by the love of ritualistic detail: class-consciousness, status symbols, tyranny, colonialism . . . anything which suggests that one man or group of men can be superior to the rest of mankind. Herr von Gerlach teaches his second son, Werner, how to dominate his subordinates: "Never look at them in the eyes. Always look at the bone in their foreheads." This domination is economically necessary to the von Gerlach family. Without it, they couldn't run the shipyards. And it is quite divorced from real merit. Herr von Gerlach is proud of the fact that he does nothing but sign letters: other people know about the shipyards and they work for him. The mistress in Genet's play *The Maids* comforts herself that she has much better taste than her servants. In his play *The Blacks* the white colonialists reassure themselves that they don't have the nasty smell of the blacks. This is the sadistic society in action: where the individual is driven by a mixture of social, economic, and private forces to prove his superiority, and because this superiority never can be proved, he is forced to magnify tiny details —these class distinctions, taste, color, smell—in order to convince himself that the superiority exists. These details in time become ritualistic, not simply because they are inflated beyond their real importance, but because men use them to convince themselves of their "divine" origins and nature. The whites assume that God has a white face. Naturally. After all, he's their god. The "divinity," the superhumanity, is what matters to them: the ritualistic details merely confirm this inner longing. In the sadistic society, one generation succeeds another by a revolution in miniature: for no one abandons his illusion of superiority except in defeat, and only victory gives the individual or the class a temporary reassurance.

Because the socialist believes that the claims of the individual or the class must be subordinated to those of society as a whole, he must resolutely oppose the sadistic society; but to believe that socialism can exist, he must believe with Sartre that sadism is the result of bad faith and can be avoided. Genet, as we have seen, assumes that sadism is innate, and so he admits that he cannot imagine what the socialist society would be like. Although he shares so many of the preoccupations of the left-wing existentialists and has been acclaimed by them, he is in fact an extreme right-wing reactionary. True, he sympathizes with the underdog: the maids, the blacks, the rebels. But when the revolution's over, the rebels become the establishment, the blacks are the new whites, and society continues in the same pattern. Society is the mass projection of the sadistic impulse. When the corrupt feudal state in *The Balcony* is overthrown by a revolution, the figureheads of the old order—the Queen, the Bishop, the General—are replaced by fantasy creations from the brothel. Private dreams become public institutions.

Nor is Genet simply shrugging away the possibility of change. He is stating a social philosophy which is the exact opposite of the Marxist. Whereas Marx believed that society is under constant pressure to adapt itself to its environment, to become, in other words, more useful, Genet assumes that men are always trying to free themselves from their environment and become useless. The man who acts the role of the bishop should be without functions, without obligations to other men. When he hears a confession, he absolves, not to relieve the sinner of guilt, but to glorify in his powers of absolution. A man mustn't become a bishop through personal merit. This would pin down God's representative to human conditions. A bishop should exist "in solitude, for appearance alone." And once the appearance has been established, the man steers a "skillful vigorous course toward Absence. Death." The divine rituals we create become our tombs, and when they're built, gently we dissociate ourselves, shrink away, and die. And so, society changes like the coral reef, in size and mutation, but not in kind. One generation of tombs simply piles upon another. In *The Balcony* the only man to produce social change is not the revolutionary, Roger, but the Chief of Police. Roger, a socialist, wants to change the *kind* of society. He would like the rebels to be useful, rational men, and he disapproves of Armand, whom he finds posturing in front of a mirror. But Roger comes to a futile end, castrating himself in the brothel he swore to destroy: whereas the Chief of Police who, through sheer terror, forces people to admire him, adds a new studio to the brothel. It is he who produces a mutation of the coral.

Expressed in these terms, Genet's vision of society seems only a more faded version of Spengler's cyclical history: itself an outworn and discredited idea. Society, like the individual, aspires toward ritual, and we call this ritual "civilization" or "culture." We only define culture in nonuseful terms: the art of the Romans is their culture, their plumbing is not. And we judge a culture, not by the way in which it reflects their life, but by the way in which it shows their superhuman control of life: their "nobility," their "wisdom," their aesthetic pleasure. A wriggling worm is of no interest: a worm which wriggles gracefully and rhythmically, which has tried to transform its instinctive movements into some sort of dance, is aspiring toward ritual. It is a cultural worm. Once this social ritual has been established, men lack the incentive to develop it further. Civilization is an end in itself, and this is where human energy stops and dies away. The Whites give way to the Blacks, who give way to the Reds and the Yellows.

The difference between Spengler and Genet lies in the intensity with which Genet perceives this need for ritual, and the degradation on which this need is based. When Genet writes, "my body is only a pretext" (for poetry), he is not only justifying his existence in terms of art. He is saying that without art, life is pointless and humiliating. The life cycle of a man or a society is like that of a plant. The thin malodorous stem which feeds on dying leaves and strangles its neighbor in its search for food has one aim: to produce a flower. And when the flower has been formed, the stem dies away and the blossom droops still glorious, until it rests on the ground. The flower, like the man, must be judged not by the morality of its growth, but by the beauty of its blossom. This is the central vision, intense, all-embracing, which floods through Genet's work. It is Lawrentian in its size and simplicity. It binds together all that multiplicity of subject matter which we find in his plays: the politics, the love-hate relationships, the social comment, the doubts about identity, the search for God and death. We respond to the vision unconsciously at first, without quite knowing why. We may loathe his characters, their degradation, their narcissism, but at the same time, something beyond the story and the people warms and excites us. Our disgust is never total. We turn a corner in the plot, and stand suddenly face to face with a vision that explains all, reconciles all, and illuminates with clarity and beauty the dark passages through which we have reluctantly trodden.

Jean Genet has been called a playwright of the Absurd. Martin Esslin gives him a chapter. I believe that this term is deeply misleading, even though we can see how it came to be applied. Like Pirandello, he writes about people who put on masks and disguises in attempting to discover their own identities. Like Ionesco, his dialogue is often nonsensical, and his scenes vivid, fragmentary, and symbolic. Like any existentialist, he denies the existence of absolute truth, doesn't believe that even partial truth can be adequately communicated, and the absence of this truth worries him.

The danger of applying the word "absurd" to Genet's work lies partly in the term itself. It can mean so many things. A distinction must always be made between a play which uses an "absurd" technique to express a simple, coherent thought, and a play which expresses the vision of an absurd universe. In Ionesco, there is usually a perfectly understandable theme: *Rhinoceros* is about the danger of being stampeded into brutality by group hysteria. When one has grasped the theme, the apparent nonsense of men turning into rhinoceroses becomes the simplest, most obvious means of expression. It is an allegory, as the *Tempest* is an allegory. In the case of Beckett, on the other hand, his vision of the universe is absurd: one never knows whether the universe is ordered or not, whether existence has any point, whether our lives may or may not be futile. Genet's plays are usually absurd only in the first sense. There is a coherent meaning, though it may be expressed in an apparently nonsensical technique.

The main reason, though, for disliking the word "absurd" in this context is that it runs counter to a perceptive response to his plays. Behind the word absurd lies the feeling of pointlessness. In whatever we do or are, our lives are equally vain. Genet's plays are, on the contrary, concerned with *justification*. In spite of the degradation of our lives, in spite of the fact that God may not exist, sanctity is still within our grasp. All of Genet's plays contain people who manage to transcend the shame of their existences: Green Eyes, the Chief of Police, Claire, the blacks, who in overthrowing the whites create a black heaven. His plays are even optimistic. *The Maids* ends with Solange saluting the death of her sister with the words, "We are beautiful, joyous, drunk, and free."

Few writers have had a greater insight into the shame of men's lives: only Dostoevsky perhaps. Much of Genet's work is, of course, the catharsis of a man whose childhood was intensely distressing and whose life is that of a social outcast. His terms of reference are those of a convict. But beyond this shame lies his belief that our humiliation can be transformed: that it is the necessary prelude to the beautiful flower of ritual, which, though pointless in the sense that it is not useful, is nevertheless the end product of our existence. He retains his faith in the ritual and communicates this faith to us. This is why his plays are optimistic: this is why they move us so deeply.

THE THEATER AS RITUAL

R. W. F. WILCOCKS

In an early essay, "The Beating of a Drum," T. S. Eliot pointed to the importance of ritual in the history and development of the theater:

> *The drama was originally ritual; and ritual, consisting of a set of repeated movements, is essentially a dance* [. . .]. *It is possible to assert that primitive man acted in a certain way and then found a reason for it. An unoccupied person, finding a drum, may be seized with a desire to beat it; but unless he is an imbecile, he will be unable to continue beating it, and thereby satisfying a need (rather than a "desire"), without finding a reason for so doing. The reason may be long-continued drought. The next generation or the next civilization will find a more plausible reason for beating a drum. Shakespeare and Racine—or rather the developments which led up to them—each found his own reason. The reasons may be divided into tragedy and comedy. We still have similar reasons, but we have lost the drum.*[1]

The ritual which Eliot has in mind is the fertility symbol of the Country Dionysia which, with its phallic processions and improvised speeches, is the prototype of Attic drama. What particularly interested Eliot was the suggestion that tragedy was related to this early ritual in the sense that its

---

1. In *The Nation and The Athenaeum* 34 (6 October 1923), p. 12.

Extracts from "Jean Genet: A Study of His Drama" (Ph.D. diss., University of Khartoum, 1966), pp. 179–192. Printed by permission.

themes and characters were symbolic of archaic seasonal rites. He is accepting the idea put forward by Sir Gilbert Murray—an idea which has been refuted by more recent scholars, but which is important none the less, if only for its effect on Eliot's dramatic output. Murray writes as follows:

> . . . *The life of the Year-Demon, as it seems to be reflected in tragedy, is generally a story of Pride and Punishment. Each year arrives, waxes great, commits the sin of Hubris, and then is slain. The death is deserved; but the slaying is a sin; hence comes the next year as Avenger, or as the Wronged one re-risen.*[2]

The element which fascinated Eliot was the ritual of the Slain God. He takes this concept as a seasonal myth; and then, of course, integrates it with the Christian myth of the Slain Saviour. For Eliot's drama to have any ritual significance for the civilization of modern Western Europe, this integration was clearly necessary. For once the basic elements of any ritual cease to form part of current belief, its powers of communion are impoverished: what had once been "the poignant drama of the sacrifice of a god," argues E. Doutté, "is no longer anything but an absurd ceremonial: the grotesque burial of a creature of fantasy."[3] Thus the ritual appearance of a god or other expiatory victim loses its immediacy once the belief necessary for such a ceremony is no longer present among the participants. The delight, for example, in the ritual sin of consummating a marriage before it is sanctified can only be enjoyed within the framework of a belief in God. This is precisely the point made by Mrs. Blankensee in *The Screens:*

> *Betrayal's not what it used to be. In the old days, as my great-grandmother used to tell me, an engaged couple would marry on the eve of their wedding. The male would gash*

---

2. *Five Stages of Greek Religion* (Oxford: Oxford University Press, 1925), p. 49.
3. *Magie et Religion dans l'Afrique du Nord* (Algiers: A. Jourdan, 1908), p. 533.

the female, and an invisible red spot under her white gown would prove that love was stronger than God. One had to believe in God, of course, and betray.[4]

Merely to believe, however, in the efficacy and value of the given ritual is not enough; it is also necessary to have a genuine victim. As soon as the living sacrifice is replaced by a pasteboard effigy, the entire ceremony degenerates—as can be seen in Roger Caillois' analysis of the modern carnival, which is

> *a sort of dying echo of antique festivals like the Saturnalia. Here you have a cardboard effigy representing an enormous King—brightly colored and comical—who is invariably shot or drowned after a period of merry-making. The ritual no longer has the slightest religious value, and the reason seems to me to be obvious: as soon as the human victim is replaced by an effigy, the rite tends to lose its expiatory and fecundating value, and to shed its double symbolism: that of past defilements, and that of a new world created.*[5]

Now, one aspect of *The Screens* is the creation of a new order through the apparent chaos of the ritual destruction of an old order. In the London production by Peter Brook and Charles Marowitz, the figures representing Western colonialism were cardboard effigies behind which the actors spoke. The effect was that of those cats on a wall which are shot down in fun fairs. The comic and at the same time pathetic nature of the characters was lost beneath this exterior. Roger Blin, on the other hand, fully grasped the ritual nature of the play, and therefore was careful to avoid this mistake. It is indeed rare in Genet that an effigy replaces the human sacrificial victim. Almost the only example is that of the Dolls representing the White Court, to which Diouf, disguised as the White Victim, gives birth in *The Blacks*. And the Dolls are not the essential

4. Trans. Bernard Frechtman (New York: Grove Press, 1962), Scene Eleven, p. 86.
5. *L'Homme et le sacré* (Paris: Editions Gallimard, 1950), p. 157.

victims in this play. Indeed, if Genet's plays are considered in the light of sacrificial ritual, then the majority of his central characters are in fact victims.

Although the structure of the plays has evolved from the classical linear action of *Deathwatch* and *The Maids* to the circular ceremony and panorama of the later dramas, there is little evidence of any change in Genet's conception of character. In all the plays there is more than one victim, but in the later plays the sacrificial roles are so diversified that the spectator is sometimes left feeling confused. In the first two plays, however, the issue is straightforward. In *Deathwatch* all the characters are in some way sacrificial victims. Maurice, who is strangled by Lefranc, is the obvious victim in a ritual whereby Lefranc hopes to be reborn as a god of Green Eyes' caliber. But Green Eyes is himself a victim, and destined to die as a sacrifice to society. So also is Lefranc. He is a victim of his own illusions, of course; but, what is more important in the present context, he has committed the ultimate act which will bring about the retribution he demanded (since he now shares Green Eyes' guilt) and a punishment which he sought to avoid, but to which his very action has condemned him—solitude. Similarly in *The Maids*, all three characters present aspects of the sacrificial victim. The spirit of Madame is sacrificed through the person of Claire in the substitution rites of the maids, and the situation is such that this ritual will infallibly involve the death of Solange. Thus, in the background to the play, we can detect an almost Wagnerian ideal of the attainment of spiritual freedom and love through the sacrifice of the flesh. Because of this sacrifice, the maids can predict that they will be "beautiful, joyous, drunk, and free." And in the English version of the play, the theme is developed more explicitly still:

> SOLANGE: . . . *Madame is dead. Her two maids are alive: they've just risen up, free, from Madame's icy form. All the maids were present at her side—not they themselves, but*

rather the hellish agony of their names. And all that remains of them to float about Madame's airy corpse is the delicate perfume of the holy maidens which they were in secret. . . .[6]

By contrast, *The Balcony* is rather more difficult to analyze from this point of view. On the one hand, it clearly deals with the sublimation of flesh into spirit, of the person into the image; and yet, on the other, there are no immediately apparent ritual victims, and certainly the structure seems to bear no relation to any recognizable ritual pattern.

None the less, a closer inspection will reveal more than one link with the world of ritual. There is, of course, the killing of Chantal, who in death will achieve the status denied her in life. The attitude of Carmen to the brothel and the language she uses to discuss her life reveal the development of an idea already expressed in the novels—namely, the identification of the brothel and its inmates with houses of religious retreat; and, suggests Genet, the mortification of the flesh in the course of the striving after an ideal is a feature common to both. Perhaps the climax of this theme is reached toward the end of the play, when Roger-the-Plumber castrates himself in the "Mausoleum Studio."

This bizarre and violent action has been variously interpreted. Some critics have seen it as an admission of the revolutionaries' defeat, while others have suggested that it is an expression of what Roger would like to see happen to the image he has chosen to incarnate. Certainly both these interpretations are justified by the text, and indeed they are complementary rather than contradictory. However, there is yet a further point to be borne in mind. We should remember that, from the sixth tableau, Roger has been aware of the failure of the revolutionary principle, inasmuch as he acknowledges that it has been necessary to construct and to believe in an "Image of the Revolt" (Chantal) in order to combat those in power, whose

6. *The Maids*, trans. Bernard Frechtman (New York: Grove Press, 1961), p. 100.

force is related to their recognition of the power of the ideal image:

> *It is so as to fight against an image that Chantal has turned forever into an Image. The battle is no longer taking place in reality, but on a pageant field. On a field of azure. It is a battle of allegories. Neither we ourselves nor our enemies can understand the reasons for our revolt.*[7]

Thus, Roger's decision to incarnate the image of the Chief of Police, and his radical severance with his past attitudes, epitomized by the self-mutilation, may be seen not merely as the acknowledgment of the defeat of his revolutionary principles, but also as a violent rejection of them, a rejection which entails an acceptance of the principles which govern his erstwhile opponents. The flesh is thus truly sacrificed for the spirit, and in a way which curiously resembles the initiation rites practiced by the ancient priests of Attis. It is a symbol of separation from the everyday world, a violent extension of the ritual offering of the wife to the warder by Green Eyes in *Deathwatch*, a sacrifice which marks his ultimate isolation. Whether Roger's action is the result of a miscalculation, as the Chief of Police suggests, or a necessary part of his own purification, the brutal and unexpected nature of the act has a dramatic intensity which is hardly relieved by the amusing reaction of the Chief of Police. This points, incidentally, to a fundamental weakness in *The Balcony*, for it is neither a *fête* (if that term may, for convenience, be applied to dramatic presentations such as *The Blacks* or *The Screens*) nor yet is it constructed within the framework of a conventional dramatic form (as were *Deathwatch* and *The Maids*). Because its structure falls between these two stools, Genet's dramatic intentions are difficult to realize on the stage. The incongruous and inventive interweaving of the grossly comic and the deeply tragic which occurs in *The Blacks* and *The Screens* is made possible by the unusual

---

7. *Le Balcon*, p. 123, translated by R.N.C. (This passage is not included in the English version of the play.)

structure of these plays. In *The Balcony* it is difficult to determine what is farce and what is tragedy; and from this it is evident that there is a wide discrepancy between what was intended and what was achieved. For we know that, for Genet, the purpose of theater is to produce an effect very close to catharsis on the audience. Now catharsis involves "purgation," to use the medical term frequently employed in discussing tragedy; but what Genet wishes to produce is that sudden clarity of perception which accompanies the emotional violence associated with catharsis. A play may present a problem, but may not attempt to solve it, since this would detract from the necessary degree of participation by the spectator. Genet states this quite clearly in the introduction to the second edition of *The Balcony;* but, whereas the intention of "having the evil on the stage explode, showing us naked to ourselves, leaving us wild-eyed if possible, and having nowhere to turn for help, save to ourselves"—whereas this intention is admirably achieved in the other plays, in *The Balcony* it fails to come to fruition.

In *The Blacks* the entire "ceremony" which is enacted before the audience is specifically presented as though it were a ritual. This ritual is a *divertissement*—or, as Genet called it, a "clown show"—designed to keep the audience amused while the real action of the play, which is peripheral to this ceremony, takes place off-stage. Now, it is the existence of this external action which prevents any direct interpretation of the play as a ritual-in-itself, and which makes it impossible for the spectator to consider himself being treated to a privileged "private view" of someone else's rites and ceremonies. This was the case with the two early plays, and also with *The Balcony* until the final speech in which Madame Irma makes it evident that the audience is not a disinterested party. In *The Blacks*, however, Genet forces his audience either to leave the theater or to enter into the ritual, which is performed simultaneously for them and against them, as communicants. The entry of the "White Court" at the beginning of the play and Archibald's speech of introduction addressed both to this court and to the spectators obliges the audience to accept that the adventures of the "White Court" and the ritual directed against it are, in reality, a ceremony in which it (the audience) is a participant congregation whose image is the sacrificed victim. This is illustrated by Genet's concern that there should be at least one white spectator present in the audience:

> *This play, written, I repeat, by a white man, is intended for a white audience, but if, which is unlikely, it is ever performed before a black audience, then a white person, male or female, should be invited every evening. . . .*[8]

Genet's last play to date, *The Screens*, is something different again: it is neither the presentation of a private ritual nor does it involve the audience in the manner of *The Blacks*. In scale it is much vaster than any earlier play by Genet. The panorama of the Algerian conflict is detailed in epic terms. But within this setting we are given glimpses of hidden rituals: the raising of Si Slimane from the dead (possibly borrowed from *The Persians*); the ritual of the brothel scenes; the murder of Warda by a group of village women with its ritualistic "*tricoteuses*" sequence, reminiscent of the mocking of Christ as well as of scenes of the French Revolution where the fallen mighty are jeered at; the French officers obsessed with the ritual details of their appearance before the battle.

Over and above these details, however, the play as a whole may be seen simultaneously as the ritual destruction of an old order and as the public agony of one family—at one point caustically alluded to as "the Holy Family"—and of one sacrificial hero, Saïd. Saïd does not join the tranquil world of the Dead after he has been shot, because he has been "alive not dead" and "dead alive," in the same way as the sacrificial saviour of any religious mythology. That Genet intends Saïd to be a modern Arab parallel of Christ is indicated by the Missionary's aside in the first half of the scene leading to Saïd's

---

8. Introduction to *The Blacks*, trans. Bernard Frechtman (New York: Grove Press, 1960), p. 4.

death: "They're organizing. That's the beginning of a ceremonial that's going to bind them together more firmly than anything else. [*He sniffs the air.*] I recognize a familiar smell. . . ."[9] Thus, while *The Screens* is in many ways very different from Genet's earlier plays, the basic structure can still be said to rely upon the concept of the ritual sacrificial victim.

At the outset of this study, I suggested certain significant parallels between T. S. Eliot and Genet; perhaps it would be as well to conclude by indicating where they differ. For Eliot, except in the cases of *Sweeney Agonistes* and *Murder in the Cathedral,* the audience is neither expected nor invited to *participate* in a ritual experience, and consequently, any form of "communion," religious or otherwise, in the theater would be alien to Eliot's demands. For Genet, on the other hand, the desire for an active "communion" between play and spectators is explicit. Obviously, it is not necessary for all "communion" to be of a specifically religious nature: what matters is the *intensity* of the involvement, whatever the actual subject matter of the representation. In addition, it is evident that the form of the play is as important as its content. A play constructed as a ritual is more likely to achieve its objective than another play with similar subject matter but a more "natural" construction. For religion is a ritual and, while it is not true that all ritual is religion, the reaction aroused by the presentation of a sacrificial ritual is closer to religious communion than to anything else.

One of the most effective forms of ritual drama ever devised by man is the ceremonial of the Mass; and Genet and Eliot alike derive a significant part of their dramatic ideal from the symbolism of the Last Supper. But here again there is a difference of emphasis. Genet, in his *Lettre à Pauvert sur Les Bonnes,* concludes his remarks on the relationship between the Mass and the Theater with the phrase: "Doubtless it is one of the functions of art to propose, as a substitute for religious faith, the efficacy of Beauty." It is possible that Eliot might have

9. *The Screens,* p. 190.

proposed to "*combine* religious faith with the efficacy of Beauty"; but even here, the divergence of opinion is not so great as might at first appear. For Eliot's own appreciation of the Mass seems to stem as much from a sense of aesthetic as from one of religious values. When he writes that "the only dramatic satisfaction that I find now is in a High Mass well performed,"[10] he seems to set a seal on dramatic satisfaction rather than on any degree of religious experience. Of course, the dramatic satisfaction is there *because* of the substance of the Mass, which is religious, but this does not alter the fact that the primary reaction is an aesthetic one. Nevertheless, nowhere does Eliot suggest, as Genet does, that art has as one of its functions the substitution of beauty for religious faith. In a way, then, it is Eliot's attitude to religion, rather than to art, which allows us to see in these two statements a difference of emphasis, and not a contradiction.

SCULPTURE INTO DRAMA: GIACOMETTI'S INFLUENCE ON GENET

ROBERT NUGENT

Today modern art and modern drama have come closer together. They treat, although employing different media, problems common to man in the twentieth century. These problems concern the view the individual takes of himself as an existent being and his view of himself as he stands in relationship to the world about him. Recent art and drama are both ways whereby the self explores such concerns. The result of this exploration is frequently the terror the individual discovers in his own apartness: he finds himself separated from the

10. T. S. Eliot, "A Dialogue of Dramatic Poetry," *Selected Essays* (London: Faber and Faber, 1932), p. 46.

From *Drama Survey* 3 (1964), pp. 378–385. Reprinted by permission.

phenomenal world for which his needs—emotional, physical, spiritual—are not the evident cause. We may say that this alienation of the individual from the world forms the basic tenet of Genet's theater. The theater, moreover, for Genet is the means of expression whereby integration within oneself may be achieved. A parallel search for such integration Genet discovers in the art of Giacometti.[11] The artist uses the piece of sculpture or drawing or painting, as the writer uses the play, to come to such a state of wholeness or completeness, though brief in actual duration. The moment of victory over suffering and solitude may be quickly gone, the acts of ritual appear temporary, the gestures of existential becoming seem deceptive, still—for that moment—we have become actors in the drama, or artists of the work of art, we create to fulfill our needs.

This fulfillment begins with the realization of the continued presence of terror. The world and its history seem always to be caught up in an inescapable, ineluctable movement. The tempo of this movement becomes always greater, and nothing but the inevitable grossness of the external appears in evidence. Nor can we rid ourselves, denude ourselves in Genet's phrase, of the external world.[12] Is, then, another adventure possible than that of the "real" world? The answer is the play within the play. The play constitutes an inner ritual played around the hard core of the outer ritual of the world's change. The external ritual always threatens to break in upon the true inner ritual, which the people turned actors are performing. This threat

---

11. Genet's essay on Giacometti was originally published together with *Les Bonnes: Les bonnes et l'atelier d'Alberto Giacometti* (Décines: L'Arbalète, 1958), pp. 8–57. All translations of passages cited are the present writer's.

12. The search for integration is tied in with the problem of sincerity: "The visible world is what it is, and our action upon it will never be able to make it be anything else. One thinks, therefore, with longing, of a universe wherein man, instead of acting so furiously upon the visible appearance, would have exerted himself sufficiently to discover that secret place, within ourselves, from which starting point a quite different human adventure would have been possible. Doubtlessly, and more precisely, moral." [P. 9]

leaves the individual-turned-actor in a state of terror. He realizes that he must face the world as "himself" since the world's inevitable movement toward grossness compels him to do so. The artist, too, is forced to turn to the outer world which he can never, visually, avoid.

Ritual, moreover, implies an escape from time into the timelessness of art. The notion of timelessness consists not in the possibility of an understanding to take place in the future (as we shall see in Genet's discussion of the sculpture of Osiris). It includes as well the accumulation of past events and people. Genet would wish to escape the inescapable course of history and retreat into a true sense of time which would be constructed from his own awareness of his existential self. Time for Genet, as for Pascal, lies at the center of terror. Man is faced with history, his own and that of others. He deals with the history of the world about him and with the world he has made by himself. For the modern artist, whether he work in painting or in the theater or in poetry, the primary wish is not to tell a "factual" story (for telling a story is an acceptance of the phenomenon of time in the external world), but to present the mood of terror. Time is, in a very real sense, terror; the spectator (or the reader or the viewer) must experience the terror of the present moment. The enactment of ritual is, in one way, an occurrence in time: the actor moves, the painter paints, each thus makes his own history. It is also an escape from the other, historical, time. Much of contemporary art (for example, Genet's theater and Giacometti's sculpture as *seen* by Genet) does not attempt to narrate. It prefers to show—or more precisely, to be—the individual separate moments of terror. A great deal of the lack of understanding of contemporary art is due, I believe, to the fact that this art is not primarily focused on the event as event, but on the event as ritual. The condition of terror is not immediately grasped because it does not insist on the necessity of cause and effect. It consistently underlines the necessity of escape from such a chain. (Genet discovers this necessity in Giacometti's sculpture, or in any significant sculpture for that matter.) The dismay that arises when the individual experiences terror is action, in that it occurs as an act of becoming. Pascal knew the absoluteness of terror because it had no history in the sense of a beginning or an end: it simply existed. To face terror was the necessary act of existence. The commitment to terror, as Genet proposes it from the opening paragraphs of the essay on Giacometti, constitutes the core of modern art. We can not change the movement of the world. The world outside ourselves *is*. It has its own essence beyond our existence or beyond our experiencing of it. Nor can we in any way modify this essence.

The dilemma for Genet, then, as for the modern artist in general, is not one of refusal or acceptance, of refusal to act and of acceptance of a kind of denuding oneself down to the act itself (as in Sartre). The fundamental question is one of identity: do we accept it from others (basically the world outside ourselves with its "history"); or do we impose our own identity on ourselves (thus the importance of mask and change of costume in Genet)? As Genet says, we must discover the secret place within ourselves where the imposition occurs. We must also invent ritual through a series of experiments involving change of character, even of outer dress and manner (as is true in Genet's drama). From this action derives a possibility of self-identity. And with self-identity comes authenticity, although this authenticity may be considered antisocial in its ritualistic functions, as inevitably in *The Maids* or *The Blacks*. Authenticity must lead for Genet (and this he finds proven in Giacometti's art) to a statement of a meaningful condition, which is the play itself or the piece of sculpture itself. It is the need for meaning that Genet admires in Giacometti when the playwright speaks of the artist's desire to get rid of appearances. For once we have achieved a meaningful condition there comes the moment of truth. The moment of truth, by its very brutality, even horror, even fascination of the perverse and ugly, creates by its intensity a very real and very pure beauty. The world within is truly then the world without, a one total and complete situation of creative potential.

Genet then asks what is the basis of creative potential; what act must be "situated" in the ritual that we make for ourselves; what relationship to another must prevail in order that such beauty might arise. Suffering, for Genet, is the response for the primary source of understanding, even of the ritual we impose on ourselves and of the manner in which we turn ourselves into, and dress ourselves as, actors.[13] Further, the impact of this beauty can be summed up in a three-part formula: *inexorable, physical, divine.* In viewing the statue of Osiris, Genet speaks of the inexorable quality of its presence. The first impact on the viewer, however, is not visual—for the statue of the god was half-concealed in shadow in a niche in the museum wall—but physical: the shuddering of the human body, the trembling sensation at the base of the neck. I think that anyone who sees a play by Genet receives a similar kind of physical shock—not from the words or the apparent distortion of phenomenal reality, but physical distress. From the fear, which is essentially physical, is brought about an awareness of something divine. The audience, in hearing a play by Genet, many times experiences the impression of a religious group looking upon the writhings of an oracle. One also thinks of the various mysterious symbols always evident in Genet's plays (the dolls in *The Blacks,* for example), as being, in some way, familiar.[14] Baudelaire's line in the sonnet "Correspondances"

---

13. "There is for beauty no other origin than the wound, strange, different for each of us, hidden or visible, that each man keeps in himself, that he keeps safe, and wherein he retreats when he wants to leave the world for a temporary but profound loneliness. There is, therefore, a great distance from what is called wretchedness [*misérabilisme*]. It seems to me that Giacometti's art wants to lay bare this secret wound of each human being and even of each thing, in order that the wound might illuminate them." [P. 10]

14. Genet speaks of the familiarity of Giacometti's statues. For Genet "they are at the further end of time, at the origin of everything, there is no end to their coming forward and their receding, in a supreme immobility. . . . Where do they go? Even though their image remains visible, where are they?" [P. 12]

comes to mind: "ils [les symboles] nous regardent d'un œil familier."

Such familiarity, moreover, is timeless: again the notion of an ahistorical concept of the cause and effect of beauty includes the structure of the play itself as well as the forms of sculpture. Related to this belief in the ahistorical is the inversion of the life-death motif. Death is a continually felt presence in Genet's plays. The preoccupation with death is not morbid; it is, on the contrary, an affirmation of the necessary escape from time. The understanding of both the artist and the playwright has to do with destiny. Destiny, for Genet, is thought of in the sense of a continued growth of the past: the statues of Giacometti escape the present. The effect on the spectator is overpowering because, once more, he approaches a premonition of the divine. The divine, in this case, can be defined as the eternal present. One experiences, additionally, a coming close to the very origin of human consciousness, which is the true stage of Genet's unfolding drama. One also has a very profound understanding of things, which is possibly similar to Rilke's poetic principle of *the thing in itself*.

The fundamental desire in Genet, in Giacometti, and in modern art as a whole, is to *know* the present moment as it can be defined within the limits of the subconscious. Various descriptions have been offered before in French literature: Renan's *l'infini réel;* Baudelaire's *le fond de l'Inconnu;* Claudel's theological *prise de conscience;* the existentialist moment of self-description (I am what I have done, I will act therefore as I have become). The veritable consciousness, at this moment, is the subconscious. The awareness the conscious individual has of his inmost self is terribly vivid in the state of terror and in the moment of creativity. The fundamental solitude of the individual is perceived in isolated clarity. Genet's plays could be defined as each individual describing his solitude by an action of creating a role or a diversity of roles. Solitude, whether it be isolation of each object or each person or each work of art (and how often we are aware of this isolation in

Genet's plays when the stage is most crowded), is—for Genet—the criterion of the work of art.[15]

Solitude can be termed, in Genet, freedom of space in which to move. The set is made to appear unreal, almost without limits, either by deliberate invention, as in *The Blacks*, or by its triteness, as in *The Maids*. The freedom of space is what each character in Genet's plays, I believe, wishes to accomplish for himself. The spatial relationship is not one which the character wishes to develop toward a future action. It is directed toward this very moment of time. The criterion of the work of art is the discontinuity or break with the normal sequence of time. Genet writes of the solitude, either of the person or of the object, that is "reconstituted" through the separation or liberation from the usual three-part division of time. Both the art object (sculpture or painting) and the person on the stage turned actor, create this kind of solitude. The individual spectator or viewer joins the "reconstituted" solitude to his own isolation; he must experience it in himself as he lives the action on the stage or takes part in the action of the sculpture or painting. Further, this isolation is characterized by the word *inaccessible*. Our solitude is continually expressed by the fact that others cannot understand it. For this reason many of the actions in Genet's plays seem inscrutable to the audience, for each person of the play is attempting to create an inaccessibility of solitude. It is described by the words *nocturne*, dark and unfathomable; *incorruptible*, pure and not influenced by others; general, almost universal, for, Genet writes, "chance is canceled out" (*l'accident est anéanti*). Yet we, as spectators, must hold ourselves ready to grasp the solitude of others. Genet speaks of going on a bus, very rapidly, through the Paris streets. He

---

15. "It is therefore the loneliness of the person or object represented that is restored to us [i.e., upon examining a painting or a piece of sculpture]; and we, who are looking, in order to perceive this loneliness and to be touched by it, must have an experience of space, not in its continuity, but in its discontinuity. Each object creates its own infinite space." [P. 20]

catches glimpses of figures in the street and holds their individual character for a moment only. He seemed, in a way, ready for this glimpse, however fragmentary and passing. The city, for Genet as for Baudelaire, is most typical of modern life and is made of solitude. Solitude, however, is the capacity to dominate a kind of secret kingdom of one's own, the mysterious strangeness of which we can never communicate. Many times there is in Genet's plays a singularity that strikes us very forcibly. It is as though the play had the curious effect of something regal: the ritual is that of the court, the set itself becomes a room in the palace set aside by its timelessness. We seem almost afraid to touch the "sacredness" of this regal chamber, so much it appears dedicated to the ceremonies of the court.

Such solitude is tied in with the whole question of the value of contemporary painting and theater, insofar as they are communication. Must the artist so live in solitude, as does his work, that it becomes impossible for others to undergo catharsis? Can catharsis be effectively communicated to someone who is not an artist? Evidently, according to Genet, in agreement with Artaud, the great achievement of modern art, including the theater, is that it shows us that our solitude is absolute, that we have escaped from history. And, by the act of recognizing our solitude, we exist, although we cannot give this existence to others. By our action, however, as a kind of symbolic gesture which is the true significance of drama, we can contribute value to the predicament of others (cf. Camus).

How then can we find, we ask ourselves with Genet, the existentialist condition where terror, suffering, and solitude have reached the freedom of having become? The existentialist act is that of gaining a reality where formerly was only absence. For example, in *The Maids*, the two women impose a reality on a situation which lacked significant meaning. The meaning is acted out. The actions become, through the motions and the words of the actor, sacred rites. The acting out is very near tragedy and is close to Baudelaire's idea of *élévation* where the viewpoint of the artist is lifted beyond the context of his work.

There is also *mystère*, something almost nonrational when the visible outline of the play-as-play tends to disappear as do the contours of a piece of sculpture or the lines of a drawing. We have, in some way, experienced value which is necessary, for Genet, in both theater and art. Further, the acting out is one directed to a unity within oneself, which proceeds from a resolution of the difference between two types of solitude: one's own, of each actor and each spectator; and another is despair and emptiness. One's apartness must become a commitment to despair. The actor of the play, too, commits his solitude to emptiness as does the member of the audience. He becomes, through the experience in the theater, such a unity within himself. The cruelty of the modern theater, in Artaud's phrase, as indeed of all modern art, is in the shock of recognition when the individual person becomes aware of his incapacity or his lack or even the occasion to resolve this double solitude. The one escape, so to speak, from complete disintegration is ritual. Genet finds that Giacometti's giving firmness to the base of his statues is a ritual act. Although—at first glance—to many viewers the seeming heaviness appears out of proportion to the height of the sculpture, the solid base unites, integrates, brings into line, the total person (or object) represented.

The result of ritual, moreover, is magic.[16] On the one hand, it is a realigning of the perspectives of reality, as is true of the characters in Genet's plays when considered superficially as characters. Genet speaks of the frame surrounding the sketch of a head: though the sketch is smaller than the actual head portrayed, the representation appears with all the force of the head because of the adjustment of perspectives and outlines

16. Genet discovers a connection between ritual and magic in Giacometti's figures: "Strange feet or pedestals! I come back to them. As much as (in any case, at first sight) to the requirement of statuary art and its laws (ideas and restitution of space), it seems here that Giacometti (I beg his pardon!) observes an intimate ritual according to which he will give to the statue an authoritative, earthy, feudal base. The action of this base upon us is magical. . . . By the head, the shoulders, the arms, the pelvis, he enlightens us. By the feet, he casts a spell upon us." [Pp. 51–52]

due to the frame. On the other hand, magic is a question of change, of metamorphosis, of underscoring the otherness possible in each individual which is very near to Rimbaud's *Je est un autre*. The change does not represent a wish, however, to escape from the confines of the reality of the external world. Nor is it an act of the will to create another world as in the angelism of nineteenth-century French poetry. No, the metamorphosis in Genet's plays, illustrated by changes in pantomime, gestures, and dress, represents a very profound need to become what one is essentially, to bring the inner world into a plastic or verbal one. It is, in a quite wonderful way, the transformation of the ugly about one or in oneself into something of beauty. We have not a restatement of eighteenth-century aesthetics (the right of the ugly as the subject of art, beauty residing in the artistic intent, process, and effect); such a transformation shows an evidence of a much deeper human need to delve far into one's psyche and find therein the true self, the authentic self. The delving into oneself constitutes the tragedy of Genet's theater. The transformation based on ritual has an aspect of sacrifice, the sacrifice of the artist to his work, of the person-turned-actor to the rite he is performing (the "altar" in *The Blacks*, for example). The final impression that Genet wishes to give is, I think, one of peace, of an "old-fashioned" tranquillity: *The Blacks* opens and ends with the minuet from *Don Giovanni*. As the ultimate meaning of the work of art is a sort of reassuring friendship and peace, in Genet's phrase, so we should realize that the ultimate meaning disconcerts us only because such works or such plays are *pures et rares*.[17] The members of the audience, as also the

---

17. "Every object drawn or painted by Giacometti suggests to us, proposes to us, its most friendly and affectionate thought. Never does it appear in a baffling form, never does it try to be monstrous. On the contrary, from a great distance it brings a sort of friendship and peace which we find reassuring. Or, if these thoughts disturb us, it is because they are so pure and rare. To be at one with such objects (apple, bottle, mobile, table, palm tree) requiring the refusal of any or all compromise." [Pp. 55–56]

"actor" on the stage, have undergone suffering, terror, solitude; the experience is total and therefore has such purity. The desire of the artist, for Genet, is to let the object speak for itself; the object is lifted to that point where it is related to other objects only in the solitude common to all objects. So the desire of the playwright, we might add, is to relate one actor to another through each individual solitude. It is an art of *clochards supérieurs*, of superior tramps or clowns.

The result of the coming together of terror, pain, aloneness, ritual, magic—which Genet calls the basis of Giacometti's art—is an ability to avoid history, change. The end which gives significance to art and theater is more than that, however. Man becomes, he is enabled to withstand the necessities of others; he can set up a ritualized becoming from which he proceeds to create and to communicate on a higher level of solitude, a level common to all men and objects. What Genet says of the object in Giacometti's sculpture is true of each actor on the stage: "I am alone, the object seems to say, therefore seized in a necessity against which you can do nothing. If I am only what I am, I am indestructible. Being what I am, unreservedly, my solitude recognizes yours." [P. 57]

THE THEATER OF GENET: A SOCIOLOGICAL STUDY

LUCIEN GOLDMANN

Until a few years ago, aestheticians, critics, and literary historians accorded sociology only marginal status. However, the availability of Georg Lukács' early work, the psychological and epistemological researches of Jean Piaget, and the acceptance of the dialectic as genetic structuralism has changed all that.

From *The Drama Review* (T38), Winter 1968, pp. 51–61, trans. by Pat Dreyfus. Originally, "Le Théâtre de Jean Genet," *Cahiers Renaud-Barrault*, no. 57 (November 1966), pp. 90–125.

Traditional sociology—which still dominates university teaching—tried to relate the *content* of a literary work to the *content* of the collective unconscious: how men think and act in daily life. Such criticism becomes more effective the more mundane is the writer being studied, content merely to relate his experiences without imaginatively transposing them. Structural sociology begins from premises that exclude those of traditional sociology. The five most important of these are:

1. The essential relation between social life and art does not lie in content but only in the *mental structures*—the "categories"—which organize both the day-to-day consciousness of a social group and the artist's imagination.

2. Individual experience is too brief and limited to create such structures. They can be produced only within a social group. Individuals within groups experience together a set of problems for which they seek solutions. In other words, mental structures—or, abstractly, meaningful categorical structures—are not individual but social phenomena.

3. The relation between the structure of day-to-day consciousness and the organization of the artist's imagination—in works that can be most easily studied—is more or less rigorously homologous. Often, however, it is a simple significative relation. Frequently, heterogeneous or contradictory contents are structurally homologous: they are related on the level of categorical structures. For example, a fairy tale can be rigorously homologous *in its structure* to the experience of a particular social group; or, at the very least, it can be related meaningfully to that experience. No longer is there anything contradictory in asserting that a literary work is closely linked to social and historical reality as well as to the most powerful creative imagination.

4. The finest literary works are especially suited for such examination. In fact, the categorical structures—which are the object of this type of literary sociology—are what give the work its unity: its specific aesthetic character.

5. The categorical structures are neither conscious nor unconscious in the Freudian sense (which implied repression). Rather, they are nonconscious processes—similar in certain ways to those mechanisms which regulate muscular and nervous activity. These are neither conscious nor repressed.

That is why discovering these structures (and thereby understanding the art work) is beyond the range of both purely literary studies and those oriented toward the writer's conscious intentions or hidden motives. Categorical structures can be found only through sociological investigation.

2.

Genet's theater offers a very interesting object for sociological study. He is the product of the French underclass of petty thieves and homosexuals; he describes and transposes his underclass experiences in his early works. But what makes Genet truly interesting (as an example of the relation between modern industrial society and literary creation) is the encounter in his work between an implicit but radical rejection of society and the problems of a still active European intelligentsia which is hostile to today's corporate capitalism. The underclass has been expelled from respectable society. But Genet has interiorized this expulsion and raised it to the level of world vision.

This encounter is complicated. The rejection of industrial society is coupled with the knowledge that this society provides a high standard of living for most of those living in it. A previously unheard-of number of consumer possibilities (cars, apartments, vacations, etc.) create an apparent unity among individuals. However, this same consumer orientation stifles the deep need for authenticity, for communication with one's fellow men, for the development of one's own intellectual and emotional life. This conflict produces a relatively broad sector of the lower middle class which, while seemingly integrated into the existing social order, feels oppressed and frustrated, particularly in its emotional life.

It would seem that the first task of a sociological analysis of modern French theater would be to relate this lower middle class to characters like Ionesco's Bérenger who, although unsatisfied and out of place, is unable to resist; indeed, he cannot even conceive of the possibility of resistance. However, alongside this widespread "Bérenger phenomenon," there are—particularly in France and Italy—strong socialist and anarchist unionist traditions. These comprise a small number of workers and creative intellectuals and a fairly large number of educated people who refuse to accede to modern capitalism. They are concerned with the problem of establishing a human order that will effectively guarantee individual liberties. The frustrated hope for a socialist revolution in the West and the development of Stalinism in the East constituted a set of difficult problems for this group. It now finds itself maintaining a genuinely negative attitude toward capitalism (which it rejects more firmly than does the lower middle class), while knowing that this rejection brings with it intellectual and practical difficulties which are incomparably serious and decisive.

The early novels of Malraux, Robbe-Grillet's fiction, films like *Last Year at Marienbad*, some of Beckett's writings, and, primarily, Genet's theater should be studied as the literary transposition of this latter group's world vision.

Genet's plays result from an encounter between the radical negative of the underclass poet who, as he says, is in no way rebelling against existing society (making no claims on it) and the consciousness which exists among progressive workers and the most radical intellectuals, who see the difficulty—increasingly evident as the years go by—of finding satisfaction through revolution. Another characteristic of Genet's theater (and one which is most interesting to the cultural sociologist) is the way in which it unintentionally incorporates certain decisive experiences of the European Left. A play like *The Balcony* cannot be understood without taking these experiences into account. The sociologist must ask, of course, how this incorporation takes place; it is important to know because one finds analogous phenomena in other authors: Gombrowicz's *The Marriage*, for example. But whatever the answer, the fact remains that Genet, the nonconformist subproletarian whose work is essentially moral and lyrical, is the only modern French dramatist who assigns a central place to the problems of history as a whole, thereby making them the key to understanding his work's unity.

3.

So far, Genet has written five plays: *Deathwatch, The Maids, The Balcony, The Blacks,* and *The Screens.* These plays show an ever richer and more complex—but also more unified—expression of one and the same problem.

Deathwatch belongs to the poetic universe of the nonconformist underclass. Lefranc strangles Maurice to win Green Eyes' acceptance and become Snowball's equal. But his act is gratuitous, for, as Green Eyes says:

> *Don't talk to me. Don't touch me. Do you know what misfortune is? Don't you know I kept hoping to avoid it? And you thought you could become, all by yourself, without the help of heaven, as great as me! Maybe overshadow me? You fool, don't you realize it's impossible to overshadow me?* [. . .] *I didn't want what happened to me to happen. It was all given to me. A gift from God or the devil, but something I didn't want.*

Later, again Green Eyes:

> *You don't know the first thing about misfortune if you think you can choose it. I didn't want mine. It chose me. It fell on my shoulders and clung to me. I tried everything to shake it off. I struggled, I boxed, I danced, I even sang, and, odd as it may seem, I refused it at first. It was only when I saw that everything was irremediable that I quieted down. I've only just accepted it. It had to be total.*

Deathwatch is already a strictly coherent work, although it is Genet's first play. It describes the individual's struggle for moral recognition where the only things of moral value are those which ordinary society condemns. This divides the world into two kinds of men: the weak, the petty thieves and crooks; and the strong, the natural murderers whose criminal character is part of the natural order.

The Maids is more complex and, in certain crucial ways, different. Although the play is as radical and nonconformist as *Deathwatch*, it is no longer set entirely within the marginal world of the underclass. In *The Maids* the opposition between the maids and Madame is central: we cannot understand Claire and Solange without knowing of their hatred for Madame. *The Maids* shows the basic structure of Genet's world, the setting for *The Balcony*, *The Blacks*, and, to a degree, *The Screens*. This world pivots on the relation between the ruled and the rulers: the maids and Madame, the rebels and the balcony, the blacks and the whites, the colonials and the colonists. It is a dialectical relationship, one of hatred and fascination. Hatred is fundamental to all these plays. It becomes love-hate only through the fascination which the ruled have for the rulers, a fascination based on the utter incapacity of revolution to succeed. It is not until *The Screens* that the rulers can be defeated. Madame cannot be killed; the revolt is put down; the whites are routed only in fantasy.

The action of these plays unfolds in a static, insufficient universe; but this insufficiency is compensated by a fantasy ritual which permits the ruled to identify either with the rulers or with subjects who end domination through revolution. In this way, the ruled—but only in their imagination—cause values to exist that are not found in the real world. In *The Maids* Claire plays Madame and Solange plays Claire. In *The Balcony* minor employees play a bishop, a judge, a general (and also, it is true, a slave). In *The Blacks* Negroes on the balcony play whites and below, on the stage, enact the purely imaginary murder of a white woman. In *The Screens*, before the revolt breaks out, Saïd plays a fiancé laden with costly gifts; later his wife and his mother play the owners of a farmyard full of poultry. On one side of the stage Warda—who, through tremendous effort, has become the perfect whore—enables the oppressed to ritualize the poetic and intensely felt communion between man and woman.

In short, in a world where the power of the rulers cannot be shaken, where the ruled are motivated by love-hate for the rulers, an inadequate reality offers the possibility of a poetic-religious ritual through which the ruled identify with the rulers and succeed in fantasy in overcoming them.

4.

Let us return to our structural comparison of *Deathwatch* and *The Maids*. The world of the first play is structurally homologous to middle-class society—not as it is but as it wishes itself to be. Only here it is presented inversely. Love is at the center, but it is homosexual love. Value and recognition are a function of the dangerous nature of the characters' lives. But danger does not consist in choosing a perilous profession or in socially recognized heroism. Rather, danger comes from crime and murder, which lead to imprisonment and death. *Deathwatch* also presents an élitist view which is confirmed by contemporary society. Green Eyes and Snowball are creatures of misfortune; their nature dooms them willy-nilly to be murderers. This is why Lefranc, who kills by intention, can never be admitted to their community. The special power of *Deathwatch* comes from the implicit criticism of the purely verbal and often deceitful values of accepted morality and the intensity which marks human experiences when they are forbidden and acted out by the outcast and condemned.

Just how different is *The Maids?* First, the world here is divided. On one side are the strong, whose lives consist of lies and prating but who are invincible: Madame and Monsieur. On the other side are the maids, authentic, intense, simultaneously hating and loving their masters. A world, therefore, where everything is positive and negative at once and where the one authentic value is the imaginary realization of love-hate in the ritual which the maids resume each evening (and which they now act out for spectators, on the stage).

The maids are authentic, while Madame—powerful and insuperable—is nothing but a puppet. Solange and Claire have a vivid fantasy of following their condemned lover into exile. Later, Madame appears and touches the same theme in almost the exact words. But her verbs are conditional, she is self-satisfied; and, anyway, Monsieur will not be convicted: her words lack all sincerity. "Of course, none of this is serious, but if it were, Solange, it would be a joy for me to bear his cross. I'd follow him from place to place, from prison to prison, on foot if need be, as far as the penal colony, Solange!"[18] The little word "Solange" at the end of the speech betrays how utterly superficial Madame's emotions are: play-acting for the benefit of the maids. But, pushing the farce to its extreme, Genet also has her say that this situation makes her "almost happier, monstrously happy!" until the moment when, exhausted, she ends her speech: "I'll simply die if I don't have a cigarette!"

The telephone call from Monsieur interrupts the maids in the middle of their ritual. He has been released from prison. Solange exclaims: "The judges have their damned nerve letting him go. It's a mockery of justice. It's an insult to us!" They will be discovered, arrested, and sentenced for libel. In *Deathwatch* Solange and Claire would have proudly accepted this as the confirmation of their existence. But the world of *The Maids* is radically different. Here the sentencing will be a shameful defeat. Thus they try to poison Madame, fail, and follow their fantasy ritual into reality. The sentence for libel is transformed into one for murder. In becoming a murderer, Solange has become "Mademoiselle Solange Lemercier. [. . .] I'm Madame's equal and I hold my head high." She has become an autonomous creature for all eternity.

Before dying, Claire says:

---

18. Translation by Pat Dreyfus from the text as printed in L'Arbalète (1963) edition. The Evergreen edition contains a variant text at this point. [Ed.]

It will be your task, yours alone, to keep us both alive. You must be very strong. In prison no one will know that I'm with you, secretly. On the sly.

In both human and spiritual terms the maids have won over the powerful puppet, Madame. They really live in appearances while Madame—lying and ridiculous—only appears to live in reality. But this has been so since the play began. Madame cannot be defeated and the maids are forced to destroy themselves in order to preserve the seriousness and authenticity of their existence. *The Maids* is an embodiment of the static dialectic of despair. By interiorizing the conflict between ruled and rulers, Genet becomes a radical pessimist for whom art and appearance are the only possible compensations for a deceitful and inadequate reality.

5.

With *The Balcony*, Genet introduces a new element: he incorporates social and political reality not merely as a framework but as a possible future. Even if this future comes to nothing, its presence brings into his work the principle of motion. *The Balcony* begins as the other Genet plays do: little people acting out their dreams inside a house of illusions. But right from the start, and particularly in Scene Five, two new tensions are present: there is a revolt which threatens the established order, and this house of illusions belongs to the chief of police and his girlfriend, Irma (who are both disappointed that no client has ever asked to play the chief's role). The play shows how the image of the chief of police penetrates the ritual of the house of illusions and how this is related to the revolt's defeat.

Scene Five takes place in the rear of the house—in the rooms of the administration. Here we meet the Chief of Police, the pimp Arthur, Irma, and Carmen, a whore whom Irma has hired to help run the house. A few words about Carmen: she epitomizes the general predicament expressed in the play (a technique repeated in *The Screens*). The rebels' struggle against the balcony is one between death and life, between an order in which values exist only in fantasy and ritual and the attempt to create a new order in which these values penetrate life itself, making it unnecessary to escape into fantasy because living at last will be authentic. Carmen, like the world, is forced to choose between her genuine love for her daughter, whom she has sent to the country, and her activities as a whore in the brothel—where she used to play the role of the Virgin. Irma tells Carmen that she will have to give up her daughter and because Carmen no longer wishes to help administer the house, she is given the role of Saint Theresa.

IRMA: *Whether dead or alive, your daughter is dead. Think of the charming grave, adorned with daisies and artificial wreaths, at the far end of the garden . . . and that garden in your heart, where you'll be able to look after it. . . .*

CARMEN: *I'd have loved to see her again. . . .*

IRMA: *You'll keep her image in the image of the garden and the garden in your heart under the flaming robe of Saint Theresa. And you hesitate? I offer you the very finest of deaths, and you hesitate? Are you a coward?*

Carmen renounces life in favor of illusion, just as the revolt will be quelled and the house of illusions rebuilt.

The revolt is doomed because it has split into two factions—one oriented toward liberty and fantasy and the other, led by Roger, organized in a disciplined, repressive way. Chantal, the girl from the house of illusions who has become the rebels' muse, is killed and her name and image glorified, inscribed on the banners of the repressive forces. In the rebuilt house there is friction between the Bishop, General, and Judge (who are now real dignitaries and therefore puppets) and the Chief of Police, who has the power. The long-awaited event happens at last: Roger presents himself and asks to play the chief of police. But Roger recognizes that this is nothing but play-acting, a ritual. His revolutionary essence consisted precisely in his efforts to create a reality which had no need of fantasy or ritual. Despairing, he castrates himself: thus fantasy accords with the reality of suppressed revolt. Roger's gesture soils the carpet. He is thrown out and the real chief of police takes his place. Outside, machine guns are heard. The Queen (Irma) asks: "Who is it? . . . Our side? . . . Or rebels? . . . Or? . . ." The answer: "Someone dreaming, Madame."

The Balcony poses a very important problem to the sociologist. The play represents a transposition of the decisive historical events of the first half of the twentieth century in a manner that is very likely nonconscious and involuntary. The theme of *The Balcony* is how awareness of the importance of the executive function develops in a society which has long been dominated by property-owners but in which people still imagine power to be in the hands of long outdated fixtures: the Bishop, the Judge, and the General. And Genet is telling us that this awareness is created by the threat of revolution and its subsequent defeat: a fairly accurate reflection of Western European history between 1917 and 1923. Although we cannot describe the mechanism by which these events were incorporated into *The Balcony*, we do know that the Polish aristocrat Gombrowicz incorporated into *The Marriage* the contrary but complementary experience of Eastern Europe. In neither case is the incorporation conscious or voluntary.

The Blacks represents another step. Here hope and the prospect of victory make their way into the world of the play, if only in a peripheral way. Outside, distantly, the blacks are engaged in a real struggle. One leader has been executed, but another has already replaced him. And this revolutionary struggle is linked to what happens on stage. "Thanks to us, they've sensed nothing of what's going on elsewhere." On stage, however, in the present world, the situation is homologous to *The Maids* and *The Balcony*. Like Solange and

Claire, like the humble clients of Irma's house, like the dreamy revolutionaries in the Andromeda network, the blacks enact a nightly ritual: the murder of a white woman. Like the maids and Roger, the only way the blacks can overcome the whites *on stage* is in fantasy. As in *The Maids* and *The Balcony*, this fantasy is comprised of revolt, hatred, and fascination.

So much for similarities. What are the differences? Everything points to the lengthening shadow of the real struggle going on outside the theater; and the revolution outside is in the interest of the blacks who charade for their white audience (both real in the theater and make-believe on the balcony). But victory off-stage is only a hope, as distant in time as it is in space.

But the nature of the onstage ritual has changed, and this is particularly evident in the way it affects the real world. Claire and Solange commit suicide, Roger mutilates himself, the blacks kill one of their own. This killing, however, is performed within the framework of a real struggle which strengthens the hope of victory. On stage *The Blacks* ends with an apotheosis, as does *The Maids*. In that play the apotheosis is a real suicide; in *The Blacks* it is an imaginary murder of an imaginary white woman but the real hope of future victory over the whites—the self-awareness of the blacks—is authentic. The play ends with Village and Virtue on stage. He wants to express his love for her but can do so only with words and images borrowed from the whites. She is disappointed, but offers her assistance. "I'll help you. At least, there's one sure thing: you won't be able to wind your fingers in my long golden hair." The destruction of the caricatured whites, even if only imaginary, will oblige the blacks to discover authentic words of love, original gestures, a truly black culture rooted in their own essence, which they have just discovered.

Nor is the relation between ruled and rulers the same in *The Blacks* as in *The Maids*. It still involves a synthesis of hatred and fascination; but in *The Maids* fascination was dominant. In *The Blacks* hatred is the authentic fact of black existence. We may now ask: what social group's point of view is represented by *The Maids, The Balcony,* and *The Blacks?* It seems at least possible that the basic structure of these three plays corresponds to the mental and spiritual structure of the French radical Left; this structure includes—among other things—these five elements:

1. Affirmation of the existence of a radical opposition between classes, and the need to strengthen that opposition.
2. Recognition of the fact that the rulers of Western society cannot be overcome by violence: this society is without revolutionary perspective.
3. Fascination with the political and technological success of corporate capitalism.
4. Condemnation in moral and human terms of the social reality created by corporate capitalism.
5. Justification, in the name of moral, aesthetic, and human values, of the radical struggle against corporate capitalism. These values—once compromise and acceptance of oppression have both been rejected—can alone give value to a society founded on minority rule, lies, and the decline of culture.

6.

We may now begin to analyze *The Screens,* which, beyond its unquestioned artistic value, has the added significance of being one of the first works of contemporary French drama to be animated by a belief in man's ability to resist regimentation and constraint. The action is divided into four stages, representing both society's development and Saïd's increasingly radical attitudes.

At first we find the ruled-ruler situation already familiar to us from Genet's earlier plays. This social order, however, is extremely provisional—the revolution will succeed—and this means that hatred is tempered and that the ritual, brothel, trunkful of gifts, farmyard, is of only peripheral importance. In the second stage, Saïd, surrounded by his wife and mother, clashes with the social order and is rejected as a thief and outsider. From that moment, the ritual loses its importance for all three of them. Saïd no longer goes to the brothel, because his struggle for an authentic life has begun. The Arab village, which still accepts the rule and morality of the colonists, at first rejects Saïd and his family. Kadidja and the village women prevent Saïd's mother from taking part in the funeral. The Mother resorts to magic and appeals to the dead man's mouth. But he too rejects her, in a scene which summarizes the entire play (the dead man was a member of the revolution and therefore incarnates the three social orders of *The Screens:* the Arab village, the revolt, and the kingdom of the dead). In prison Saïd and Leila grow closer to each other: they go together toward radical politics, monstrosity, evil, and negation.

The third stage begins with the outbreak of the revolt. Kadidja, who is the incarnation of the village, is killed. But before yielding to death she exhorts the village to revolt and thereby embraces the position she condemned in Saïd and Leila.

I'm dead? So I am. Well, not yet! I haven't finished my job. So, Death, I'll fight it out with you! Saïd, Leila, my loved ones! You, too, in the evening related the day's evil to each other. You realized that in evil lay the only hope. Evil, wonderful evil, you who remain when all goes to pot, miraculous evil, you're going to help us. I beg of you, evil, and I beg you standing upright, impregnate my people. And let them not be idle!

But Saïd, Leila, and the Mother—who started the resistance as thieves and arsonists—will withdraw from it now that it is organized and taken over by the entire community. Their action was personal. They will pursue their course of negativity and evil to its absolute limit. Saïd poisons watering troughs, an act which harms the rebels more than the colonists. The

Mother kills a soldier, apparently by accident. Later, in the kingdom of the dead, she admits that it was intentional. She denies taking part in the resistance, even when her deed objectively defines her as a participant.

Stage four: the revolt is successful and a new order has been created, one which has neither oppressed nor oppressors and which Genet describes in a manner that is no longer caricature but serious and dignified. Still, it is an order and it will necessarily reappropriate many elements of the order it has replaced.

As the revolutionary social order adopts the patterns of the order it has replaced, the third and last social order appears: the kingdom of the dead. It is beyond contradictions and all those who previously were enemies exist in harmony before entering the true realm of the dead: Nothingness. The Mother arrives here to wait for her two children. Like Kadidja she is replaced on earth by a mythic figure, Ommu, who declares: "Kadidja! Kadidja! They say you're dead, since you're in the earth, but enter my body and inspire me! And as for Saïd, may he be blessed!" Later, in the kingdom of the dead, Kadidja will say to the Mother: "Ommu has taken over from us, from you and me. . . ."

Saïd returns to the village and meets the representatives of the new order. Ommu, who incarnates the expectations of the village, notes that Saïd did everything he could to betray them but that he "didn't achieve much." She says that she will be able to disappear if—in the new revolutionary order—there is a place for Saïd, whose truth is not of those which must be realized in action, but which alone can become song and give meaning to the new society. ". . . There are truths that must never be applied, those that must be made to live through the song they've become." The revolutionary leaders offer to pardon Saïd. Saïd is ready for one last act of treachery. "I'm very much in demand. I can set my price. . . ." But the Mother cries out from the realm of death:

Saïd! . . . Saïd! . . . you're not going to give in? She-dog that I am, she-dog big with a mongrel pup, I kept you in my guts not to become one more one less! A dog's life, kicks in the ribs and maybe rabies! Less than a patch of nettles, less than what you're worth, until noon today—it's noon sharp —I thought it was hatred that was leading me, *Saïd!*

Saïd reconsiders. He is about to leave when he is killed by one of the Arabs. There is still no place for him in the new order, as there was none in the old. Ommu—representing the hopes of the village—must remain on earth. "Burying this one, screaming at that one: I'll live to a hundred." The Mother waits for Leila (who died earlier) and Saïd. But they do not come to the kingdom of the dead. All that gets there of Leila is her veil. As for Saïd, he has bypassed the kingdom of the dead and entered Nothingness direct.

So as not to be guilty of omitting a particularly important element from this schematic picture, I would like to add that the development of the brothel—the house of illusions—runs parallel to the other events in the play. With the revolt and the resistance the prostitutes—who were essential and autonomous in the society of oppressed and oppressors—become the same as all the other members of the community: respected citizens who fight and whose function is recognized and respected. But after victory there is no place for them in the new order. Warda is killed by the village women: she carries Leila's veil to the Mother in the kingdom of the dead.

How does *The Screens* fit into Genet's development? It would be both easy and inadequate to say that Genet here returns to his point of departure: anarchy. Saïd does, to be sure, share many features with the narrator of *The Thief's Journal* and the attitudes which shaped *Deathwatch*. But there are fundamental differences, too. The problem of the meaning and the quality of social orders which is so important in *The Screens* is not even mentioned in the early works. The characters in *Deathwatch* are nonconformists, outcasts. Saïd is a universal figure, moral to be sure, but through his negativity, also political. As Ommu says to the soldiers of the victorious revolution: "You and your pals are proof that we need Saïd."

Some of the decisive experiences of the European Left have been incorporated into the play. First of all: the possibility of a successful revolt in Algeria, and in other countries throughout the world as well. Then: victory alone will not guarantee men happiness and freedom, nor secure a place within the new order for those values which, as Ommu says, are not to be realized in action but are to become song. The play's three social orders correspond to three basic concepts of European socialist thought: the class society based on oppression; the society born of the successful revolt which does away with oppression but is still rooted in constraint; and the vision of a classless society with no restraints. This last serves the same need for socialist thought as the Kingdom of Heaven does in Christian eschatology.

Saïd and through him Genet refuse to participate in these three orders. There is another path which must be followed if we wish to remain men. *The Screens* is the first French theater work to describe the possibilities that men still have intact and—paradoxical as this may sound—to put on stage a hero who, in and through his negativity, is ultimately positive. For whatever one may think of Saïd's values (and needless to say they are not ours) they are authentic and undisputed within the world of the play. And, unlike Solange and Claire, unlike the rebels of *The Balcony*, unlike the blacks, Saïd fulfills his ideals outside of ritual, in his life: he remains unbowed and intact to the very end. Having freed himself of all fascination and all hatred for both the old and new rulers, he follows his own path and enters Nothingness naturally and undefeated.

Is it coincidence that *The Screens* was written recently? Is it just a result of Genet's intellectual evolution, or is something much more at stake: the first symptom of a historical turning point? Difficult as it is to answer this question, let us note that a current has developed in Western European Marxist thought whose objectives will dominate any discussion of socialism's prospects in today's world. This current affirms the inadequacy of the old revolutionary schema and, in particular, the impossibility of revolution within contemporary Western society. This current also sees the dangers to liberty inherent in old revolutionary ideas and the need to replace these ideas with something better adapted to the evolution of modern industrial society. Of course, those who support the new ideas sense that estrangement from the traditional position constitutes a grave and painful predicament. Transposed to politics, this feeling corresponds to a "betrayal" of the old point of view (it is not really, however: Saïd "did not achieve much" in the way of treason) and the stock it put in revolution. Also, insofar as these thinkers are really socialists, they know that the new point of view runs a considerable risk of being compromised and integrated into the existing capitalist order. They know that any reform action, whatever its nature, involves the danger of corruption and that the only defense against this is a radical rejection of any compromise with the technocratic society.

Until now this predicament has been purely theoretical and conceptual. Things, however, are changing; and the cultural sociologist will find the following facts to be of particular significance:

1. That a writer whose last plays were focused on the problem of history can now put a character on stage who, although no longer involved with the traditional path of revolt, rejects the three orders of socialist thought without, however, putting them all on the same level. Indeed, it is not possible to put the caricatured order of the oppressors and colonists on the same level as the successful revolt or death—which are also rejected but treated in a dignified and serious way.

2. That this character, whom nothing has been able to break, maintains his negativity to the very end.

3. That without making the slightest compromise, he is still

unbowed when he leaves the world where Ommu (and, with her, the entire village) must wait for a future in which another Saïd will at last have a place.

Is *The Screens* an isolated, accidental occurrence? Or is it the sign of a turning point in our intellectual and social life?

Epilogue

THE ANARCHIST AND THE PLAYBOY

PLAYBOY: . . . In the sixteen years since you were pardoned from a life sentence for repeated burglaries and released from prison for the last time, have you gone straight—or are you still a thief?

GENET: Are you?

PLAYBOY: We'd prefer to ask the questions, if we may.

GENET: All right. I don't steal the same way the average person does. In any case, I don't steal the way I used to. I receive big royalties from my books and plays—at least they seem big to me—and the royalties are the result of my early thefts. I continue to steal, in the sense that I continue to be dishonest with regard to society, which pretends that I'm not. . . .

PLAYBOY: Now that you've achieved international eminence as an author, however, haven't you become, at least, a sought-after guest at literary teas?

GENET: Not at all! Society knows what it's doing. People don't invite me, because they sense very quickly that I'm not one of them. But the truth of the matter is that I don't like to go out.

PLAYBOY: You say you're "not one of them." Do you mingle socially, then, with ex-cellmates and criminal associates?

Extracts from interview in *Playboy*, April 1964, pp. 45–53. Reprinted by permission. According to J.-M. Magnan, this interview, the only full-scale one that Genet has ever granted, was given with the encouragement and on the advice of Simone de Beauvoir.

GENET: Certainly not. Consider the situation. I receive royalties from all over the world. You come to interview me for *Playboy*. Whereas they're still in prison. How do you expect us to maintain relations? For them, I'm simply a man who has betrayed. I had to betray theft, which is an individual action, in the interest of a more universal operation, namely poetry. I had to betray the thief that I was in order to become the poet that I hope I've become. But this "legality" hasn't made me more cheerful.

PLAYBOY: You seem to feel that you are regarded as a pariah both by society and by the underworld. How do you feel about living in this state of general reprobation?

GENET: I don't mind, but it's a matter of temperament. I like being an outcast just as, with all due respect, Lucifer likes being cast out by God. But it's out of pride, and that's not my good side. It's a bit stupid. It's a naïve romantic attitude. I oughtn't to stop there. . . .

PLAYBOY: What do you do with all your income?

GENET: That's none of your business.

PLAYBOY: Well, here in this sparse room, apart from a few pieces of secondhand furniture, we see only seven books, an alarm clock, a valise, a suit and three shirts—in addition to the clothes on your back. Is this all that you own?

GENET: Yes. Why should I have more? Mine is the poverty of the angels. I just don't give a damn about possessions and the like. When I go to London, my agent sometimes reserves a room for me at the Ritz. But what need have I for objects and luxury. I write, and that's enough.

PLAYBOY: Toward what end, if any, are you directing your life?

GENET: Toward oblivion. . . .

AT THE SORBONNE

"I refuse all complicity in the establishment of a new order. Everything that I have seen here gets me worried. The whole thing stinks of glue—glue, clogging up the whole works."

With these words, the *poète maudit*, Jean Genet, author of *The Screens*, stalked out of the Sorbonne.

A few minutes earlier, the poet had been having a discussion with a score or so of students in the library of the former Institute of Philosophy which, like the majority of lecture halls, has been transformed into a permanent Forum—if not into a living room or even a dormitory. Indeed, nothing is surprising any more, at the Sorbonne. Meanwhile, between the tables of the library, a student, stretched out on an inflatable rubber mattress and well hidden under his blankets, saw no reason to interrupt his sleep to listen to Jean Genet. "If I write," said the poet to a student, "it's more or less by mistake. If I have one advantage over you, it is because I am uneducated. I don't give a damn whether what I write is published or performed. In France, in recent times, I have done everything I could to stop any of my plays being performed. Of course, abroad, it's more difficult!"

"I can't say how delighted I am," added Jean Genet, "that a youngster with red hair should finally have forced General de Gaulle to retire to Colombey!"

Then a young man with a notice hung across his chest carrying the simple words, POETRY COMMANDO, silently handed Jean Genet a telephone directory. Meanwhile, on one of the walls, a poster proclaims: SILENCE! ACTION, NOT WORDS!

Next Jean Genet was taken to the main lecture hall, where his arrival had been announced to loud applause. In front of the platform, beneath the frescoes by Puvis de Chavannes, a

---

Nicole Duault, in *France-Soir*, 31 May 1968. Reprinted by permission. Translated by R.N.C.

group of journalists from the Television Service—Roger Couderc, Robert Chapatte, and Frédéric Pottecher—were outlining to the students their plans for reforming the French State Broadcasting Services. While this was going on, in quietly walked Jean Genet. But, confronted with the students on the one hand and the television stars on the other, he could endure it less than five minutes—and then he fled from this lecture hall, where, exactly a week earlier, Sartre had brought the house down.

A student drew the final conclusion:

"Sartre was an opportunist. Genet is a poet."

*Bibliography of Works in English**

WORKS BY JEAN GENET

Plays (standard editions)

The Balcony. Trans. Bernard Frechtman. New York: Grove Press, 1958; revised ed., 1966.

The Blacks. Trans. Bernard Frechtman. New York: Grove Press, 1960.

Deathwatch. Trans. Bernard Frechtman. In *The Maids and Deathwatch*. New York: Grove Press, 1954; revised ed., 1962.

The Maids. Trans. Bernard Frechtman. In *The Maids and Deathwatch*. New York: Grove Press, 1954; revised ed., 1962.

The Screens. Trans. Bernard Frechtman. New York: Grove Press, 1962.

Novels (standard editions)

Funeral Rites. Trans. Bernard Frechtman. New York: Grove Press, 1969.

Miracle of the Rose. Trans. Bernard Frechtman. New York: Grove Press, 1965.

Our Lady of the Flowers. Trans. Bernard Frechtman. New York: Grove Press, 1963.

Querelle of Brest. Trans. Roger Senhouse. London: Anthony Blond, 1966. To be published by Grove Press, trans. Ralph Manheim.

---

* For a full bibliography, see Richard N. Coe, "Jean Genet: A Check-list of his Works in English and German." *Australian Journal of French Studies*, VI, 1, 1969, pp. 113–130.

Various (standard editions)

The Funambulists. Trans. Bernard Frechtman. *Evergreen Review* (April–May 1964), 45–49.

Giacometti's Studio. Trans. Terence Kilmartin. *The Observer Colour Supplement* (London) (11 July 1965), 27–30.

[Interview with Jean Genet]. *Playboy* (April 1964), 45–53.

Letters to Roger Blin. Trans. Richard Seaver. New York: Grove Press, 1969.

Mademoiselle: A Letter to Léonor Fini. Trans. Bernard Frechtman. *Nimbus* 3, no. 1 (1955): 30–37.

A Note on Theater. Trans. Bernard Frechtman. *Tulane Drama Review* (Spring 1963), 37–41.

Something which seems to resemble decay. . . . Trans. Bernard Frechtman. *Art and Literature* (Lausanne) (March 1964), 77–86.

The Thief's Journal. Trans. Bernard Frechtman. New York: Grove Press, 1964.

To a Would-Be Producer. Trans. Bernard Frechtman. *Tulane Drama Review* (Spring 1963), 80–81.

What I like about the English is that they are such liars. . . . The Sunday Times Colour Supplement (London) (24 February 1963), 11.

CRITICISM

Full-length general studies

Coe, Richard N. *The Vision of Jean Genet*. New York: Grove Press, 1968.

Driver, Tom F. *Jean Genet*. New York: Columbia University Press, 1966.

Knapp, Bettina L. *Jean Genet*. New York: Twayne (Twayne World Author Series No. 44), 1968.

McMahon, Joseph H. *The Imagination of Jean Genet*. New Haven: Yale University Press, 1963.

Sartre, Jean-Paul. *Saint Genet Actor and Martyr*. Trans. Bernard Frechtman. New York: George Braziller, 1963.

THODY, PHILIP. *Jean Genet: A Critical Appraisal.* London: Hamish Hamilton, 1968; New York: Stein and Day, 1968.

WILCOCKS, R. W. F. "Jean Genet: A Study of his Drama." Ph.D. dissertation, University of Khartoum, 1966.

Interpretations

ABEL, LIONEL. "*Le Balcon:* Metatheater." *Partisan Review* 27, no. 2 (1960), 324–330.

BARBOUR, THOMAS. "Playwrights or Play-Writers." *The Hudson Review* (Autumn 1954), 473–475.

BLAU, HERBERT. *The Impossible Theater: A Manifesto.* New York and London: Macmillan, 1964.

BONOSKY, P. "The Blacks." *Mainstream* (February 1962), 61–62.

BRUSTEIN, ROBERT. "Genet's Call to the Colors." *The New Republic* (29 May 1961), 21–22.

———."Antonin Artaud and Jean Genet: the Theater of Cruelty." In *The Theater of Revolt. An Approach to the Modern Drama,* pp. 361–411. Boston and Toronto: Atlantic Monthly Press, 1964.

CALARCO, N. JOSEPH. "Vision without Compromise: Genet's *The Screens.*" *Drama Survey* 4 (1965), 44–50.

CHIAROMONTE, NICOLA. "Jean Genet: White and Black." *Partisan Review* 28, nos. 5–6 (1961), 662–668.

CLURMAN, HAROLD. "The Blacks." *The Nation* (20 May 1961), 447–448.

———. "Theater." *The Nation* (6 July 1957), 17–19.

COE, RICHARD N. "Unbalanced Opinions: Jean Genet and the French Critics." *Proceedings of the Leeds Philosophical and Literary Society,* 1970 (in press).

CORRIGAN, ROBERT. "The Theater in Search of a Fix." *Tulane Drama Review* (June 1961), 21–35.

ESKIN, STANLEY G. "Theatricality in the Avant-Garde Drama: A Reconsideration of a Theme in the Light of *The Balcony* and *The Connection.*" *Modern Drama* 7 (1964), 213–222.

ESSLIN, MARTIN. "Jean Genet: A Hall of Mirrors." In *The*

Theater of the Absurd, pp. 140–167. New York: Doubleday, Anchor, 1961.

FOWLIE, WALLACE. *Dionysus in Paris*, pp. 218–222. New York: Meridian Books, 1958.

———. "The New French Theater: Artaud, Beckett, Genet, Ionesco." *The Sewanee Review* (Autumn 1959), 643–657.

———. "New Plays of Ionesco and Genet." *Tulane Drama Review* (September 1960), 46–48.

FRECHTMAN, BERNARD. "Genet's Exercise in Black Magic." *Herald Tribune* (30 April 1961).

FRISCH, J. E. "Ironic Theater: Techniques of Irony in the Plays of Samuel Beckett, Eugène Ionesco, Harold Pinter and Jean Genet." Ph.D. dissertation, University of Wisconsin, 1965.

GASCOIGNE, BAMBER. *Twentieth-Century Drama*, pp. 191–192 and *passim*. Revised ed., London: Hutchinson, 1963.

GROSSVOGEL, DAVID I. "Genet; The Difficulty of Defining." In *Four Playwrights and a Postscript*, pp. 133–174. Ithaca: Cornell University Press, 1962.

———. "The French Dramatist: His Limits Are Those of Man." *Saturday Review* (27 December 1958), 14–15.

———. "Ritual and Circumstance in Modern French Drama." *L'Esprit Créateur* (Winter 1962), 166–174.

GUICHARNAUD, JACQUES. *Modern French Theater from Giraudoux to Beckett*, pp. 168–172. New Haven: Yale University Press, 1961.

HOBSON, HAROLD. *The French Theater Today*, pp. 120–127. London: Harrap, 1953.

HUGHES, CATHARINE. "Jean Genet and his World of Illusion." *The Critic* (August–September 1961), 20–21, 71–72.

KILLINGER, JOHN. "Jean Genet and Scapegoat Drama." *Comparative Literature Studies* 3 (1966), 207–221.

LUKAS, M. "The Blacks." *The Catholic World* (October 1961), 63–64.

MACARTHUR, R. "Kaleidoscope." *Theatre Arts* (January 1950), 40–44.

MAILER, NORMAN. "The Blacks." *The Village Voice* (May 11 and 18, 1961).

MARES, F. H. "Genet's *The Balcony.*" *Meanjin Quarterly* (1965), 354–356.

MARKUS, THOMAS B. "Genet, the Theater of the Perverse." *Educational Theater Journal* 14 (1962), 209–214.

MAROWITZ, CHARLES. "The Revenge of Jean Genet." *Encore* (September–October 1961), 17–21.

MELCHER, EDITH. "The Pirandellism of Genet." *French Review* (October 1962), 32–36.

PRITCHETT, V. S. "Black and White Murder Show." *The New Statesman* (9 June 1961), 928.

PRONKO, LEONARD C. *Avant-Garde: The Experimental Theater in France*, pp. 140–154. Berkeley and Los Angeles: California University Press, 1962.

———. "Jean Genet's *Les Paravents.*" *L'Esprit Créateur* (Winter 1962), 181–188.

STREM, GEORGE C. "The Theater of Jean Genet. Facets of Illusion—the Anti-Christ and the Underdog." *Minnesota Review* 4 (1964), 226–236.

SWANDER, HOMER D. "Shakespeare and the Harlem Clowns: Illusion and Comic Form in Genet's *The Blacks.*" *The Yale Review* (December 1965), 209–227.

Tulane Drama Review, Spring 1963. Special number devoted to Genet and Ionesco. Contains:

KNAPP, BETTINA. "An Interview with Roger Blin": 111–126.

NELSON, BENJAMIN. "*The Balcony* and Parisian Existentialism": 60–79.

PIERRET, MARC. "Genet's New Play: *The Screens*": 93–97.

PUCCIANI, ORESTE F. "Tragedy, Genet and *The Maids*": 42–59.

SVENDSEN, M. M. "Corydon Revisited; A Reminder on Genet": 98–110.

TAUBES, SUSAN. "The White Mask Falls": 85–92.

WELLWARTH, GEORGE E. "Jean Genet: the Theater of Illusion

and Disillusion." In *The Theater of Protest and Paradox*, pp. 113–133. New York: New York University Press, 1964.

———. "The New Dramatists; 3. Jean Genet." *Drama Survey* (Winter 1962), 308–320.

Yale French Studies, Spring/Summer 1962. Special issue devoted to "The New Dramatists." Contains:

EHRMANN, JACQUES. "Genet's Dramatic Metamorphosis: From Appearance to Freedom": 33–42.

MCMAHON, JOSEPH H. "Keeping Faith and Holding Firm": 26–32.

RECK, RIMA D. "Appearance and Reality in Genet's *Le Balcon*": 20–25.

ZIMBARDO, R. A. "Genet's Black Mass." *Modern Drama* 8 (1965), 247–258.